The Precarious Migrant Worker

THE PRECARIOUS MIGRANT WORKER

The Socialization of Precarity

Panos Theodoropoulos

polity

Copyright © Panagiotis Theodoropoulos 2025

The right of Panagiotis Theodoropoulos to be identified as Author of this Work has been asserted in accordance with the UK Copyright, Designs and Patents Act 1988.

First published in 2025 by Polity Press

Polity Press
65 Bridge Street
Cambridge CB2 1UR, UK

Polity Press
111 River Street
Hoboken, NJ 07030, USA

All rights reserved. Except for the quotation of short passages for the purpose of criticism and review, no part of this publication may be reproduced, stored in a retrieval system or transmitted, in any form or by any means, electronic, mechanical, photocopying, recording or otherwise, without the prior permission of the publisher.

ISBN-13: 978-1-5095-6498-9
ISBN-13: 978-1-5095-6499-6(pb)

A catalogue record for this book is available from the British Library.

Library of Congress Control Number: 2024947470

Typeset in 11.5 on 14 pt Adobe Garamond
by Cheshire Typesetting Ltd, Cuddington, Cheshire
Printed and bound in Great Britain by TJ Books Ltd, Padstow, Cornwall

The publisher has used its best endeavours to ensure that the URLs for external websites referred to in this book are correct and active at the time of going to press. However, the publisher has no responsibility for the websites and can make no guarantee that a site will remain live or that the content is or will remain appropriate.

Every effort has been made to trace all copyright holders, but if any have been overlooked the publisher will be pleased to include any necessary credits in any subsequent reprint or edition.

For further information on Polity, visit our website:
politybooks.com

Contents

Acknowledgements — vii

Introduction — 1
   Building on failures and gaps — 9
   Precarity and resistance — 15
   Borders in the social body — 20
   Precarious migrant work in the UK — 22

1. 'We Were Always Migrants' — 27
   Development, underdevelopment and migration — 29
   'We were always migrants' — 34
   The first steps — 40
   The dual frame of reference — 49

2. The Precarious Condition — 52
   The kitchen — 57
   Informality and abuse — 68
   Health and safety — 73
   Alienation — 78

3. The Socialization of Precarity — 83
   Behind Amazon's smile — 84
   The agency arena — 91
   The socialization of precarity — 96
   Isolation, competition and conflict — 105
   Resisting alone — 110

4. The Precarious Migrant Subject — 115
   'Just a foreigner': migration and the dual frame of reference — 116
   Perceiving difference — 126
   Contradictions of the 'Good Migrant' — 130
   Becoming a migrant worker — 136
   Class — 144

5. Solidarities and Resistances — 150
   Hierarchies and precarious solidarities — 152
   Precarious solidarities — 157
   Collective resistances — 162
   Workers' experiences with mainstream unions — 170
   Distance and absence — 175

Conclusion: Towards Community Embeddedness — 187
   Migration and the socialization of precarity — 190
   Notes towards embeddedness — 196

Notes — 204
References — 208
Index — 219

Acknowledgements

I never intended to write an acknowledgement section. However, the more I thought about it, the more I recognized that there are people without whom such a project would have never been conceived, and whose lives and insights are reflected in the ensuing pages. There are also those who played a crucial role in the development of my ideas, and yet, for various reasons, we no longer speak that often. And people whose presence, at the precise moments that they happened to be in my life, helped me remain relatively sane whilst researching and writing this book. We are products of our environments, and I have been fortunate enough to have some powerful humans next to me.

Thanks to every worker that gave me the gifts of their time and insights during our interviews.

Thanks to Professor Andrew Smith for believing in me and for convincing me that I have something to offer. For helping me understand, through your writing and our conversations, that sociology is much more than a sterile academic exercise. For reading and commenting on the various iterations of this project multiple times between 2017 and 2024, always contributing something that lay just beyond my grasp.

To Valia Mastorodimou, my therapist. The years leading up to the writing of this book were difficult. There is no way that I would have done this without your support.

Thanks to Jonathan Skerrett at Polity for your invaluable guidance and assistance in every aspect of writing and producing this book, and to the academic reviewers who commented on its previous versions.

Thanks to Cathy and the School of Social and Political Sciences at the University of Glasgow for the support of the Neil Davidson Postdoctoral Fellowship, without which the decisive steps to produce this book would probably not have been possible.

To Odysseas Kamarinos, my brother, the most inspiring fighter that I know.

ACKNOWLEDGEMENTS

To Dr Emily Foley, for commenting on this entire manuscript and for the endless ranteractions.

To the Interregnum collective, for helping create a platform where we put our ideas into practice.

To Darren Gillies. For the availability of your sofa bed. For countless conversations, countless challenges, but most importantly, for knowing that you got my back in Glasgow.

To Nafsika Zarkou. For your critical brain and the power and conviction with which you live your life. Most importantly, for helping me negotiate the difficult process of growing up.

To all my friends in Glasgow for making it feel as close to home as is possible for a migrant.

To Dr Diego Maria Malara, for expanding my horizons, showing me the limitless possibilities of our disciplines, and supporting me even in times that I could not reciprocate.

To Vyronas Kapnisis, for dropping the spark that made me fall in love with sociology.

To a friend that is no longer with us, and was involved in my first serious attempt at organizing with other migrant workers.

To the 1in12 Club in Bradford, for teaching me the potential of self-organization and for allowing me to work on, and in, the Albert Meltzer Library. The hours I spent in there were undoubtedly the most important in my theoretical and political development.

To Dr Francesca Stella for co-supervising my PhD and for your insightful comments at every stage.

To the Industrial Workers of the World (IWW).

And, of course, thanks to my parents. For ceaseless inspiration, love, solidarity and guidance.

Introduction

Alexia works while her son is dreaming. She dreams – can she remember her dreams? – while her son is at school. She wakes up around two hours before he returns; just enough time to cook something and share a few words about their day. She will then take a strong painkiller to ignore the pangs in her back and in the nerves of her arms, get dressed, and slide into Bradford's neglected landscape for another twelve-hour night shift.

She worked next to me for a few nights. I was struck by her smile: a ray of light amidst decay, the hope that was the last to rise from Pandora's box. Nobody smiled here. The production line and the earplugs never allowed for much conversation, but the mere *existence* of a smile in this environment that was built to drown all manifestations of human warmth was soothing. Yet, one night, the smile crumbled. Unnoticed by everyone else – the production line, alongside stifling conversation, is also proficient at stifling humanity – and while maintaining her excellent production rate, Alexia was crying. At around 2 a.m., during our single half-hour break, I approached her and asked what was wrong. Thinking back, there was probably a selfish element to my impulse – I *needed* that smile to survive the shift – as much as genuine care. Her reply was simple and devastating: 'I am thinking about my son. And I am thinking that by the time I will be able to really get to know him, and enjoy him, I will have already grown old.'

We are in a large printing press in Bradford. The year is 2014 or 2015. All around us, the howl of machines and the icy glare of fluorescent lights, contrasting sharply with the darkness outside the windows. Throughout the warehouse's many crevices, precarious migrant workers – mostly from Eastern Europe, their high-vis vests harshly demarcating their status as non-permanent staff – are feverishly working in the different stages of printing, cutting, checking and packaging a beloved product that features in every British household: greeting cards. Their colourful layout and cheery inscriptions are so contradictory to the anxiety, alienation and exploitation that are imbued within them that, when looked upon from the perspective of a worker, it seems as if they are jeering at you: as if they are laughing at your pain. I do not remember the precise words on the greeting cards. However, the feeling of revulsion towards them is unforgettable.

This is one of the first jobs I accessed as a migrant worker in the UK, and one that I would keep on returning to when I couldn't find anything better. It is a place where the asphyxiating working conditions ensure a constant turnover of staff, and the company is always in need of more fodder for its production lines. This fodder – us – is sourced from two employment agencies, who have stretched their tentacles deep into migrant communities and supply a steady stream of precarious, dependent, disoriented and exploitable migrant workers. Production never stops, which is why this dreary machine needs workers around the clock: there is almost always work, and, in those pre-Brexit years, there are always more migrant workers coming in that need it. As is typical for these types of jobs, we are paid the minimum wage.[1]

Everyone working alongside me is a migrant. We are all on zero-hours contracts, our lives tethered to the business's epochal fluctuations. If they receive a big order, we might be required for a few weeks; in the months before Christmas, work is almost guaranteed. We also know that we can be replaced at any moment. As non-permanent staff, we cover most of the posts that are designated as 'unskilled' – for me, this mostly means packing the various greeting cards in plastic sleeves, separating the cards from each other after they have been printed, or wrapping thousands of cards on pallets, ready for them to be shipped to stores across the UK. We don't really speak to the permanently employed, British workers operating the printing machines, and, when we enter the workplace, they rarely acknowledge us. We are but objects that cover a specific need – once it has been addressed, we are thrown back into the labour agency's pool of available workers, to be shunted to the next workplace. Sometimes the agency will call you without warning and demand that you present yourself for work in a few hours; once that phone rings, you must be ready to upturn your whole life. If you aren't, they'll just hire someone who is.

Our presence there is contingent upon our performance. The production line's pace does not stop, and if you cannot keep up you are replaced. Yet, we have more reasons to overexert ourselves than simply fulfilling this specific order: we know that there is a small, yet important, chance that we might impress one of the British managers and be offered a permanent contract. We also know that we are building a reputation: if the agency considers us to be 'good workers', our chances of being offered future jobs *before other workers* are increased. We are therefore compelled to work as efficiently as possible, with the constant threat of dismissal – and the latent sense of competition amongst ourselves – saturating our every moment.

Precarity breeds insecurity and feeds a constant cycle of anxiety that is *intrinsically* disempowering. One day, I noticed a problem in my payslip: I had been deducted half an hour's wage for every shift I had done that week. Upon asking the agency why this deduction had been made, they told me that it was because I received two unpaid, half-hour breaks per shift. Yet, the workplace only allowed us one half-hour break. When I asked my fellow temporary colleagues about this, it emerged that everyone had been subject to the same deduction and had received the same explanation. I was dismayed at their acceptance of the situation: wage theft was perceived as just another lousy aspect of a generally lousy job. The most common response was a shoulder shrug: 'they do that all the time'. When I suggested bringing a union in to help us reclaim our stolen wages, I was met with anxiety, abjection and apathy: nobody was willing to even consider doing anything that they feared would jeopardize their already precarious job. This is when I began to think about the socialization of precarity: it seemed that precarity does not simply ensure a steady supply of insecure workers – it *creates* a specific *type* of worker. Once you realize that everyone else has accepted these conditions – and that you are therefore alone in opposing them – you quickly fall in step.

The cameras above our heads that monitor our performance transmit the image of workers bent over a production line, hastily performing nimble movements and sorting through thousands of cards an hour. What they don't show are the physical and mental outcomes of this labour: the thumping aches in our calves and the back pains that result from standing and performing very specific, repetitive motions for twelve hours; the blue veins staining the backs of our legs; the bleeding fingers from the paper-cuts, which we must quickly bandage up and keep on working; the piercing fatigue that stems from monotonous night-shifts; the deep, dark circles around our eyes; the papery taste of dust that we inhale; the humiliation of being screamed orders at by the British managers, of not being able to respond in the way that they deserve; the gnawing sense of stress at having to blindly fight for a job that is never guaranteed; the fear of falling sick and missing a shift, which means that you will be replaced; the anxiety every single evening of waiting for the bus, knowing that if it is late, your tardiness will at the very least cost you an hour's wage, or, at the very worst, your job; and the misery of isolation that comes with working the night-shift. Finally, they don't show the critical mental recalibrations that operate inside our heads in order to allow us to survive these conditions whilst maintaining our senses of self and dignity.

As I am struggling to ignore my throbbing joints, I wonder if the consumers realize the amount of pain that has gone into these greeting cards. I wonder whether a greeting card tainted with blood from a frantic finger has ever made it through the checks, and whether it has been opened by someone wanting to surprise a person they love. I wonder whether, if people knew about the pain behind the words, they would still buy them. To my dismay, I think I know the answer.

Will Alexia ever give her son a card for his birthday?

This is another book about migration. Migration is as old as humanity itself, inseparable from our collective history, firmly engrained in our myths and our collective narratives. It involves a departure and a becoming, an immersion into the unknown that leads to knowledge and experience, an adventure that also longs for stability. It is personal, and yet reflective of wider, collective forces; simultaneously, it is spurred by those collective forces and is still – always – intimately personal. Its essence contains the material of our greatest stories, and no matter how much we discuss it, analyse it, historicize it, glorify or vilify it, it still stands shoulder to shoulder with war and love in capturing our imaginations in a way few themes can. Our need to wrap our heads around its constantly changing nature leads to the development of archetypes, in a doomed attempt to control the uncontrollable: the Economic Migrant; The Refugee; The Fraudster; The Smuggler; The Stranger. Migration induces the writing of books, the production of songs and movies, the publishing of legislation, the organization of protests and campaigns, the patrolling of borders, and the deaths and sufferings of so many within and in between them. It also helps people build their lives. And yet, no matter how much work is being done on migration, it seems that the questions – and answers – never cease.

So, what is the use of yet another book on migration? For the lay reader, what will it tell you that you don't already know, that you haven't already picked up through the social osmosis of existing in a world in which migration is seemingly at the forefront of every second public debate? For the scholar, what contribution can it make that has not already been touched upon by a myriad of articles, conferences and canonical texts?[2] For the activist, how could it possibly enhance the understandings that you have developed through a history of standing in solidarity with the marginalized and oppressed, of listening to their stories, and partaking in their struggles? And, for the migrant, what could it provide that you haven't already perceived through experience, having *lived* the issues that it discusses?

My goal was never to provide *the* definitive answers, solutions or pathways towards the emancipation of migrant workers. I firmly believe that these only emerge collectively, through the activities of the working, oppressed, precarious and marginalized sections of society in their daily attempts to negotiate and escape the economic and cultural shackles that organize our collective existence. Yet, in order to do so, we need to be aware of precisely what we are escaping, as well as of the ways in which our current existence confines, directs, and ultimately owns our imaginations and our ideas about ourselves. I attempt to contribute to these efforts by drawing upon a sliver of our collective social reality – working alongside, and speaking to, migrants in precarious occupations in Glasgow – to explore how migration and our daily experiences in precarious work structure our understandings of ourselves as migrants and as workers. Similarly, by looking at our society from the standpoint of the migrant worker, we might be better equipped to critically analyse the social realities that *all* of us are confronted with. This is not just a theoretical exercise: by exploring how precarity socializes us, we might be better equipped to think – and act – beyond it.

This book is thus also necessarily about work. Work is an aspect of humanity as old, and as complex, as migration. However, in contrast to migration, the everyday aspect of labour does not animate the public imagination with the same vivacity. Gone are the days when, in the West, one's status as a worker formed the basis of imagining an alternative future in which the working class – by virtue of its position as the producers of what society needs to survive – would liberate the whole of humanity. Instead, the defeat of mass working-class movements and the triumph of neoliberalism have dispersed us into a multitude of individuals. We think of ourselves as businesses, projects, works-in-constant-progress, with our status as workers being perceived as the most banal – and shunned – aspect of our lives. And yet, this change in our imagination is a product of a momentous mystification, because the cogs of the world *still* turn thanks to the labour of billions of workers, while the profits of this labour are *still* appropriated by a meagre minority. And what is more heroic, more tragic, more adventurous than workers' repeated, dismissed, arduous struggles to make ends meet – amassing a plethora of physical and mental ailments in the process – in order to secure an existence that should have never been in question?

Work remains the quintessential feature of our reality; our need for wages organizes our lives – when and where we wake up, when and what we eat, whether we have the energy to play with our children – and this work makes possible the lives of everybody else (whose work, in turn, makes our own life possible). And yet, despite its totemic role in arranging our existence, work has become more precarious, insecure, dangerous and taxing across the Western world. In contrast to the previous epochs of historic working-class struggles, it is no longer something that is perceived as having the potential to liberate us; it is simply something that we must survive through. Alone.

Migration and work come together in the figure of the migrant worker, the child of wider geopolitical injustices and relations that traverse the world and lead to humans leaving their homes to sell their labour in other lands.[3] The poverty that underdevelopment creates – the same poverty that is the condition for other nations' development – fuels ever more profits for the businesses of the receiving countries, as migrants are swiftly inserted precisely into the most precarious, underpaid and highly exploitative occupations, their lack of secure labour rights making it possible to use and dispose of them according to the fluctuations of an intensely competitive and unregulated neoliberal market economy. Indeed, despite vehement official proclamations to the contrary, Western economies are organized in a way that umbilically depends on the labour of precarious migrant workers. Crucially, precarious workplaces are often also completely bereft of any form of trade union presence. Migrant precarity also extends beyond the workplace, as migrants often must grapple with a myriad of other factors such as citizenship and residency restrictions, housing barriers, racism and xenophobia, language and cultural barriers, and a disorientation produced by their arrival in an unfamiliar country. In short, while precarity in the West increasingly touches everybody, migrant workers are *more* exposed to its most destructive, and most acute, manifestations. Any attempts at thinking and organizing around social justice therefore necessarily pass through the sphere of migrant work and migrant precarity.

We thus come to the gaping question that has been haunting social movements since at least the Industrial Revolution: *how do we organize?* The seas of ink that have been spilt over this question, the historical splits in the labour and radical movements, and our current impotence in the face of a rampaging neoliberal assault suggest that we are still far away from developing adequate answers (or, at least, agreeing to them). Rather than examining the rare successful instances of migrant-led collective struggles in the West in order to contribute to these explorations, I opted to analyse their wider absence: what prevents some of the most exploited sectors of society from seizing the power that their objective position in the economy affords them? As a migrant worker in precarious occupations myself, I was convinced that any answer would be incomplete if it did not depart from the corporal, minute, banal, but cumulatively decisive effects that labouring under conditions of insecurity and overexertion have on the bodies and psyches of workers.

These threads bring us to the book's subheading, the socialization of precarity. All labour regimes socialize workers: they aim to sculpt specific behavioural traits that will increase workers' productivity. I argue that the insidiousness – and, perhaps, the relative novelty – of the current conditions of precarity *amidst a wider absence of collective narratives that foreground an alternative to this mode of existence* lies beyond the anxiety, stress and bodily harms that labouring under its shadow produces. The fact that class no longer forms the basis of an inspiring, radical collective identity does not mean that it is no longer *felt*; in the context of our daily labour, class is now experienced individualistically rather than as an aspect of a wider collective identity and narrative.[4] This is a structural feature of precarious contractual relations: it breaks workers into units, atomizes them, and renders them individually responsible for rights and securities that were previously guaranteed. Workers are thus forced to continually and frantically overexert themselves under conditions of competition with their peers for a limited number of limitedly secure occupations, mirroring and responding to a wider mass culture of competition and individualism. This suffering – both dull and intense – is presented as the only pathway towards security, in an endless Darwinian rat race where the strongest and most efficient live to work another day. The bonds that lead to affinity and solidarity between workers are thereby ruptured, and the glimmers of solidarity that emerge are also precarious.

In the absence of any other collective forms of security, one's individual capacity to labour *becomes* one's security. The scars, pains, fatigue, anxiety and isolation experienced in the course of daily precarious labour thus turn into badges of self-worth: this is the socialization of precarity. It is a socialization that, beyond forming workers that are trained to respond to the demands of flexibility, availability and overexertion, leads to a proud internalization of, and identification with, the precise conditions that one is attempting to overcome.[5] In so doing, the foundations of neoliberalism are fortified, having emerged victorious as unchangeable. In the absence of inspiring contestational narratives that offer alternative imaginaries, the socialization of precarity sculpts workers whose identities are attached to *surviving* conditions, rather than *changing* them.

Therefore, while the research that informs this book focuses on precarious migrant workers in Glasgow, the implications of recognizing the socialization of precarity extend to all precarious workers in the West. They point to seemingly insuperable difficulties in the emergence of radical, emancipatory identities, since they suggest that neoliberalism grounds itself in workers' psyches and tightens its grasp on the imagination even *through* attempts to escape the precarity that it has created. And yet, not all is lost. Because, as I will argue in the forthcoming pages, neoliberalism is unable to circumvent workers' experiential awareness of class-based injustice, daily confirmed through the fatigue of the mind and the body. For migrant workers, despite all its proclamations at equality of opportunity, it is similarly unable to dispel the knowledge that their intensified exploitation is connected to their status *as migrants.*

While this might initially seem like a trivial insight, it is vastly important in the context of the retreat of social movements from most workers' everyday lives. The disparate identities that proliferate in the absence of a wider working-class identity and the transience, isolation and disconnection induced by precarious lives are *still* connected through workers' common, daily experiences of the injuries emerging from their class status. Precarity, and the socialization it produces, has succeeded precisely in rupturing the *feeling* of this common predicament; it has not succeeded in changing its reality, or dulling workers' awareness of injustice. It thus becomes possible to imagine new, intersectional solidarities and alliances, whose embeddedness in the social reality of migrant workers and other precarious groups has the potential to highlight the precise connections that precarity so insidiously mystifies. As always, these initiatives must depart from the objective labour conditions, and communities, within which workers find themselves.

Building on failures and gaps

These objective labour conditions that structure precarity in the UK form the foundations of this book. Escaping the Greek economic crisis, I started working in the migrant-dense city of Bradford in 2013. Bradford is one of the UK's most deprived areas, and this dubious accolade was reflected in the available jobs. My obvious foreignness (most people thought me to be Polish) immediately positioned me at the lower rungs of the labour ladder: indeed, not a single employment agency whose office I entered ever bothered asking me for a CV, instead almost immediately assigning me to a warehouse with many other men who looked like me. These travels included various stints as a kitchen porter (a job I revisit in the subsequent pages), a long stint in a shelf-making factory, numerous emergency pit stops at the printing press presented in the first pages of this book, bartending and leafleting simultaneously, and a dramatic exit from the hellhole of a factory that produced medical furniture after they refused to give me a day off to attend a friend's funeral. These were the years that Nigel Farage and his nationalist party, UKIP, were rising, Brexit was brewing, and migration was widely portrayed in the media as a plague that was almost exclusively responsible for Britain's declining standard of living. Fascist marches were regular occurrences, and our British colleagues' attitudes towards us mirrored the violence that we were threatened with on the streets.

Instinctively, my group of friends and anti-fascist comrades began organizing something like a labour and social solidarity initiative around 2015. The aim was to establish a migrant-led group that would offer advice and support against labour exploitation, alongside maintaining a physical space in the community that would allow migrants to autonomously organize (I would later find that such formations figure prominently in the relevant scholarly literature as supporting some of the few victorious instances of migrant mobilization). Despite our best efforts, we failed magnificently, marking the first of many unsuccessful or mildly successful attempts that I would be involved with concerning the organization of migrant workers. Paradoxically, despite the glaring exploitation and mistreatment migrant workers in precarious jobs were experiencing, both trade unions and *most workers themselves* seemed uninspired to do anything more than saying that it was 'about time' that someone did what we initiated. In the meantime, mistreatment at work, the withholding of wages and holiday pay, and punitive dismissals remained daily occurrences of our precarious lives.

This passive acceptance of reality perplexed my early-20s brain and became the trigger for me to venture more deeply into theory. In contrast to the UK, Greece is a society where memories of revolution coexist with our daily realities. My grandmother's side of the family was heavily involved with the Communist Party of Greece; her father had participated in the revolutionary process of the mid-1940s, and had been punished by imprisonment, torture and exile. When she refused to denounce his beliefs, she was denied access to university and entered the textile industry, proudly participating in historic strikes. My own father – a lawyer supporting the rights of refugees – was active in the movement that toppled Greece's military dictatorship in 1974, eventually meeting my mother – a schoolteacher and organizer – in a Free Mandela group in 1990. Such family histories are firmly rooted in Greece's collective memory. Their legacies were still being expressed when I left Greece in 2011, with millions of people on the streets resisting austerity.

The sharp contrast between my home and host countries was extremely difficult for me to digest. How could one of the most exploited and stigmatized sectors of society not rebel? I worked the same long hours and lived in the same decrepit, rat-infested neighbourhoods as them; were our different attitudes merely attributable to divergent levels of politicization? Moreover, how could trade unions, those organizations that supposedly existed to serve the workers, not be passionately and ceaselessly active to support the class's most exploited segments? The more I found out about Bradford's radical history and the role of migrant and Black Power movements within it, the more I struggled to comprehend the glaring retreat of these empowering narratives from our lives.

I decided to study the theory of organizing migrant workers in order to answer these questions and inform my organizing activities. However, the more I read, the more convinced I became that both scholarly and movement literature was ill-equipped to understand the complexity of the forces that structure migrant workers' choices in the current precarious socioeconomic context. I observed that the literature that did exist was either completely detached from the working realities of migrant workers, did not actually speak to those workers, or was concerned with only surveying the rare success stories of migrant mobilizations while overlooking the vast, much bleaker reality of defeat that permeates most parts of the West beyond the metropoles.[6]

This lack of migrants' participation in the research that directly concerns them leads to the omission of valuable nuance. Such exclusions also contribute to further perpetuating the marginalization of oppressed groups, as their perspectives are implicitly or explicitly relegated, their interpretations of their own experiences silenced. According to Paulo Freire, a foundational feature of oppression is that the oppressed have had their means of articulating their reality 'stolen from them' (1993 [1970]: 115). The reclamation of speech, discussion and self-organization emerges as a prerequisite for empowered political action. Regrettably, much of the literature that explores the lives of migrant workers partakes in excluding their voices.

I also noticed that the bulk of the writing that explored the barriers that precarious migrant workers experience in mobilizing was generally split into two strands, both of which lacked an analysis of how precarity socializes workers. The first tended to look at how the architecture of precarity makes it difficult to organize migrant workers. This strand would, for example, note how labour insecurity makes workers reluctant to organize for fear of being fired from their insecure jobs, or how the transience associated with precarity – with workers never staying in a workplace for long – curtails the development of bonds of solidarity. The other strand focused on factors emanating from the condition of being a migrant. This generally looked at elements such as the fear of deportation, the short-term, economistic outlook that is associated with the initial stages of migration, or aspects such as language barriers and migrants' unfamiliarity with the host country's labour market. It was very rare to encounter a text that connected these realms: namely, how do structural features (such as precarity or the lack of secure residence status) interact with subjective factors (such as the disorientation one experiences post-migration) and the wider cultural associations of migration (which migrant workers do or do not internalize) to reinforce the exploitability of migrants? More importantly, how does working daily in acutely insecure conditions, while being a migrant, impact migrants' ideas of themselves as workers, as migrants, and as migrant workers?

Another set of questions that led to this research involved whether migration could be the impetus for forging communities of resistance. As a migrant worker who was also involved in anti-fascist organizing, I did perceive my migration through a political lens – but was this a wider reality? I wanted to understand whether migration had the potential to develop into a 'politicized identity' – an identity encompassing political understandings that leads to organized action (Bradley 2016). I also wanted to investigate whether the accentuated xenophobia and social marginalization experienced by EU migrants during and after Brexit had the potential to forge links between them and other exploited and historically racialized migrant groups. Finally, I wanted to find out simply whether the naturalization of their inferiority as 'migrants' played a role in their accepting of exploitative conditions.

When I was offered a PhD scholarship by the University of Glasgow in 2017, I was afforded the rare privilege of having money and time to explore these precise questions.[7] Following the work of others such as the Angry Workers group (2020), Seth Holmes (2013) and Barbara

Ehrenreich (2021 [2001]), I assumed work at a total of six precarious workplaces in and around Glasgow.[8] These included kitchens, factories and warehouses.[9] After formally concluding my research, and with my PhD funding running out, I accessed an Amazon warehouse and had the opportunity to explore one of the richest and most controversial companies in the world.[10]

These immersions were critical for developing the concept of the socialization of precarity. They enabled an in-depth exploration of precarious jobs, disturbing popular conceptions of 'skilled' and 'unskilled' labour and highlighting how these definitions – which directly determine conditions and remuneration – correspond to norms that disempower workers and migrants (Anderson 2013; Bauder 2006). The experience of actually performing the tasks that I was analysing helped me understand the roles of dignity and ability in forging our senses of self, even in the most exploitative conditions (Sennett and Cobb 1972). Paradoxically, one of the key elements that is missing from academic and social movement analyses are discussions of *pain* and *fatigue*. The issue of how we experience our bodies during work – and, in turn, how this experience is metabolized in our conception of ourselves – is central in developing my understanding of the socialization of precarity. Finally, the everyday aspect of working alongside other humans was perhaps the most important feature of this process: the jokes, the exasperated proclamations, the sighs expressed over a cigarette break, and the way that people carried themselves conveyed a universe of signals about how work and migration are individually negotiated in the contemporary neoliberal landscape.

From 2017 to 2021, I also interviewed other precariously employed migrant workers to ensure that their voices formed a central pillar of whatever analysis I would go on to write. I conducted twenty-one formal interviews – most of which figure in the subsequent pages – and hundreds of informal discussions across the UK.[11] Whether we were sharing a coffee in someone's living room or a pint in a noisy Glasgow pub bent over a portable recorder, it became apparent that people very consciously wanted to speak; they *wanted* to be heard. What always started with the intention of lasting about an hour would become a two- or three-hour conversation as they recounted their stories of work, migration, nostalgia and struggle, as well as their hopes and desires for the future. These exchanges revealed the ways that migrants experience their own identities as migrants in the UK. However, their most critical contribution was in helping me understand that no matter how deeply the socialization of precarity penetrates our senses of self, it cannot dispel our awareness of the fundamental inequalities that we are subject to.

This research was made possible because of my position as a migrant worker who was already familiar with the landscape of precarious employment. However, this precise position also limited my reach. Western labour markets push certain migrant groups into specific sectors, in a dynamic that reproduces itself. As a white man from Southern Europe, this meant that I generally found work in places that were largely staffed by migrants from Eastern and Southern Europe. The labour process in each workplace significantly impacts its ethnic composition. In Amazon, the workforce was diverse because of the high turnover and the very little need for in-depth communication between workers. However, precisely because Amazon represents the most isolating and intensive of the labour regimes that I accessed, it was where the fewest conversations could be had.

Similarly, because I was relying on various personal informal networks to interview migrant workers, most of the people I spoke to are white, status-secure European immigrants. This does not mean that they were not precarious or marginalized; everybody's working lives had resulted in adverse physical and mental impacts. Furthermore, particularly during the years before and immediately after Brexit, European workers were the most vilified social group of the UK's public sphere, regularly experiencing violence in the context of their daily lives. However, it does mean that most of the workers I interviewed did *not* experience the haunting effect of having migration controls – and the spectre of the detention centre – determining their every move in society and in work.[12] Also, even though their whiteness in the UK is perceived as a 'degenerate whiteness' (Anderson 2013: 45) similar to that of the Irish in the nineteenth century, it still affords them certain privileges – or a respite from certain attacks – that other migrant groups do not experience.

Despite the limits of my reach, I believe that the focus on these groups of workers is particularly useful for examining the socialization of precarity. As Bridget Anderson writes, status-secure European workers in the UK 'are a group where it is possible to examine migratory processes separately from immigration controls because, as EU nationals they are not subject to immigration controls' (2013: 82). Their experiences in precarious work are therefore connected to two factors: migration *as such* – the feeling of being foreign, of having left your land in search of something better, of attempting to negotiate the new landscape you find yourself in – and precarious work. One can only presume that, if the traumatic effects of racism and deportability are added to the equation, the debilitating effects of the socialization of precarity become even more potent.

Precarity and resistance

Migrant labour in the West takes place within a wider environment structured by neoliberal economic policies. It is therefore imperative to develop a foundational understanding of what the context looks like before delving into the more specific details of migrant labour. Inside a capitalist system that is based on the unequal access to resources between labour and capital, neoliberal policies introduced since the late 1970s have accentuated class inequality and disrupted the post-Second World War Western class-collaborationist infrastructure. Austerity policies, particularly intensified following the 2008 economic crisis, disproportionately affect minorities and those in the working class and lead to ever-increasing pressures to accept whatever work is available, irrespective of conditions or wages. In the sphere of work, these changes are most directly experienced as a rise in insecure and exploitative labour conditions.

The concept of 'precarity' has become increasingly used by theorists and social movements to describe these converging processes (Jørgensen 2016; Casas-Cortés 2014; Standing 2011).[13] The violent disruption of previous, Fordist labour regimes in the West, especially in the lower rungs of the job hierarchy, forms a central facet of the turn towards precarity. Many industrial occupations have closed, with capital moving to other parts of the world that offer cheaper production costs. They have been replaced by a proliferation of jobs in the service sector, including in hospitality, logistics and care. These changes are characterized by part-time, flexible, individualized contracts (as opposed to collective agreements), the outsourcing of employees and the stripping back of labour rights. As we shall see in chapter 3, precarious work is often complemented by the incorporation of performance monitoring technologies. These additions aggravate an already insecure contractual relation, as workers are ceaselessly compelled to overexert themselves for a limited number of jobs.

The rapid growth of employment agencies providing temporary labour to businesses is another exemplary feature of precarity. Agencies further fracture the already insecure capital–worker relation by supplying contingent, flexible labour that is largely deprived of the rights of a contracted worker; the worker is thus disposable and completely subordinate to the short-term 'needs of the business'. This flexibility is more important to employers than the cost of hiring an individual worker from an agency, as the business is completely absolved of most contractual obligations towards them. In 2005, employment agencies were employing 86% of all workers on temporary contracts in the UK (McKay and Markova 2010: 447). This increased following the economic crisis of 2008. The number of agencies operative in the UK saw a 46% increase in 2018 alone, with 39,329 separate companies registered since 1990 (Sonovate 2019). Reflecting years of government-abetted labour market dysregulation, the United States, Japan and the UK are the three largest markets for employment agencies in the world. In 2021, the sector generated more than $132 billion in the United States (World Employment Confederation 2023).

Precarity extends beyond the workplace, impacting every aspect of social life (Hardt and Negri 2017; Federici 2012). The erosion of previously secure class positions brought forth by the neoliberal restructuring of the economy has fractured the sense of solidarity and mutuality associated with stable class-based identities. It has also triggered – and been exacerbated by – a collapse of trade union power across the West. The individual becomes increasingly isolated in the face of social forces beyond their control. As economic polarization deepens, it is complemented by cultural narratives that demonize and further exclude those who already suffer most directly from the deleterious effects of that polarization, such as the working class. These mentalities of 'responsibilization' (Melossi 2008; Garland 2001) blame the poor for their poverty; they also partake in crafting and reproducing wider hegemonic narratives that compel those in disadvantaged positions to blame themselves. A social and cultural landscape is thus established where workers are compelled, both by structural and cultural pressures, to accept the first available jobs they can secure, while the wider weakening of class-based institutions and empowering narratives ensures that the conditions of these jobs are seldom challenged.

The objective experience of contractual and psychological precarity has become a rallying point for various social movements, and scholars and activists contend that the experiences of precarity can be used to connect, rather than divide, people across cultural backgrounds and classes. Marcel Paret and Shannon Gleeson (2016: 280) therefore argue that 'the central significance of the precarity concept lies in the way in which it connects the micro and the macro, situating experiences of insecurity and vulnerability within historically and geographically specific contexts'; the concept makes possible specific lines of analysis, and, consequently, illuminates new avenues for action.

Yet these new avenues generally remain to be found, and the rise of precarity both depends on, and worsens, the decline of the power that trade unions in the West previously had. This is most acutely illustrated by the collapse of trade union membership: indicatively, in the proportion of UK employees who were union members having fallen to 22.3% in 2022, the lowest on record; even more worryingly, almost 40% of members were above the age of fifty (Department for Business and Trade 2023). In the US, union membership stands at a meagre 10% (US Bureau of Labor Statistics 2023). Fundamentally premised on the Fordist model of a geographically proximate, tight-knit community that is securely employed in a single industry, trade unionist solidarity emanated from the already existing connections between neighbours and co-workers. With the current environment displaying the exact opposite features, workers have been disconnected from the instruments that had previously formed the foundations of their collective struggles. Furthermore, there is a discrepancy between job security, remuneration and union membership: people in more secure and higher-paid occupations are more likely to be members of unions, while in occupations that need representation the most unions are disproportionately absent.

The space for action and solidarity that has been vacated by trade unions and other class and community-based institutions has been largely turned over to charities, NGOs and state-associated remedial processes such as employment tribunals, whose aims and methods largely complement the modern capitalist structure. Their existence and operation mirror the wider proliferation of control throughout society, since they rely on the disempowerment of the groups they profess to help: at the same time that the welfare and penal systems place the individual in a series of conditional relationships relative to the State and fail to address the social, rather than individual, origins of poverty, these organizations come in to provide a form of relief that (1) does not challenge the foundations of the economic or social system, and (2) hinders the possibilities of autonomous community empowerment. Addressing social issues is reduced to a service provision, and humans are reduced to 'beneficiaries'. This description, rather than being confined to official NGOs and charities, also applies to the biggest trade unions, which have moved away from mutual organizing to a service-based approach geared towards individual representation. To this end, Natasha King (2016) draws the important distinction between solidarity and charity: charity presumes a hierarchy where one party 'gives aid' to the other, whereas solidarity foregrounds a non-hierarchical shared interest and involvement to resolve the issue at hand. The latter is thus the basis for shared, intersectional struggle, while the former is a by-product and extension of the consumer-oriented and depoliticized modern public sphere.

Alongside the erosion of class-based politicized identifications, another result of the hegemonic neoliberal culture is the linguistic erasure of the vocabularies of resistance and an almost all-encompassing absence of alternative imaginaries. Herbert Marcuse's (1991 [1964]) one-dimensional man becomes a generalized social reality: detached from their collective identities, excluded from representational organizations and denied the linguistic, cultural and institutional tools to imagine a different social order, the alienated individual succumbs, and by doing so participates in the reproduction of the ensemble of social structures that further atomize and alienate them. Mark Fisher's analysis of capitalist realism (2009) adds a contemporary dimension to these ideas by examining how the impoverishment alongside the fervent commercialization of popular culture has almost entirely exhausted people's capacities for imagining alternatives to the dominant social reality. When the resignation of the imagination is combined with objective insecurity, sustained labour mobilizations are rendered increasingly difficult, sporadic and unfocused.

Racism, xenophobia and the widespread 'culturalization' of politics that have emerged from the combination of institutionalized insecurity and the retreat from class identifications further impede the rise of sustained mass mobilizations. In the UK, this was most poignantly expressed through the politics surrounding the Brexit vote, with hostility to migration playing a crucial role in voters' decision to withdraw from the EU.[14] Indeed, direct attacks against EU-migrants increased significantly during the Brexit years (Rzepnikowska 2019). Satnam Virdee and Brendan McGeever (2018) thereby identify the Brexit process as combining an imperial, racist, nationalist sentiment with a desire to protect a normative conception of the 'English' nation from the assaults of globalization, thus drawing a clear connection between culture and economic anxiety. These pressures exploded again in 2024, with a wave of anti-immigration riots across the UK.

Similar trends are observable in the United States, with anti-migrant narratives being central components of Trump's campaigns (Milkman 2020). Around the world, these trends could be described as exemplary of 'misplaced alliances' (Mayo 2016) since they often involve groups of indigenous workers identifying more closely with far-right parties than with migrant workers, with whom they share an objective economic affinity. This is legislatively expressed by right-wing assaults on migrant rights, underpinned by a range of policies that aim to make it difficult for non-status-secure migrant workers to live and work.

As will be explored below, these policies result in pushing people to ever more insecure sectors of the labour market. (However, it has to be noted that not all migrants are inserted in the worst jobs: for example, migrants from outside the EU make 18% of the total workers in the science, research, engineering and technology sectors [Fernández-Reino and Brindle 2024].) What differentiates migrants from the British white working class are their increased likelihood to be placed in precarious employment in combination with additional barriers such as social exclusion, deskilling, language difficulties, lack of access to support and a migration status in an increasingly hostile environment.

To summarize, migrant workers inhabit a Britain that is characterized by: (1) deepening class inequality; (2) the increasing penetration of precarity in all aspects of social existence; (3) the erosion of class-centred identities and unions; and (4) the rise and consolidation of immigrant-blaming xenophobic narratives. These are important contextual points that must underpin any serious analysis of migrant labour and collective resistance to precarity. Contrary to simplistic, underdeveloped understandings of migrant labour being used by elites to destroy labour rights and weaken unions, the reality is that migrants enter a situation that is *already* entirely saturated by poor conditions and weak unions.

Borders in the social body

The politics of migrant labour in the UK are intimately connected to wider global processes of uneven development rooted in colonial and post-colonial relations. The labour requirements of specific economic sectors that were previously filled by a reliance on migration from the former colonies were, until 2021, largely succeeded by the migration of EU workers. As we shall see in the next chapter, this is a migration that is itself spurred by a variety of push-factors in their countries of origin such as debt crises, austerity and lack of opportunity. Predictably, the UK is already facing acute labour shortages as a result of Brexit, and its labour requirements are precisely the reason that, despite the government's overt hostility to migration, more than 5.3 million EU citizens had been granted status to remain in the country as of March 2022 (Migration Observatory 2022).

Countries and businesses around the world, including the UK, depend on migration and directly factor it into their economic planning (Milkman 2020; Boswell and Geddes 2011). The politics of migration control therefore emerge as fundamental operations of national states and supra-national entities such as the European Union. Jane Hardy (2014: 148–9) encapsulates the relations between states and the world market by writing that they 'are mutually constitutive in a process whereby nation-states are constrained and shaped by the parameters of the accumulation process in the global economy, but at the same time the strategies of states and capital reshape the accumulation processes in the global economy and forge a new set of parameters and dynamics'.

While many scholars as well as Marxist social movements have argued that globalization and financialization have led to the retreat of the State's power, other voices instead maintain that the State continues to perform a fundamental regulative and productive role in the workings of the capitalist economy (Lazzarato 2015; Anderson et al. 2011). In tracing the development of the intrinsic logics and ideas of neoliberalism,

Michel Foucault would argue that competition – the basic tenet of neoliberal theory – rather than being perceived by neoliberals as a 'natural' state of affairs, above and beyond human control and therefore infallible, is instead thought of as constantly under attack and necessitating protection. The State's role, therefore, becomes one of attentively regulating all aspects of society that might impede competitive market activity. In order to allow competition to thrive, it is impelled to manage all non-economic spontaneity, leading to a situation of deep social control: 'neo-liberalism should not therefore be identified with laissez-faire, but rather with permanent vigilance, activity, and intervention' (Foucault 2010: 132). This process has increasingly come to involve the management and repression of everything considered detrimental to profitability, with a resulting rise in the penalization and control of poor and immigrant populations in the West (Melossi 2008).

Bridget Anderson has done extensive work (2013, 2010) on how the State, and specifically its operations vis-a-vis territorial and imagined borders, *produces* migrant vulnerability and precarity. She writes that 'through the creation of categories of entrant, the imposition of employment relations and the construction of institutionalized uncertainty, immigration controls work to form types of labour with particular relations to employers and to labour markets' (2010: 301). For example, most worker visas in the UK depend on the worker having secured a job prior to entry and are revoked once the job is lost or completed. As a result, non-status-secure migrant workers are directly dependent on their employer's goodwill and might be reluctant to unionize or otherwise claim better conditions. Citizenship and migration restrictions could therefore be seen as ways of regulating the labour market: not only do they provide a clear way of establishing a primary differentiation between 'included' and 'excluded', but they afford the possibility of further qualifying this initial division and thereby distributing different ethnicities according to the requirements of labour markets and popular stereotypes. Simultaneously, the spectacle of detention and deportation, the ultimate expression of the State's power over migrants, is constantly operative in the background and imbues every moment with fear of expulsion. This experience is increasingly beginning to apply to previously status-secure EU migrants.

The State's functions of bordering not only create migrant vulnerability through their direct operations, they also contribute to migrant oppression through their ideological articulations. Since ideas of the State are inherently tied to a particular normative conception of the 'people', which includes an imagined conception of their common values, mentalities and aspirations, citizenship becomes associated with inclusion and shared participation in this ideological mix. Concurrently, these operations produce bodies that are codified as 'foreign', with all the added weight that 'foreignness' carries in a structurally racist society. This means that, even if a migrant succeeds in jumping through the hoops required for a nominal acceptance in the 'community of value', they 'must endlessly prove themselves, marking borders, particularly of course by decrying each other to prove that they have the right values' (Anderson 2013: 6). Bordering is therefore reproduced in the very interactions and self-awareness of the people it regulates, and whose oppressions it structures.

Precarious migrant work in the UK

Despite the fluctuations induced by Brexit, migrants continue to staff some of the most exploitative, symbolically stigmatized and arduous jobs of the UK's labour market. These occupations are often characterized by intense pressure to perform at the highest level of one's capacity, by instability and the constant, overhanging threat of dismissal.

The latest statistics available at the time of writing covered the period until the end of 2022, where migrant workers made up nearly a fifth of the UK's total working population and figured prominently in the most precarious sectors of the labour market.[15] Indicatively, migrants made up 15% of the construction sector, 22% of the health and care sector, 27% of the hospitality sector, 18% of the retail sector and 27% of the transport and storage sector. While Brexit had the impact of reducing new migration to the UK from the EU, a substantial portion of EU workers still staff the most precarious occupations of Britain's economy. Paradoxically, the new points-based system that followed Brexit did not reduce migration levels in total, with the majority of visas being issued for workers in care. Out of all migrant workers, those from the Czech Republic, Estonia, Hungary, Latvia, Lithuania, Poland, Slovakia, Slovenia (referred to as EU8 countries) and Bulgaria and Romania (referred to as EU2 countries) were found to be overconcentrated in the lowest positions of the labour market; they also had the lowest median earnings of all ethnic groups in the UK, and worked the longest hours. Illustrating the reality of the non-recognition of qualifications, *all* migrant groups were more likely than the British-born to work in jobs that they were overqualified for. This is particularly true for workers from EU8 and EU2 countries, Pakistan and Southeast Asia and Sub-Saharan Africa. Migrant workers are also significantly less likely to join unions: only 16.2% were members of unions, as opposed to 25% of the UK-born.[16] Furthermore, it is important to note that these data only refer to workers in formal or declared work; the vast numbers of migrant workers in informal or undeclared employment – where there is even less protection and precarity is experienced at its most forceful iterations – are missing.

Due to a combination of factors stemming from the immigrant experience, such as deskilling, legal status, lack of familiarity with the new labour market they find themselves in, language barriers, and an initial need to access quick jobs to establish themselves in the host society, migrants provide a supply of easily exploitable labour (Bauder 2006; Holgate 2005). As we shall see in the next chapter, the choice to migrate frequently entails the acceptance of a trade-off whereby one exchanges one's higher social status in one's home country in favour of a higher salary in the country of destination. This exchange is often conceived of as a temporary and merely instrumental one: many migrants enter the host society with an economistic outlook, aiming to collect as much money as they can before returning home (Sayad 2004; Piore 1979). Not expecting to stay for long, they may tolerate substandard labour conditions and employ a 'dual frame of reference' whereby they compare their current occupation favourably in relation to the objectively worse economic situation that they emigrated from.

In his seminal study of migrant labour, Michael Piore (1979: 53) argues that 'from the perspective of the migrant, the work is essentially asocial: It is purely a means to an end. In this sense, the migrant is initially a true economic man, probably the closest thing in real life to the *Homo economicus* of economic theory [author's italics].' While this argument does not currently apply to as many migrant workers as it did in the late 1970s, the need to make quick money to establish themselves is an important factor in the considerations of many migrants.

Operating in a tight and competitive market, employers deeply rely on this stable supply of precarious, flexible and obedient labour. This becomes even more urgent in sectors that experience high turnover rates. The most important consideration for employers hiring migrant workers is flexibility, allowing them to direct their labour supply through uncomplicated hire-and-fire practices in tune with changes in production, unconstrained by unions. Indeed, recruitment agencies are frequently the first organizations through which migrants become introduced to the UK labour market, thereby also directing their distribution. Upon interviewing agency recruiters, David McCollum and Allan Findlay (2015: 439) found that employers have a conscious understanding of how intimately their business depends on employing migrants; they conclude that labour markets and migrant labour are connected by a mutually reinforcing relationship where 'flexible labour markets create a structural demand for migrant labour and a ready supply of migrant labour allows flexible labour markets to flourish'.

In their important book *Who Needs Migrant Workers?*, Martin Ruhs and Bridget Anderson therefore argue that, in contrast to dominant narratives about migration, it is not migrant workers who fill vacancies undesired by the locals; rather, the real reason 'typically underlying employers' calls for migrants to help fill vacancies is that the demand for labour exceeds supply *at the prevailing wages and employment conditions* [authors' italics]' (2010: 4). Indeed, a sizeable proportion of the business community vocally supported, and still supports, the free movement of labour enabled by the European Union's internal border policies precisely because of the flexibility offered by newly arrived precarious immigrants (Greene 2019; Boswell and Geddes 2011). Post-Brexit, and conscious of the economy's deep dependence on migrant labour, the UK government allowed EU citizens already in the UK to apply for settled status, guaranteeing their right to remain. While migration rates have fallen after Brexit and COVID, this dependence on migrant labour has remained unaltered.

The distribution of migrants within an already precarious labour market is heavily gendered and further structured by the interplay of essentialist stereotypes that attach certain characteristics to specific migrant groups (Anderson 2013; Acker, 2006; Bauder 2006; Miles 1982).[17] As previously held stereotypes converge and interact with wider structural forces to concentrate a population within a given sector or range of jobs, the jobs themselves become associated with the groups performing them.

INTRODUCTION

Essentialization thus functions in ways that ultimately close off significant segments of the labour market while opening others up, *ultimately confining migrants to specific occupations without the requirement for overt legal interference*. However, rather than essentialist notions simply functioning to foreclose access to migrants, Bridget Anderson (2013) argues that corporeal signifiers of difference may in fact be specifically required in certain markets such as in hospitality services, which rely on selling a fetishized 'experience' of difference (as, for example, do many restaurants that employ particular migrant groups). These combinations of culture and the economy craft a popular conception of the migrant as *essentially, intrinsically* a worker, as opposed to a complete human being (Bauder 2006; Balibar and Wallerstein 1991). This is most clearly reflected in the binary that I call 'The Thief and the Cash Cow':[18] in dominant narratives, migrants are either presented as thieves or as 'good for the economy'. In both cases, they are dehumanized and solely viewed on the basis of their perceived capacities to feed the cogs of Britain's precarious labour market.

The ensuing pages will explore how these threads of geopolitical relations, precarity, cultural representations and migration are experienced in the daily life of precarious labour, and how these experiences contribute to crafting the socialization of precarity. The next chapter starts – as all migratory journeys do – from the homeland, surveying the geopolitical conditions that underpin migration from impoverished to wealthy nations and migrants' first steps in their new societies. Chapter 2 focuses on the plethora of ways that precarity is manifested in the UK labour market, foregrounding the roles that labour insecurity, overexertion and alienation play in structuring migrants' experiences. Chapter 3 then investigates how precarious labour socializes workers – it is here where the socialization of precarity is fully defined and explored. Departing from an understanding of how precarious conditions infect the mind and the body, chapter 4 explores what this means in terms of how migrant workers *perceive themselves* as migrants, workers, and migrant workers. Chapter 5 relates these threads to how migrant workers experience solidarity and resistance inside a wider environment of proliferating precarity and the absence of unions from their workplaces and communities.

This book concludes with a discussion of what the socialization of precarity means in terms of organizing alongside migrants and other precarious groups. The socialization of precarity is a concept that allows us to understand the ways in which wider social structures such as the economy and migration regimes interact with subjective factors like workers' hopes, dreams and senses of self, in an amalgamation that is forged through the daily experience of precarious employment. The implications of this understanding also point to ways that we could fight against precarity by foregrounding alternative horizons and alliances, deeply embedded in the daily lives of the groups we are organizing with.

After understanding, we must act. And through acting, we will understand.

1
'We Were Always Migrants'

Every voyage has a beginning, a spark, a set of contextualizing elements; without these factors, a migrant's subsequent journey becomes incomprehensible. While it is common to discuss migration and migrants' experiences from the perspective of the difficulties they face once their journey begins (and here, we may think of factors ranging from checkpoints and deaths in border crossing zones to more 'benign' difficulties such as language barriers), we must also understand the conditions from which they left. A key argument of this book is that migrant workers are not empty vessels that 'become' subjects[1] only after the act of migration: their lives and the structures within which they grew up before migrating are important in explaining their motives and mentalities in the new society. What myths do migrants carry with them? How do they imagine their lives in their country of destination? Why do so many people accept working in worse conditions than they are qualified for? Why does one of the most exploited segments of the workforce not rebel? Finally, are migrant workers simply responding to the situation they find themselves in, or do they somehow partake in reproducing it?

Most people do not *want* to migrate. Rather, their journey begins spurred by what they believe will be achieved *through* the act of migration. The act itself, a violent, sad separation from family, loved ones and settings steeped with memories, is rarely joyous. For days, weeks or months, the migrant prepares their departure. The final weeks are frenetic, and they begin to understand – whether they are fully aware of it is always a mystery – that their life has already been split between two worlds (Sayad 2004). Still in *their* city, they are dealing with the logistics of both departure and arrival. Today, they are searching for accommodation in a place they have never even seen, in streets they have never walked; a few hours later, they are sharing some last drinks with their friends, with the weight of their imminent disappearance already felt, but not mentioned, by everyone at the table. In these discussions, there is hope, but the dominant sensation is that of loss. It is a feeling that expands and saturates, until, by the time the migrant leaves, they are already long gone; a memory amongst memories, a symbol that grows stronger as it fades. At some point, the hugs have been given, the promises of return exchanged, the possibilities of delay exhausted; there is nothing else to do but turn around, board the bus, enter airport security, leave. As you walk away, you feel your family's eyes touching the back of your coat. You do not stop; you do not return. And it is this moment, this pivotal decision to proceed despite the feeling that you are tearing yourself away from everything that makes you *you*, that underpins the entire complex of emotions and dispositions that a migrant will carry with them from now on. This moment is powerful enough to deeply impact the ways in which we think about ourselves.

As I am writing these lines, I am re-experiencing my own migration, in 2011. A heated discussion about the future with a lover under the covers; my mother, struggling to process my departure; trips to the Athens flea market, scrambling to find cheap, 'suitable' clothes for the British winter; a final, extremely drunken outing with faces from my youth, until my best friend drove me to the airport in the early morning hours; the strong hug, the goodbye. Despite having studied migration for almost eight years, it is only now that I am realizing the enormous weight of this final departure moment. And I am wondering why I didn't ask my interview participants – the people who we will meet in the subsequent pages – to talk to me about it. How did they experience the piercing feeling of their loved ones' eyes on their backs? Did they want to turn back, or did they proudly proceed? Did they leave intending to return, or out of a desire to escape? In the next pages of this chapter, you will read about what they felt, what they thought, before the actual act of migration and immediately after. But this specific interregnum, the gap between two realities, the precise flash when one literally *becomes* a migrant, when the past is closing and the future is a gaping, incomprehensible struggle, has been missed. Experiencing the resurgence of so many buried sentiments, I think I know why I neglected to ask: this moment is a birth. It is painful, dreadful, and hopeful; it is a change without a direction, as you do not know what you will be confronted with. You have not *become* yet; or more specifically, you have become a migrant – but right now that only means that you are no longer who you were. Once you arrive at your destination, the rebuilding process begins. But do you remember your birth?

Development, underdevelopment and migration

While migration is one of humanity's most ancient practices, in the last centuries it has been inextricably linked to the long shadows of colonialism and imperialism. These legacies still impact how migration is lived in our current epoch. Far from delivering on promises of prosperity, capitalist development has worsened inequalities between and within nations. In relations of unequal exchange between countries, a variety of interrelated processes combine to extract funds, resources and labour power from one country and transfer them to the other (Rodney 2018 [1976]). Recent years have seen the hierarchy of global and national spaces become more complex (Mezzadra and Neilson 2013), but traditional circuits of labour and capital remain powerful. These unequal exchanges lead to imbalances between 'developed' and less developed economies, and to masses of workers ready to migrate between them. Despite the wealthier nations' official anti-migrant proclamations, these migratory patterns suit the ruling classes; they provide cheap, flexible and exploitable labour for their businesses, while at the same time creating an 'Other' against which the passions of the electorate can be rallied whenever there is a crisis.

These migrations frequently follow blueprints established by previous colonial relations. An observer will notice that a large portion of the populations that are classified as 'foreign' in countries such as France, the UK, Portugal and Spain tend to originate from countries that were once colonized by these powers. Always hungry for cheap labour, the ex-colonizers have established a variety of deals and pathways with their former colonies to facilitate migration between them. As Abdelmalek Sayad has shown in his seminal study *The Suffering of the Migrant* (2004), moving to their old colonizer makes a degree of sense for migrant workers because of a relative lack of linguistic and cultural barriers, as well as the potential existence of familial networks that they can rely on for support. This attraction is further complemented by the long-term effects of colonial ideology that foster a representation of the colonial metropole as a symbolically and materially privileged space. The needs of the 'host' nation for cheap labour, therefore, interact with the needs of workers in impoverished nations, who choose (is it really a choice?) to migrate for better prospects and wages.

The experiences of migrant groups are therefore determined by an interplay of both the demands of British capitalism and an imperial ideology of racial difference and superiority that enabled and justified their exploitation and socio-political marginalization (Miles and Brown 2003). In the early 1900s, minorities in the UK consisted mainly of West Indian, Caribbean, Asian and Irish populations, all of which arrived through the networks fostered by Britain's expansive imperial activities (Ramdin 2017; Virdee 2014). Alongside these groups, a sizeable number of Jewish workers came to the UK, fleeing persecution from other parts of Europe (Rocker 2005). Migrants were swiftly inserted in those occupations that demanded workers or were otherwise kept as a reserve army of labour until demand rose again (Tabili 1994). Mezzadra and Neilson's (2013) concept of 'differential inclusion' is important here, as they argue that, in contrast to theories that argue that migrants are excluded from social participation, what in fact occurs is the meticulous management, through legislation and employment practices, of the precise form and function that their inclusion assumes. That is, cultural, political and economic factors combine to render migrants exploitable and collectively produce regimes whereby their inclusion is regulated and directed towards servicing the labour requirements of the host society.

Similarly, Bridget Anderson (2013, 2010) has argued that border controls such as visa restrictions do not simply prohibit workers from working; rather, they render them more precarious and exploitable. As Hsiao-Hung Pai (2008) has shown in her important explorations of the experiences of undocumented Chinese workers in the UK, when one needs to work, there exists a vast parallel economy that will readily exploit their necessity. Status restrictions do not prevent that worker from working; they simply mean that they are pushed to a darker area of the economy, where they are more vulnerable to intense exploitation. The concept of 'differential inclusion' is thus important in clarifying the ways in which various structural and juridical elements combine to produce exploitable, precarious migrant workers.

Britain has a long history of utilizing such forms of 'differential inclusion'. For example, a sizeable wave of Irish migrants arrived at the peak of the Industrial Revolution to fill the ever-expanding demands of a developing capitalism (Virdee 2014). Black seafarers from the Caribbean and the West Indies, travelling across the empire, gradually began to settle in the nineteenth century around ports and docks in the UK – joining the already established Black communities centred around London – and became part of a growing Black population that included students and other professionals (Ramdin 2017). A wave of pogroms against Jews across Europe led to a significant influx of hungry, poor and readily exploitable Jewish immigrants in the late nineteenth to early twentieth centuries, most of whom immediately contributed to the burgeoning British textile industry in cities such as London, Manchester and Leeds (Virdee 2014; Rocker 2005). Similarly, as British workers moved away from heavy manufacturing into more service-oriented occupations in the mid-twentieth century, the Attlee administration actively encouraged migration from Europe and the former colonies, including that of 125,000 West Indians and 55,000 Indians and Pakistanis who were brought to Britain in order to fill the vacated posts (Virdee 2014: 100). The 1950s also saw an increase in West Indian migration to the UK as individuals and families utilized their right of free entry as British subjects (Ramdin 2017). Throughout these developments, migrant groups were vilified, ostracized, controlled and regimented, *at the same time* as they were deemed necessary for servicing the demands of the British capitalist machine. The endurance of these legacies can be confirmed when one looks at the most recent discussions around migration and Brexit.

Colonialism and imperialism are not the only factors that trigger, and sustain, migration from underdeveloped to developed nations. A key mechanism that maintains the development of the dominant nations and enforces the underdevelopment of the dominated ones is debt, managed through international institutions such as the International Monetary Fund (IMF) with the complicity of national governments (Harvey 2005). Institutions like the IMF and the European Central Bank have imposed a range of policies on countries that are directly responsible for triggering migration. For example, Central and Eastern European countries that entered the EU experienced an array of conditions imposed on them by way of structural adjustment programmes following the collapse of communism in the 1990s and subsequent exploitative accession requirements, ultimately fostering insecure working and living conditions (Samaluk 2016; Hardy 2014).

The term 'structural adjustment programmes' refers to a series of demands that organizations such as the IMF impose on countries whose debt is deemed unsustainable, as a condition for loans to allow them to stave off bankruptcy. Beyond debt, similar 'adjustments' can also be imposed as a condition for a country to be able to access other benefits, such as trade deals – which also create networks for the circulation of specifically 'skilled' labour – or EU membership. These usually involve commitments to liberalize the market (such as easing restrictions on trade, reducing public spending on areas such as health, education and welfare, decreasing wages and curtailing employment protections), which almost inevitably lead to an intensification of poverty for the majority of workers. Instead of being directed towards servicing society's needs, any surplus generated by the country's economy is now directed towards debt repayment; however, exorbitant interest rates mean that the debt can never be repaid. It becomes a stranglehold on the economy, preventing even progressive governments from implementing the policies needed to exit the spiral of underdevelopment. At the same time, market liberalization opens the country even more to foreign capital; as wages are falling, unemployment is rising and workers are compelled to work ever harder for less, a significant amount of capital produced in the indebted, 'underdeveloped' nation is transferred to the wealthier countries. Soon, this capital is accompanied by humans, who migrate in search of better wages, employment conditions and life opportunities.

For Southern Europe, this process was exemplified in the aftermath of the economic crisis of 2008, where intense structural adjustment and austerity measures were imposed on virtually every European country. The conditions imposed on countries such as the PIIGS (a term referring to Portugal, Ireland, Italy, Greece and Spain) caused an explosion of unemployment while, at the same time, preventing any future substantial development from taking place since large proportions of countries' surpluses were directed towards debt repayment (Lapavitsas 2012). Within the space of a few years, the PIIGS witnessed a sharp rise in unemployment – in some cases reaching above 30% – while GDP contracted, prices rose, rents became unaffordable and public infrastructures such as schools and hospitals decayed. These developments forced hundreds of thousands of workers to migrate to countries such as the UK. I was one of them.

Beyond analysing the ways that material conditions trigger migration, it is important to understand how they impact workers' perceptions of emigration. These neoliberal and neocolonial structural changes have been accompanied by corresponding ideological projects that symbolically construct the local working classes as under-developed and under-civilized, in contrast with the societies of core European economies that are perceived as more 'modern' and 'European'. These are similar to the myths around British, French or Spanish cultural supremacy and 'civility' that dominated their colonies. The underdevelopment one experiences and has grown up in has become naturalized: rather than being viewed as the result of a *process* of underdevelopment that results from unequal geopolitical and economic relations, it becomes perceived as a product of the nation's 'backwardness', 'corruption' or 'inefficiency'. In contrast, even if one does not believe in the myths of a developed nation's cultural superiority, it might still be viewed as a place that offers more stability, 'discipline' and 'rule of law'. Ideas, cultures, stereotypes and imaginaries all combine with concrete geopolitical relations to create dreams of migrating.

As people migrate and become established, networks are formed: the younger brother follows the older brother, the nephew follows the uncle, leading to the emergence of migrant communities. In some cases, emigration can become a fundamental aspect of the national culture (Sayad 2004); in various countries around the world, from Mexico to Poland to the Philippines, it is widely expected that a significant portion of the younger workforce will work in other countries. On the other side of the equation, receiving countries such as the UK actively structure their economies expecting migration to address specific needs in specific sectors (Boswell and Geddes 2011). These combinations of structural and cultural factors, present in varying degrees across the world, spanning old colonial networks and newer, neoliberal assemblages, continue to sustain migration from 'underdeveloped' to 'developed' economies.

Such geopolitical relations result in a constant transfer of resources that include people and their labour power. This process is accentuated by national debt, the decimation of the welfare state, the loss of jobs and the proliferation of unemployment, and the wider lack of hope that eventually takes root. When hope is lost, people's labour power, their capacity to work, becomes the latest export in the cycle of unequal exchange: it will be used to create ever more profits for companies in the receiving countries, while paying taxes and supporting the wider social fabric of those countries. In the meantime, their countries of origin are progressively deprived of the human and technical contributions that could be used to re-balance the scales, were the local authorities willing to do so. Berger and Mohr (2010: 72) write that 'migration involves the transfer of a valuable economic resource – human labour – from the poor to the rich countries'. Most importantly, however, it involves the transfer of the unquantifiable raw materials of human hope, fantasy and desire – qualities that are strong enough to maintain one's persistence and willingness to work even in the most adverse conditions.

'We were always migrants'

We are in the dusty, expansive second floor of a factory that manufactures large commercial radiators and other appliances near Glasgow. The business has seen better days, as evidenced by its collection of seldom operated machinery or by the vast emptiness of the third floor, which is no longer in use. Nevertheless, the company continues to produce at a rate that requires at least fifteen shop floor workers. Most of them are Polish (while the management is exclusively white Scottish) and have been made permanent after initially being sent there by an employment agency.

I have just arrived on a zero-hours agency contract. After having a coffee with James, the white Scottish manager, and quickly being given to sign a series of documents confirming my attendance of a health and training session that never happened, I am now being mentored by Kris.[2] He is an energetic, tall Polish man who is taking great care to make sure I learn the job. We are at the first stage of the labour process: we must construct the radiator's core. A worker operates on a table upon which this central, 'core' part of the radiator is fixed. It consists of thin sleeves of metal with a hole in the middle, which we delicately position next to each other. At eye level, the core kind of looks like a row of tunnels. Depending on the size of the radiator (and how many tubes go through the core), the number of tunnels increases. Our section is lined with six such tables of different sizes: the larger the radiator, the larger the table and the more difficult the task. After constructing the core, we must put some long tubes through the holes in the middle of the sleeves. These are the tubes that fill up with hot water and make the radiator warm. The worker must put a 'sword' through the tube and thrust it inside the core, which is held firmly in place by the table. It is very easy to make a mistake here and tear the fragile metal sleeves, an infraction that usually results in the whole device being thrown away. After the core is completed and the tubes are inserted, the product moves to the next stages of the labour process.

This work is anything but 'unskilled', despite its designation as such by the employer, the agency and our position in official government statistics. Indeed, Kris was extremely proud of his proficiency at finishing the most complex, nimble constructions. It requires excellent arm–eye coordination, a combination of firmness and delicacy, acute attention to detail and above-average fitness to be able to stand up for so long while performing this repetitive thrusting motion. This is clearly the most difficult job in the factory, and, unsurprisingly, is the one where the most migrant workers are located; indeed, this is the only department where we are the vast majority, with only one Scottish worker working alongside us.

As we work relentlessly and I am trying to follow Kris, I am also trying to talk to him and understand how he perceives himself as a migrant and a worker. He is strict, confident and focused, but he has already indicated a degree of criticism underneath his professionalism: when James entered and gave everyone a couple of sweets, he told me 'Here, take one. This is what they pay us for our work.' This cynical statement betrayed a world of frustration at the discrepancy between his importance in the labour hierarchy (he was one of the most crucial components of the labour process, as only he and another Polish worker could be trusted with the most difficult radiators) and his low, minimum-wage remuneration. Despite his seniority, he was paid the same as I was, and much less than the few Scottish workers on the shop floor (who were also positioned in more 'skilled' departments). Nevertheless, he was proud of his work. At some point, we took a quick break, and he started telling me about his migration from Poland.

He pulled out his phone and started showing me pictures that I initially perceived as entirely random. 'Look at this', he would say and showed me a picture of a pothole; it was followed by a picture of a broken telephone booth, and a few pictures of closed, boarded up shops. I asked him what he was trying to show me. 'This is my city', he said. 'I left because there was nothing to hope for there.' He then told me that there were only three functional factories left in the region that he comes from, and that their pay is abhorrent. When I tried to continue the conversation, he suddenly told me to stop. 'These political topics' were making him 'angry'. We continued working, and I attempted to connect the dots between his experiences in the two countries. Despite being critically aware of the injustices he experienced as a low-paid worker in Scotland, Kris held on to this job through an incredibly proficient cultivation of skill; but this job was not important *in and of itself,* as his cynical remark about wages illustrates. Rather, the job symbolized an escape from the *nonexistence* of jobs and from the wider deprivation that characterized his home region.

As Lois, a hospitality worker who came to the UK from Greece to study journalism, told me during an interview, one's hopelessness regarding the situation in the country of origin is combined with one's hopes for the opportunities of the host society. Despite finding herself in intensely precarious occupations in the UK after her studies, she still believed that her life was preferable to what it would have been if she had returned home. Most importantly, she contrasted the possibility of being 'autonomous' with the lack of freedom that is associated with living in Greece.

> *Q:* Why did you not want to go back to Greece?
> *Lois:* Because Greece, in Greece we are experiencing a financial crisis at the moment and it is very difficult to find a job where it pays even like a good wage, a wage good enough to be able to sustain yourself and be autonomous. Here, even if you do a job that is a very precarious job, you may at least be autonomous. Have your own house and pay a rent. And also, there were other factors as well; I had my partner, I wanted to try and gain experience in journalism before I go back to Greece, save some money, pitch some articles to some papers while working in other jobs. So, I was hoping to build up some profile as a journalist.
>
> *Lois, Greek woman, late 20s, hospitality/freelance journalist*

As the socioeconomic conditions that create and sustain migratory circuits become increasingly permanent and accepted as a part of daily life, a culture of emigration begins to establish itself as a feature of the home society's collective consciousness (Sayad 2004). Sayad has described this process in depth, in relation to the economic-migratory chain connecting France and its former colony of Algeria. As the first generation of emigrants communicate their experiences in the new country to those back home, an entire mythology emerges; emigration becomes naturalized. As more people emigrate, networks of migrants are established in the destination countries, which significantly reduces the anxiety of moving to a new and strange society. Migrant groups gradually become associated with specific jobs and, in some cases, begin to be able to facilitate the entry of newcomers into these jobs (Vasey 2017; Bauder 2006). As the economic situation in the country of origin remains stagnant or worsens, emigration–immigration slowly develops its own dynamic and becomes inseparable from the myths and dominant narratives that circulate amongst the country's working- and middle-class populations. Those who can migrate, normally will. The economically well-off will go to study in the receiving country's universities, spurred on both by the lack of opportunities in their home country and by a culturally relativistic belief in the destination's country superiority; meanwhile, the working classes will migrate in search of better wages, better conditions, and the hopes of building something for themselves.

Q: Does Lithuania have a culture of migration?
Emma: Yeah, very big.
Q: Could you talk to me about that a little bit? How did you feel about migration, try to disentangle this concept.
Emma: Yeah, I feel like, when Lithuania was separated from the Soviet Union, it was chaos. [. . .] So I feel like that's when people started migrating to Western countries. I feel like in the 2000s a lot of people couldn't migrate to the UK because at that time Lithuania was not in the EU, it was really difficult. Same with me going to the USA now, I could have a visa and everything, but if they don't like me at the border, they send me back. And so, a lot of people started migrating to Spain, like my parents in this case. It was also a possibility to kind of avoid that chaos. And we would go to another

country, like my dad and mom, they started working in orange fields in Spain.

Q: And you expected to face difficulties with contracts and employment conditions?

Emma: Yeah. Not like I was aware of them, but it doesn't surprise me. I think it was because in Spain I was already an immigrant, and I could see that is the situation that my parents would face. They would like to find a job and everything. So I'm like 'OK, if I am going to be a migrant that is what will happen'.

Emma, Lithuanian woman, early 20s, hospitality

A similar perspective was offered by Viktor in the radiator factory mentioned above. Viktor is a Polish worker in his early 20s. While his whole attitude and demeanour make one think that he would be much more at home in one of Glasgow's famous underground raves than in a dark, cold factory, as soon as he starts to work he enters a zone of absolute focus, agility and productivity. He informs me that he had been a migrant worker since 'basically forever', having worked in many different European countries close to Poland on his school holidays. During these jobs, he was living in accommodation provided by labour agencies. This is indicative of a wider culture in migration-sending countries such as Poland, where labour migration is seen as something quite unspectacular and can even be incorporated into one's holidays. It is expected that precarious, exploitative and highly controlled conditions will prevail, and people grow up with this awareness. The decision to migrate already includes an understanding of the difficulties that one will face. In Emma's words, it is a brave, empowered act where one consciously inserts oneself into a precarious condition to 'avoid that chaos' of one's home country.

Migrating to avoid chaos is something that Greek workers can acutely relate to. While I was working in a Mediterranean restaurant as a kitchen porter in Glasgow, migration was a topic of daily conversation. The kitchen was staffed by mostly Albanian males, many of whom either were born or had lived in Greece, and with whom we could therefore converse in Greek. One of the people I became closest to was John, an Albanian male in his mid-20s who, like Kris, was energetic and skilful despite his almost incessant criticism of the job's many injustices. He mentored me during my first two shifts, and throughout my time there we would engage in many conversations over our limited breaks or on quiet periods. John had grown up in Athens after his family emigrated to Greece in the early 1990s. Following the collapse of the Greek economy after 2008, he took the decision to migrate again. One day, I mentioned my surprise at how many Greek Albanians live in Glasgow.

> *Q:* There is a lot of Albanians here in Glasgow, I've seen many of your compatriots.
> *John:* What can you do man, you can't live in Greece.
> *Q:* Yes, it's bad. I am just thinking about how difficult it is to migrate again.
> *John:* Fuck it, man. We were always migrants. *[Translation mine from Greek]*

This last sentence reveals both the depth of the culture of emigration and the conscious pain associated with it. Before the collapse of the Albanian communist regime, Albanians were already clandestinely crossing the borders to Greece. When the regime fell and the borders opened, many thousands migrated to Greece alongside their families. At that time, the Greek economy was booming, and the new workers quickly became manual labourers, while simultaneously experiencing intense xenophobia and exclusionary practices at all levels of Greek society. Just as the second generation of Greek Albanians had begun to establish itself in the new country, the economic crisis of 2008 and the ensuing social collapse led many to mobilize their extensive European networks in search of new employment (Gemi 2017).

The lyrics of Eni-D, an Albanian rapper and close friend of mine who grew up in Athens and recently moved to Hamburg, encapsulate what John was saying: 'my brothers are migrants, for a second time/ a cheap offering to the international market' (Eni-D 2016). There is an acute awareness amongst Albanians of the reality of the precarious migrant condition; yet, over time, it has become naturalized. In their seminal text on migration, *A Seventh Man*, Berger and Mohr (2010: 115) write that 'if he is aware of a current, a tide which is stronger than his own volition, he thinks of it, in an undifferentiated way, as Life [. . .] that is not to say that he will never resist, that he will accept every injustice. It is to say that tragedy is more real to him than explanations.' In the above quote, this tragedy was most visibly expressed by John's 'fuck it', encapsulating the combination of resignation and anger at the exploitation that many migrant workers experience.

However, I believe that this statement hides more than exasperation and pain: it is also an affirmation of endurance and strength. 'Fuck it' criticizes both the structural and geopolitical conditions that force Albanians to migrate, but it also dismisses the difficulties associated with migration by positing 'we' (Albanians) as a nation that has learnt to endure it. In this statement, Albanians are equated with migration. And they are also equated with having cultivated the necessary strength not only to survive it, but also to be able to dismiss it as just a fact of life. This mentality forms a critical component of the socialization of precarity: in an attempt to wrest a degree of agency and dignity from objectively exploitative and unjust conditions that span generations, one's understanding of migration has fused with one's ability to survive the difficulties that stem from this migrant condition. In essence, the socialization of precarity involves both a resigned awareness of structural domination, as well as an empowered decision to survive as best as one can within these confines. More importantly, for groups that have a history of migration such as the Albanians, Eastern Europeans, or the Algerians interviewed by Sayad (2004), this identity has begun to be fomented even *before* they literally migrate.

The first steps

Migration under conditions of neoliberalism involves more than just searching for jobs; for many newcomers – especially those with limited resources – the search for their first occupation is interwoven with the intense precarity of finding suitable, cheap accommodation and establishing some degree of stability in their new environment. Precarious jobs are often the first occupations accessed by migrant workers, and one of the reasons for this is precisely the need to make some quick money in order to be able to organize all the other components of one's livelihood. This objective need on the part of migrants neatly interacts with wider social and cultural processes, including the economic demands of employers, to create a vicious cycle that makes migrants particularly vulnerable to finding themselves at the lowest rungs of the labour market.

'WE WERE ALWAYS MIGRANTS'

Escaping the economic crisis in Greece, Takis arrived in Glasgow without any links to the city, essentially having to start from nothing. While staying in a hostel, he immediately began looking for a job, and found one in a Greek restaurant for which he was paid cash-in-hand. His first apartment was accessed through the ethnic and social network that was centred around the restaurant. Takis introduces two points that will figure prominently in subsequent discussions: the first concerns the role of ethnic networks in assisting immigrants to cover some basic immediate needs following migration, such as finding a job. The second is the fact that it is not uncommon for established migrants to exploit newcomers in a multitude of ways. The segment below illuminates some of the overlapping webs of informality, precarity and ethnicity that migrant workers might find themselves in.

Takis: I worked in a Greek restaurant for a month, and they found me a house. They said, 'we have a landlord, so you stay somewhere for a start, make some money, and then you can leave'. I wasn't fooled, I could tell there was some dirty business going on. They know that people will come, and they say, 'we will pass you on these guys so you can make money also'. And the room was horrible, very small, and the guy was completely untrustworthy. Once something was broken, he never used to come, until I started threatening him, 'you will either do something or I am leaving today'.

Q: Was he also Greek?

Takis: He was Algerian.

Q: Strange!

Takis: And then I am considered a racist!

Q: Alright. . . *[I can see that he is visibly uneasy]*. Come on man, what's the matter?

Takis: I feel that everyone who is here, other than the British, the other ethnicities that are here for years and have set themselves up nicely, they are all exploiters! I clearly consider them exploiters. They have all become landlords and things like that, they have all opened businesses and now, whoever comes that is new, they will drink his blood. That's it!

Takis, Greek male, mid-30s, hospitality
[translation mine from Greek]

As we shall see in the next chapters, affinity through shared experiences of migration is clearly not enough to disrupt class-based and other forms of exploitation. Hierarchies and exploitative practices exist between migrant groups, and the forces that push precarious populations towards degrees of informality may lead to even more informality, which may be exploited. Unsatisfied with the hours and prospects he was receiving, Takis decided to find a different job, and he found one handing out leaflets. Once again, this was arranged through informal channels, but this time the boss was Scottish.

> *Q:* Was this job under the table also?
>
> *Takis:* No, the payments came through the bank, but you know, basically it's black money, I didn't pay taxes, nothing, it was just a deposit in my name, nothing more. I worked in leaflets for one and a half years. I can say that, as a boss, the guy was straight with me. He didn't make you work overtime with less money, the payment was every Friday, I always received the money I was supposed to get. It was a hard job and essentially it really is a job for immigrants that don't know English.
>
> *Q:* And how much did you get paid?
>
> *Takis:* In the beginning it was very low, at £45 a day, so. . .
>
> *Q:* So, they paid you daily and not hourly?
>
> *Takis:* They paid you by thousands. Which was never a thousand. We handed out about 850, but it was £45 for the thousand. If it was a good area we finished in six hours; if it was a bad area, in eight.
>
> *Q:* Were your colleagues also immigrants?
>
> *Takis:* Yes, the main ones were Hungarians. I had spoken to the boss. Scottish people had also come, but these guys never came for work. They came to make a quick catch for one week, make £300 or something and disappear. I personally told the boss to not get Scottish people for the job. He told me 'I know, I know, I want to work with Scottish people, but they don't stay.' [. . .] I started with £45, then they became £50 and the last three months they had become £55. I can say that when they were £55, I was economically satisfied.
>
> *Q:* But you didn't have any of the rights of a contracted worker.

Takis: No, no, but as a first job, because this is what I consider to be my first job, it was good.

Takis, Greek male, mid-30s, hospitality
[translation mine from Greek]

Here, it is evident that Takis made various trade-offs. Firstly, he chose to be paid illegally, and frequently under the minimum wage: £45 for eight hours amounts to £5.60 an hour, which is less than the minimum wage was in 2012 (UK Government 2020). Secondly, his employment relation left no space for the defence of any labour rights. However, these risks were calculated as necessary in the context of getting a 'good first job'. This was because it was stable, 'the boss was straight', and the non-payment of tax meant that his final wage was close to what a contracted worker would make on minimum wage. As will be discussed in the following chapters, in informal occupations interpersonal relations replace contracted employment relations. Workers' relationships with their superiors therefore assume an overwhelming significance in forming their experiences, and many choose to stay in these jobs precisely for those relationships. Cognizant of the adverse conditions in various agencies, warehouses and similar precarious occupations, Takis chose to enter this type of employment and told me that he would have stayed there if it wasn't for the Scottish weather. Takis's example illustrates that precarious workers are not *only* fashioned through 'hard' migration controls such as visa schemes and their potential detention; precarity and illegal employment are also conditioned by the multiplicity of other borders and instances of differential inclusion (Mezzadra and Neilson 2013) that collectively structure labour markets, nurture these spaces of informality and direct workers in various ways towards them.

Other mechanisms such as the non-recognition of foreign credentials – determined by the interplay of professional associations, licensing bodies and other actors – also play a role in directing this segment of the workforce towards insecure and 'unskilled' labour.[3] Every sector has different restrictions on the recognition of foreign qualifications, and they fluctuate internally depending on where the migrant is from. For example, while getting a foreign nursing qualification recognized in the UK is a lengthy process, it becomes even harder for migrants from outside the EU. Such mechanisms of differentiation permeate the entire labour market, and they are not confined to highly prestigious jobs such as those in the medical or legal sectors – indicatively, foreign licences to operate forklift trucks are not recognized in the UK. This becomes particularly problematic in the lower rungs of the labour market because, for example, having a forklift licence is one of the few avenues for workers in warehouse/factory settings to increase their wages and approach a semblance of security. Bauder (2006: 43) sees the non-recognition of foreign credentials as a process that represents 'the collective labor market interests of nonmigrant professionals and solidifies the grip of nonmigrants on the primary segment of the labour market'; these restrictions, which do not reflect an objective assessment of competencies, further interact with a multitude of other cultural and social processes – such as the fact that specific groups of workers are perceived as *essentially* better 'suited' to certain sectors – that confine populations to specific jobs.

Importantly, the non-recognition of foreign credentials does not *exclusively* stem from legal mechanisms. Non-recognition can also refer to a process that is much more difficult to identify empirically, in that it is not reflected legally. Foreign qualifications might not be accepted by individual employers simply *because they are foreign*; what is frequently valued by employers is having 'local' working experience (Bauder 2006). The task, therefore, for a new migrant, frequently becomes one of amassing the 'local' working experience that would allow them to better establish themselves in the future.

According to statistics compiled by the Scottish Government (2019: 14), 65.5% of EU nationals and 62.3% of non-EU nationals with degrees were employed in 'high or medium-high skill level occupations (e.g., nurses, health associates, construction trade requiring a body of knowledge and above)', compared to 81.2% of British nationals. While there nevertheless exists significant scope for a rise up the occupational hierarchy through the acquisition of qualifications, migrant workers remain more prone to finding themselves at the bottom of the labour market *despite* their credentials. And, of course, accessing these qualifications requires an investment of capital that many migrant workers lack upon entry. The acquisition of precarious jobs, therefore, is frequently seen as a critical first step in allowing one to amass the funds necessary to acquire the qualifications that would allow a more stable income; beyond that, it is also seen as the first step to *eventually* pursuing work that is somewhat meaningful to them. This is the dream of migration at work.

The non-recognition of qualifications was mentioned by most of the workers that I interviewed during my research. Anna, a jurist from Guadeloupe, recounts a story that is exemplary of this wider phenomenon.

> *Anna:* I came because I lost my job as a lawyer and jurist in France. I wanted to go back to my island – Guadeloupe, in the Caribbean – so I thought about Miami because is not far away, but I thought about Donald Trump and he changed all the immigration laws. I didn't know what to do. I got a friend, we used to work with the Foreign Ministry in France, and he just told me 'maybe you can go to the UK', like a step, you know.
>
> *Q:* You are still an EU citizen in Guadeloupe. . .
>
> *Anna:* Absolutely, absolutely. I'm French. And he said, 'you can go to the UK and maybe find some work or an American company and then maybe they can send you to Canada or Miami or something'. Yeah, why not, but there is the Brexit. And I came here 10 years ago to visit Scotland, and I knew that they rejected the Brexit, so I just said, 'I'm going to Scotland, just for me, to try to maybe go back to uni.' Because I knew that I couldn't work as a lawyer or a counsel here.
>
> *Q:* Why?
>
> *Anna:* Because I have to go back to uni.
>
> *Q:* They don't accept your qualifications?
>
> *Anna:* Exactly, or even my experience. I can work. I can work as a legal counsel in a legal firm or something like that, but they just don't want me.
>
> *Q:* Why?
>
> *Anna:* Because I have more experience and qualifications than the people I have in front of me. I speak several languages.
>
> *Q:* So, they told you that you were overqualified?
>
> *Anna:* Yeah, all the time. And that they need Scottish degree or a Scottish Master in Law. And I was, 'but you know, I got international degrees, international Master, international law and human rights'. I can work here. Because I can work in England. Even I can

work in New York as a legal counsel, and go for the bar in New York, but not here.

Q: How did that make you feel? When you came here, and you found out that your qualifications will not get accepted?

Anna: I knew that, since I came here. I knew that it's. . . it would be difficult. But I didn't expect that it was so much difficult.

Q: How many interviews did you have?

Anna: Maybe 10. Just for law firms. For me, each interview is like an experience. You know? I discover new things and I improve myself all the time, so for me it was good.

Q: So, what did you do once you didn't get these jobs?

Anna: I started looking for a job, like bartender, things like that, because I needed money. Until I. . . I wanted to go back to uni, so I applied to do a Master with British and Scottish Law in Edinburgh, but there were kind of problems. They asked me, 'we can't say yes for your application for the moment because you need to go pass the TOEFL test'. And I was just, 'yeah but I'm here almost one year and a half, I speak English all the time'. And they said 'no, it's like that for everybody, because you are not a native English speaking'. And I was 'fair enough', but it was complicated because when they told me that, it was, maybe the 20th of November and they said you have until the 27th to give us the results of your test, and it wasn't possible *[laughs with exasperation]*. So yeah, and I just try to stay positive and say 'ok, I'm going to do things after, and the Brexit is not even here for the moment, so maybe is a good thing that I didn't go for that'. So, I don't know what to say. . . The more days come and things like that, the less I want to go back to uni. Because it costs money. And I don't find any job in my area. I'm just working in hospitality, it is the only, as an immigrant, is the only chance that people give me.

Anna, Guadeloupean (French) woman, late 30s, hospitality

Many workers also mentioned direct discrimination as a factor that confined them to the most precarious rungs of the labour hierarchy. Arjun, a Sikh worker in his 40s, is a qualified lawyer who at the time of the interview was working as a carer due to the non-recognition of his qualifications. In the various jobs that he had traversed in his time in the UK, he had also experienced the harsh reality of being repeatedly excluded from employment.

> *Arjun:* We wear the turban. We are identified from that. You don't have to say anything, people judge you. So, this happened to me, I worked in Sainsbury's *[a supermarket chain]* in Southampton for about two years on the tills. When the recruitment process began, I. . . there is a procedure. First you do the online test. If you pass the online test, then they call you to the interview. There are two tests in the interview, and if you go through that, you pass. I did online test and I scored the highest, so I got called for an interview. I applied for the customer service job, they didn't select me. I know my answers were correct. I didn't have a job, so I applied second time. Second time also didn't select me. I applied part-time. Not selected. I applied full time. Not selected. At the fifth time, I got the manager who was in the first interview. So I said 'I am not going to give you the test. Just tell me what was wrong in my first interview.' So he was quite ashamed. He told to me 'your first exam you scored 100%'.
>
> *Q:* He didn't even try to have an excuse?
>
> *Arjun:* Yes *[laughing]*, no excuse. And even the fifth time he didn't take my written exam. I without shame, I know the questions. Because I was taking them a fifth time *[laughing]*.
>
> *Arjun, Indian male, late 40s, care sector*

Apart from the non-recognition of qualifications and the multitude of other ways in which migrants are denied equal participation in the labour market, it could be argued that some migrant workers with qualifications are put in a position of performing an 'unskilled' identity in order to conform to perceived or real requirements held by employers. These performances are interwoven with the stereotypes and racializing processes that determine the position of migrant workers in the labour market (Miles 1982); 'enacting' deskilling thereby further accentuates the processes that confine migrant workers to precarious jobs. This is detrimental to the long-term interests of migrants, but acquiring a job without reproducing this performance could be difficult. Employers fully partake in crafting and reproducing this essentialization by connecting specific migrant groups with specific behaviours and thereby 'naturalizing' their suitability for certain jobs. In essence, migrants respond to the situation they find themselves in upon arrival; however, at a certain point their collective responses also contribute to structuring the socio-economic reality of the host country.

For example, in my first precarious job in the UK, in a factory that was assembling shelves for commercial giants such as Tesco and Superdrug, I remember being impressed by a Kurdish colleague's deep knowledge of theoretical economics and political philosophy. Once I asked him about it, he told me that he had three Master's degrees. His aptitude at the subjects we discussed left little reason to doubt this claim. When I naively enquired whether our superiors knew about his impressive CV, he laughed and told me that he had learnt to hide his qualifications. After being repeatedly rejected from jobs that he was qualified for, he realized that employers in 'unskilled' occupations would not give work to someone they deemed as 'overqualified'. After a decade in the UK and having given up on any hopes of pursuing his discipline, his focus was on making money to support his family: to do that, he had to become 'employable' in the only jobs that would accept him, and this involved hiding his degrees.

This act of deception is something that I also quickly learnt was the only way to gain access to precarious jobs. As soon as I graduated with a Bachelor's in 2014, I found that its inclusion in my CV prevented me from accessing the occupations that I could easily find before my graduation. I realized that in order to be employed in the specific sectors, looking the way that I look (visibly not British, with many people's first thoughts being that I come from Poland), I was expected to perform certain traits that corresponded to the established norms of the context. I started hiding my qualifications and any other experience that could disrupt the image that was required so employers would hire me: that of an 'unskilled' worker who is flexible, docile, and comfortable with intense physical labour. For example, I also hid employment experience that would be perceived as anomalous, such as working as a translator for the Greek Refugee Council or as a fundraising coordinator for the Campaign for Nuclear Disarmament. In short, I had to fit with the stereotypes of a 'migrant worker' that already existed in the dominant narratives of British culture. These were tactics that I employed in accessing every workplace that will be discussed in the subsequent chapters. This is not to say that migrants are *responsible* for being in precarious jobs – it would be more accurate to argue that the structure creates almost insuperable barriers that induces specific behaviours and survival mechanisms.

The dual frame of reference

The 'dual frame of reference' (Piore 1979) is an important concept in explaining how migrant workers rationalize and tolerate the new conditions that they are confronted with. It refers to an attitude prevalent in recently arrived migrant workers whereby one's current situation is judged based on understandings and criteria imported from their country of origin. In this sense, it corresponds to Sayad's (2004) assertion that a migrant is also an emigrant: this means that one's subjective transformation to conform with the standards and mentalities of the new country is a *process* rather than an instant development. The dual frame of reference may encompass a variety of factors: for example, one might be satisfied with receiving a higher wage in a precarious job, since it would be better than working in much worse conditions in the home country – this was clearly mentioned by Emma in relation to the 'chaos' in Lithuania. Or, one might have higher levels of trust in the totality of the British system, a belief that, in the new country, everything just works better (Samaluk 2016; Sayad 2004) – for example, this was clearly felt by Kris. Contrary to common narratives that paint migrant workers as cogs in the international machinery of capital, an understanding of motivations and existing ideas illuminates the exercise of agency at all levels of their – objectively – intensely exploitative trajectories in their new labour markets. When I first met John in my role as a kitchen porter, we briefly touched upon these issues:

Q: Are you also Greek?
John: Yes, I was baptized in Greece, in Athens.
Q: And what are you doing here?
John: What am I doing? For the money man, what are you doing here?
Q: The same! *[we laugh]* How do you find it over here?
John: The money, man. Fuck it. There's no sun here, there is no fun, but the money is very good. I can work for five years and make

about £100,000. You go back to Athens and you are set, you can establish a small business.

Q: What are you talking about, man? £100,000 in five years? How much do you intend to work, 80 hours a week?

John: As much as I need to man, you'll make £70,000 to £100,000.

Q: Yeah, but only if you don't do anything else.

John: What else is there to do? This is why you are here!

Q: So you are telling me that you want to put your head down and do nothing else, just work and sleep.

John: Yes, exactly. *[Translation mine from Greek]*

Here, the comparison between Greece and Scotland, and the meanings attached to each of these locations, is evident. Greece is seen as a country with sun and fun but lacking in opportunities. In contrast, in Scotland 'the money is very good', and John hopes to save up enough to become fully autonomous in the future. He wanted to work as much as possible and welcomed the gruelling 14.5-hour shifts that we were regularly assigned to. However, he didn't expect this to last forever: he had a clear plan in his mind to work as much as possible for five years, expecting to amass an objectively huge amount of money for someone who is only paid £8.21 an hour (the minimum wage at the time). Attesting to the dual frame of reference's power were his beliefs that in the UK, contrary to Greece, employers couldn't arbitrarily fire workers, and that Employment Tribunals were there to support the most vulnerable. He erroneously believed that it was possible to claim unfair dismissal after two months of employment, when in reality one needs to be continuously employed for two years. Furthermore, in his precarious, zero-hours contract, firing him would not be necessary; many employers decide to simply reduce workers' hours to the extent that they are forced to look for another job by themselves. This is a practice that is common amongst employers in both Greece and the UK, yet in John's mind it was something that he had left behind, alongside the sun and the fun.

Despite a desire for economic security and a relatively uninformed understanding of labour rights, John did not passively accept the hegemonic neoliberal social narratives that exist in the UK and had an acute perception of class and hierarchical inequalities. For example, in my last day at that workplace I bumped into him as I entered; he had just been told to leave because it was a quiet day. He told me that 'these fuckers don't care, but in December they will be begging us to do 14 and 16 hours'. He then went on to tell me that the only reason he kept this job is because he wanted to improve his English and gradually rise up the job hierarchy to become a chef.

This conversation encapsulates many of the theoretical points outlined above: the trade-offs many migrant workers make in accepting unfavourable working conditions in order to gradually move up the labour hierarchy, gain some stability and learn skills; the unrealistic expectations that are born out of a mythologized comparison of the home country's conditions to those of their new environment; the short-term inclination to work as much as possible in order to secure a livelihood in the long term; and, concurrently with all these, an acute awareness of the exploitation that permeates their working lives.

The last point is the most important component to begin understanding the socialization of precarity, which is an infinitely more complex process than a simple internalization and reproduction of the demands and ideas of the dominant economic system. Recall the *moment* of migration: the moment when one leaves behind everything that has formed the fabric of one's existence, one's loves, passions, memories. This is the moment where one *resolves to endure* for an unspecified amount of time, as long as one is moving towards a goal that makes migration tolerable. For migrant workers, significantly more so than for workers that have never been uprooted from their home environments, the socialization of precarity is slowly nurtured in the course of their lives leading up to that moment. It becomes stronger the more difficulties one experiences after emigration, *alone*. Absent an inspiring, unifying narrative that provides alternative modes of thinking, hoping and imagining, the dreams of the precarious migrant worker are circulating around this individualist survivalism. It is not that one does not understand that one is being exploited as a worker, as an immigrant, and as a migrant worker. It is that the migratory act in itself was conceived with that exploitation already in mind; surviving through it is simply the affirmation of the promise that was made when one *became* an immigrant. And, of course, this promise was not made autonomously, but in response to a plethora of geopolitical and cultural circumstances.

2
The Precarious Condition

It was around 6 a.m. when I left my flat in the Govanhill neighbourhood of Glasgow to catch two buses and commute to a nearby town. A few days earlier, in an online search for vacancies, I had encountered an agency advertising for 'flexi-workers'. Although I had been employed in similar jobs for years, I had never experienced this extreme extent of objectification; the introductory phone call lasted less than a minute, with the harsh, Eastern European woman at the other end of the line enquiring only about whether I had the right to work in the UK. As soon as she heard that I did, she gave me an address and a time for my 'induction'. This was clearly a job for workers that were not expected to make even the most basic of demands. Information is superfluous; the objective is money, regardless of how it is made. If you were privileged enough to expect details (as if you had the luxury of weighing your options) or if you expected the agency to make allowances for your schedule (as if you had something to do that was *more* important than finding a job), then you should have probably looked elsewhere. Accompanied by a sense of foreboding, I entered the dark dampness of the Glaswegian morning.

Around an hour later, I was in the cramped waiting room of an employment agency *that was attached* to a huge warehouse. Here, the connection between employment agencies and bosses was blatant; the agency was literally an extension of the employer, existing shamelessly to staff the workplace with precarious and exploitable workers. Around me were about thirty people from Scottish and migrant backgrounds. As far as I could pick up, the different languages and accents were discussing similar issues, either poking fun at the 'flexi-worker' description or enquiring about the job. The word 'fish' was repeatedly mentioned. The office door opened, and a striking and stern Eastern European woman came in and almost threw a wad of papers at the table in front of us. She curtly instructed us to complete 'the tests' after cursorily reading some Health and Safety documents. It was only at this point that I learnt that I would be working in a fish processing unit that supplied salmon products to one of the UK's biggest supermarket chains. We were given twenty minutes, more than enough for the simplistic information that we were required to learn. Indicatively, there were questions like 'why should foreign bodies be prevented from contaminating the food'; I had to stifle a sarcastic chuckle upon realizing that the correct response was that 'because if someone gets sick, the company might be fined'. Many workers did not speak English, and I helped a few with their papers. Apparently, we were now Health and Safety experts.

After completing the tests, those of us that passed were invited into the office for a two-minute interview, which basically consisted of the woman (who never introduced herself – she was our superior, and that was all that we needed to know) asking how long I had been in the UK and how many hours I was looking for. I was given a contract, which in itself contained various strange clauses such as one which stated that, by signing, we agreed to waive our rights as agency workers to receive the same pay as permanent staff after 12 weeks of employment; once again, these concerns were clearly perceived as a luxury for the workforces that this agency aimed to attract. We also apparently signed away our right to a fair disciplinary process, as we agreed that being *suspected* of bringing nuts – a food highly associated with allergies and the possibility of cross-contamination – on site would result in our instant dismissal. Once we were officially employed, our supervisor asked us to follow her to the warehouse for a tour. We had still not been given any concrete information as to what we would be doing.

She scanned her finger in the sensor that opened the main doors and escorted us to a large preparatory area, where we were instructed to put on some white protective overalls, replace our shoes with boots (black for the permanent staff, blue for the agency workers), and put a protective net around our hair. This large cupboard led to a disinfection chamber, where we were sprayed with vapours containing cleaning products. The whole experience felt dystopian, and I had to remind myself that this process was something that everybody in this workplace went through multiple times a day. Eventually, we followed our leader to the main part of the building, where she hurriedly walked us through the main parts of the salmon processing procedure. The demographics of the labour force were consistent with that of our group of newcomers: in an expansive warehouse, struggling between salmon carcasses, pools of blood, the overwhelming odour of fish, and loud machines, you could hear a colourful mix of Scottish, Slavic and Eastern European languages, Spanish and even Arabic. After a very quick tour – at no point of which were we given any further specifics as to what we would be doing – we were told to present ourselves the following day at 07:45.

The workplace is huge and chaotic. The first thing you notice is the stench of dead fish, which permeates everything. There are many different departments, each with 10 to 30 people in them. I would estimate that the factory has around 200 workers there at all times; it continues to operate in the night. The logo of the main supermarket to which the salmon is supplied can be seen everywhere, accompanied by a variety of signs screaming orders at the workforce and threatening serious consequences if mistakes are made.

All around me, the overhanging smell of dead fish. As you walk through the factory to go to your position, you pass through the various stages of production. Dead fish are hanging, like glistening rows of sharp knives. Dead fish are being chopped up. There are buckets with bits of fish that are discarded, there are fish remains on the floor. I was placed on a production line at the last stage of the process, where salmon fillets were packaged in plastic containers, ready to be shipped off. The job was extremely repetitive and was the worst production line I had ever been in, because, other than the constant standing, the mechanized movements, and the boredom, it was also very cold. Having to move in a very precise, constrained manner while simultaneously shivering entails a level of difficulty that I could not foresee. We were assigned tasks without any opportunity to have any understanding about what our schedule was. My colleagues told me that 'they don't talk or explain anything, they just expect you to get on with what they tell you'. This results in a feeling of disorientation which in turn fosters resignation and submission, since it reinforces the already prevalent feeling that you are nothing but a cog in the machine. The isolation of precarity is omnipresent: we don't talk, we don't exchange names. We simply put our heads down and try to think of something else.

There are immigrants from everywhere, but the majority are Polish. There doesn't seem to be a clear distinction in terms of gender roles, with both men and women assuming management and line-manager

'Fuck the Poles', etched into the bathroom of a fish product manufacturer on the South Side of Glasgow. Xenophobia is an everyday reality, quietly present in many precarious workplaces.

responsibilities and both being largely equally present in the various departments of the workplace. This is also true for the migrant/local distinction. In my production line I was working with two locals and the rest (about six people) were Polish. The line manager was a Polish woman with almost perfect English. The Scottish people were not treated preferentially, and were even in a social disadvantage since they didn't speak the language and couldn't understand what the Poles were saying amongst each other. In the toilet, a small graffiti revealed a strong current of underlying xenophobia.

A Scottish man in the production line was constantly making snide remarks about the language difference, visibly offended at his lack of privilege. However, this should also be seen through the prism of the experience of precarity and the fact that the local working class has lost significant power since the years of Thatcher; these feelings of anger and injustice can easily be harnessed by racist and xenophobic narratives in the absence of an inspiring social movement. In general, everyone is negatively equalized as cogs in the capitalist machine: everyone is interchangeable.

> Despite this negative equalization, it is clear that the sector relies on migrants rather than locals to maintain its staffing requirements. There is also a clear disparity between how hard and fast the Poles worked in comparison to the Scottish, as if it is a particular socialization and a sense of self that empowers them to work so fast and hard; there seems to be a complete acceptance and internalization of the 'good worker' stereotype. There was one woman who was working with me who was around 50, had two children, and was working in a way that was perceived to be disruptive by the Scottish workers, who were a lot more laid back. She kept on wanting to do everything as fast as possible. Being on a production line, this meant that everyone had to accommodate her speed. However, when we had a moment to speak, she was amicable and it became apparent that her rush only stemmed from the fear of losing her job and being unable to feed her children.
>
> There is only one half an hour break per eight-hour shift, and it is thrown at you arbitrarily and purely based on the requirements of production. We were instructed to go for our break at around 10, after about two hours of work. Then we had to work non-stop from 10.30 to 16.30. They simply don't care about you. If you can't handle it, they will just find someone else. (Fieldnotes, 28 November 2018)

I did not last long in that place. To be honest, the shift described above was the first and last one that I did for this company. The main reason for my departure was the smell of fish; when I returned home, I could not get rid of it, no matter how many showers I took. It enters your pores, you sweat it out, it fuses with the fabric of your clothes. I was also living with a partner, and this smell was not something I would want to subject another human to. However, my choice to leave that workplace was indicative of my relative privilege: my command of English and my deep knowledge of Glasgow's labour landscape made me confident that I could easily find another job elsewhere. Someone without these resources or who had vital caring responsibilities would not have been in the position to make such 'choices'.

Indeed, structural inequality is so pervasive that this workplace was reliably staffed with workers who were forced to subject themselves to these disgusting, alienating and disempowering conditions. Disempowerment was the quintessential experience of the fish factory, from the minute you went to your induction to the minute you slept – the experience followed you *even after work*, because apart from the fatigue and the mental exhaustion, the stench of the dead fish was a stamp, making you feel sick of yourself and disqualifying you from most social interactions. While I did not stay there long enough to be able to make any substantial conclusions, I have included this brief anecdote in order to highlight the immense variety of precarious occupations, and the multiple positionalities that migrant workers can occupy *within* the precarious condition.

Experience is ultimately subjective; yet conditions are social. Precarity is a continuum. From zero-hours contracts to employment agencies, fixed-term postings and under-the-table, verbal arrangements, neoliberalism has birthed a vast array of ways to exploit workers. Even lower in the labour hierarchy than the fish factory, one can find the worlds of takeaways, carwashes and domestic work; even beneath that, yet with very thinly defined borders that are highly permeable, the UK consumer can benefit from largely 'illegalized' sectors such as the drug and sex trades. This book is limited to the (semi) legal side of the equation, which still presents a wide range of experiences and conditions. Despite the differences, all the workplaces I accessed and all the workers I interviewed expressed certain fundamental commonalities that are key building blocks of the socialization of precarity.

The precarious contractual relation breeds insecurity; indeed, this is its *raison d'être*. This insecurity is experienced as powerlessness and alienation. It breeds overexertion, as workers must force themselves to perform above and beyond formal requirements, competing with each other *and with themselves* for a limited number of permanent positions. This overexertion, combined with the informality and abuse that are frequent characteristics of precarious occupations, leads to acute physical and mental stress. As the body and mind tire, workers are compelled to develop personal resilience. It is at this point that the socialization of precarity begins to entrench itself.

The kitchen

Bustling with commotion, its modern, glass-laden architecture uneasily coexisting with grandiose, imperial red-brick buildings, Glasgow is an excellent location to study migrant labour. It was one of the first British cities to attract large-scale labour migration in the 1840s, when thousands of starving Irish peasants, their livelihoods decimated by the British imperial machine, escaped the Irish famine to become proletarians in its shipyards and factories. In his seminal *The Condition of the Working-Class in England in 1844*, Engels (1952) would comment on the brutal labour regimes they were relegated to, accompanied by squalid living environments, epidemics and premature death. Under such constant diminishment of human dignity for the sake of someone else's profits, it seemed unsurprising that workers in Glasgow filled their free time with drink; this is a reality that still permeates the city's streets. Nowadays, harder drugs such as heroin have been added to the menu, disrupting the sanitized image of prosperity and development that the ruling class intends to portray.

Substance abuse and the imperial buildings were probably the only noticeable signs of continuity between Engels' time and the summer of 2019, when, CV in hand, I embarked on the search for a hospitality job. Everyone that has worked in the many facets of the industry – whether it be bars, hotels or restaurants – will recognize the dismissive phrase 'this is hospitality', a reference that signifies a resignation to the cumulative effects of dysregulation, informality, abuse, long hours and injuries. Hospitality is a battlefield, and the various layers of informality that saturate the sector leave both physical and psychic marks on those who participate in it. Close to one of Glasgow's most central locations, surrounded by the towering relics of imperial nostalgia, there is a Mediterranean restaurant (we will call it La Dama) that encapsulates all the aforementioned characteristics of the industry. This is the restaurant I referred to in the previous chapter in which I met John, and it is here that I understood the socialization of precarity more explicitly than anywhere else.

I had already distributed multiple CVs by the time I approached La Dama. Of course, my CV was carefully amended, foregrounding my time in bars, kitchens, factories and warehouses, excluding all academic achievements past undergraduate level, and accounting for my then one-year PhD research by writing that I was working in olive farms in Crete. I had entered Greek restaurants, attempting to draw on my background to find a quick job; I had entered Asian places, from which I never heard back; and I had gone through two unpaid trial shifts as a kitchen porter at a Spanish and an Italian restaurant, which I had abandoned due to their limited number of staff and limited research opportunities. I was looking for a location with enough migrant workers to be able to observe social dynamics beyond interpersonal relations, and I had a feeling that this restaurant, near a very busy junction filled with shoppers, tourists and commuters, would be the 'lucky' one.

I entered and asked if they required a kitchen porter (KP). I was not surprised that the waiter, upon hearing my accent, responded immediately in Greek and asked me to take a seat and wait for the manager. A terse, perfectly dressed and groomed Italian emerged, grabbed my CV, and left. Five minutes later, a man in his mid-30s appeared, immediately introducing himself as the 'head chef'. He had a short but powerful physique, his arms lined with scars and tattoos. This was my first meeting with Drago, who I would come to think of as the 'God of the Kitchens'. After a firm handshake, and never breaking eye contact, he asked me what hours I wanted. I knew the script and replied that I would work as much as he needed. I was invited for a one-hour trial shift the following day, after which I was taken to an upstairs office to sign the most generic zero-hours contract that I have ever seen. A few hours later, in a short text message, Drago informed me that I would be working between 15:00 and 23:30 the next day.

My first impression of the workplace concerned the physical and symbolic subordination of the kitchen in relation to the rest of the restaurant. As soon as I entered from the front door for my first shift, the Italian manager (who never introduced himself) immediately grabbed me and aggressively told me that I should never be seen in the main area of the restaurant; he gestured to a series of steps next to the door that I was supposed to use to make a discreet entrance, safeguarding the blissful separation between the clients' consumerist experience and its literal underbelly.

Beneath the restaurant, a clatter of pots and pans, the smell of butter, smoke, and a mixture of Albanian, Greek, English and Slavic languages. Hearing my mother tongue, I immediately felt at ease. A strong hand grabbed my shoulder, and I met Manos, a stocky twenty-five-year-old man with warm, blue eyes, who immediately welcomed me in Greek. I asked him if he was from Greece, and he told me 'yes, from Patra'. Before he even finished his phrase, he was interrupted by one of the sous-chefs, another Albanian by the name of Ben: 'You are not Greek motherfucker, you are Albanian!' 'But I grew up in Patra', he retorted. 'Get out of here with that bullshit, you are Albanian!', came the swift response. The kitchen erupted in laughter.

As politically incorrect as this exchange might sound to an external observer, it was actually amicable. In the previous chapter, I briefly sketched the history of Albanian migration to Greece and their subsequent second migration to other parts of Europe. Manos, like John, grew up in Greece; the pressures of marginalization and discrimination in Greece, alongside the objective fact of growing up inside the Greek culture, had led many Albanians to extrinsically identify as Greeks. Conversely, many other Albanians, in defiant resistance, maintained a strong association with their Albanian heritage. This exchange illustrates the complex ways that identity, exclusion and migration are negotiated; the humorous banter between the two Albanian workers served as an amicable outlet to express the contradictory effects of decades of oppression, uprootedness and survival. At the same time, it was a way for Ben to attempt to ground Manos in the reality of the migrant condition: you might feel Greek, but society will always view you as Albanian. Recall John's statement: *'we were always migrants'*.

In contrast to the waiting staff, the kitchen was almost exclusively composed of Albanian males, with the exception of myself, a Polish sous-chef, a South African sous-chef who was childhood friends with Drago, a Jamaican KP who was swiftly fired, and two Polish women who would only be called on extremely busy shifts and helped with every aspect of the labour process as and when required. Drago was almost never there as he was constantly jumping between more than five other establishments, and the main head chef duties were assumed by George, a tall, boisterous Scottish man in his 50s who related to the rest of us – depending on his mood – with a mixture of humorous superiority and overt racism. Other than George, the only other Scottish worker was a retired chef who only worked the mornings and left as soon as the clock showed 12 p.m. Almost all the Albanians could speak some degree of Greek, and so communication with them was much more intimate and easy than my other interactions in my time in Glasgow. This intimacy was enhanced by the cultural proximity that they shared with each other, as well as by the cramped space of the kitchen, which allowed for the emergence of a certain familiarity; no matter how busy the day got, there

THE PRECARIOUS CONDITION

A hasty photograph of two of the three sinks that I was working with. The last sink is directly behind me as I am taking this photograph. Despite the bad angle, the cramped conditions are noticeable. On a normal shift, about three people would be working in this space, preparing food. About another three would be working in the stoves that are behind the shelves on the right side of the picture. At busy periods, these numbers could rise to eight or ten workers.

was always room to scream a joke, intended for everyone at once, above the cacophony of the pots and pans.

Whether through banter or overt aggression, this familiarity also became grounds for enforcing or competing over notions of masculinity, productivity and self-worth. The kitchen was an ecosystem of its own, almost entirely separated from the outside world (and, indeed, from the rest of the restaurant). The many hours spent inside it meant that workers' everyday perceptions of themselves seemed to become intimately associated with the restaurant; rarely did anyone speak about their personal lives, and almost all discussions, whether serious or amusing, circulated around the kitchen. However, these relationships were not taking place in a neutral environment: all interactions were both subtly and overtly structured by the overarching precarity and differential positions of authority and ethnicity in the hierarchy. Most fundamentally, these involved George at the top, with the other migrant workers below him in a hierarchy that was itself internally hierarchized by the different levels of respect that one's length of tenure acquired for them.

> *I overhear George speaking to Ben about his previous day's experience of working alongside John. In purposefully broken English, he exclaims 'I couldn't communicate at all, he no understand anything! Always "speak slow", "speak slow". Fuck off!' This is an expression of exasperation at having to work with migrants, as well as a tactic of division between the migrant workforce and an extreme exercise of authority, since the Scottish chef is utilizing his right to criticize workers in front of everyone else without any repercussions. The Albanian fellow worker, upon hearing these comments about his compatriot and friend, just kept silent and stared straight ahead as if he were focusing on the dish rather than on the conversation. What could he say? If he agreed, he would sell his friend short. If he resisted, he would be jeopardizing his job security and his favour with this extremely powerful individual in the restaurant hierarchy. (Fieldnotes, 11 July 2019)*

Critically, all the Albanians had arrived at the restaurant through some form of extended familial connection to Drago, relying on the extensive pan-European network forged by migrating Albanians since the 1990s. Beyond finding them a job, Drago would assist them with every other aspect of the migratory process: he would pick them up from the airport, help them with the logistics of securing a flat and setting up a bank account, and generally guide their navigation of Glasgow. Drago himself had significantly more cultural capital than his compatriots: he had arrived in Glasgow as a teenager and therefore had excellent command of the English language; he had finished college and secured a diploma as a chef which is fully recognized in the UK, thereby avoiding the process of deskilling; he had fully secure citizenship status; and, most importantly, he had worked for the same employer for more than ten years, gradually rising up the occupational hierarchy and assuming an authority that was only second to that of the owner. In fact, he was the most important piece of the company's infrastructure: a worker, a manager, a head chef and an administrator, Drago jumped between multiple branches of the franchise, organized every kitchen worker's rota, was almost exclusively in charge of hiring and firing, and was the quintessential authority of our labour experience.

We are alone in the kitchen with Drago, at around 11 p.m. Throughout the course of the day, I have been trying to learn about his life. He is expressively proud of his socioeconomic ascent, telling me that he came to Glasgow at the age of 14 and had become a head chef by 17. Hard work and resilience were more than slogans for him: they were adopted as inextricable aspects of his identity and were the measures by which he judged everyone else. With Tupac Shakur blasting from a cheap Bluetooth speaker, he tells me stories about his life as a young immigrant in Glasgow, involved with gangs and the drug trade. It becomes apparent that from the very start of his arrival, he was shunned by most of society ('they called me a black bastard, and I was whiter than them'), prompting him to find solidarity and community in local gangs alongside other young people from around the world. At the same time, he was making sure to 'not miss a day of work'. These two extremes are not as distant to each other as they may seem: they both represent visions and performances of the same survival-oriented, money-making identity. He tells me that 'we were partying and coming to work with half an hour sleep, and then partying again'. I reply that, 'you must have been on coke to do stuff like that'. 'Yeah, that's true, coke kept us going', he responds with a big smile and laugh. (Fieldnotes, 24 July 2019)

Most readers with experience of precarious hospitality work will broadly recognize this kitchen's conditions. The mere mention of a union or a strike was perceived as a joke, and everyone other than the two alternating head chefs was on zero-hours contracts. The rhythms of labour were intense, the work was both mentally and physically taxing, and the acquisition of future hours exclusively depended on your ability to impress the two head chefs, but particularly Drago. To do so, you had to constantly express the usual characteristics that cumulatively structure the 'good worker' stereotype: agility, flexibility, availability, and a capacity to endure above and beyond what would be required to simply get the job done (MacKenzie and Forde 2009). In the absence of contractual security, your interpersonal relations with those in positions of authority and your ability to 'get the job done' became the only guarantees for more hours.

As with the radiator factory, the designation of these occupations as 'unskilled' is highly misleading and functions to hide the social relations that underpin workers' destinies in today's economy. While only the position of the chef is recognized as 'skilled', the various posts directly beneath it require substantial levels of mental and physical dexterity: from learning how to move your body in order to maintain the requisite rhythms of production while minimizing injuries to memorizing the plethora of minute details associated with specific plates, recipes, ingredients and timings, the kitchen could only operate through the (relatively) harmonious cooperation of various workers, each individually proficient at their tasks.

Aiming to extract as much profit as possible, the workplace was permanently short staffed, with between three and ten workers working up to 14.5-hour shifts, cramped in the undersized kitchen and scrambling to feed hundreds of customers above our heads. These long shifts were sometimes on back-to-back days and resulted in an inescapable burden of fatigue that was shared by the entire workforce; yet it was hours that you were there for, and the only reason to complain was for the lack thereof, not their overprescription: upon notifying me of my first week's shift pattern, which included three successive 14.5-hour posts, Drago paternally told me 'you see, I take care of you'. This notion of care was apparently not shared by my friend John, who constantly complained about the long hours, but nevertheless accepted them because that was what he was

The back alley of La Dama

in Scotland for. Over a smoking break in a back alley brimming with garbage, rats and needles where the restaurant had its bins, he looked at Glasgow's black sky as he stepped on the butt of his cigarette: 'You enter at night, and you leave at night. There is no time for anything else.'

My position as a KP was the lowest in the kitchen hierarchy, but every other worker, including Drago, had started from there; as in many other hospitality settings, the KP post is a rite of passage, a filtering mechanism that sorts out the 'good' workers from those perceived as inadequate. One's capacity to survive the physical intensity demanded by the post alongside the symbolic aspect of doing the 'dirtiest' work of the labour process was instrumental both in securing more hours and in ascending the occupational hierarchy. Nevertheless, an improvement in one's rank from KP to kitchen assistant or sous-chef did not lead to better wages; other than Drago and George, every other member of the kitchen staff was paid the legal minimum. An improvement in one's position signified something more important than money: it was proof that you had become an integral part of the kitchen ecosystem, and this was associated with security. This security did not manifest itself in the form of a permanent contract – it was your acquisition of expertise on other aspects of the labour process and your continual demonstration of your 'good worker' credentials that somehow signified that you could hope to stay, hope to keep on rising. Contractual precarity, combined with a necessity to keep up with the constant circulation of orders, dishes, preparatory equipment and other occurrences in an excruciatingly understaffed environment created an overarching atmosphere of intensity, pressure and stress. This in turn led to fatigue and various injuries, which every worker was expected to manage *individually and productively*; a cut, a bruise or a burn became not reasons to stop work, but opportunities to demonstrate durability by continuing to work *despite* them.

> *It is a very busy day, and I didn't get the chance to sit down at all throughout the 14-hour shift. The morning preparation was very hectic and I had to repeatedly take the garbage outside, in a skip that was overflowing and on which I had to perform a very delicate balancing act. As the rhythms of work are incredibly intense, my apron has inevitably become saturated with leftovers, fats, and juices from all types of food, leading to a very characteristic smell that resembles a mixture of vomit and the interiors of a dirty dishwasher. The floor below me is full of puddles, and I have ripped up and laid some cardboard boxes on it so that nobody trips and falls. The outside summer heat seeps into the underground kitchen, fuses with the cooking fumes and makes my soiled clothes stick to my body.*
>
> *I have sustained a few more cuts and burns. The cuts are particularly problematic because they are on my fingers, which always are in use and in contact with warm water, chemicals, and leftovers. It means that almost every action that I have to perform hurts, and I have to just keep working ignoring the pain. Apart from these injuries, I have been working with cramps on both my calves as a result of not having a chance to take a seat, and my shoulder blades are burning from the constant lifting of heavy plates. As I look at my arms and hands, I can't help thinking about the fact that these conditions are directly attributable to the rhythm of the work, combined with contractual precarity and the business's unwillingness to pay more staff. Everyone is complaining about the day's intensity, yet there are no attempts to get the managers or boss to tone down the expectations. While various colleagues have told me that the KP post is a two-person job, they only bring an extra person on specific Fridays and Saturdays. I wonder if the clients above our heads, stuffing their faces with the results of our labour, have any idea about the conditions that make their leisure possible. (Fieldnotes, 17 July 2019)*

THE PRECARIOUS CONDITION

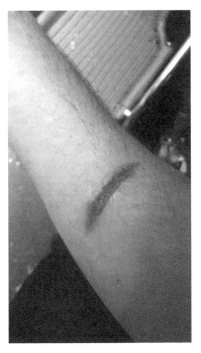

Photo of the the first 'serious' burn I sustained, while balancing multiple scalding pans in the sink. After I screamed, Afrim, an Albanian in his late 20s, triumphantly patted me on the shoulder and told me that this was my official 'welcome' to La Dama.

In one of the last conversations that I had with George, he complained that despite his privileged position, he was suffering from chronic back pain, swollen arteries in his legs and anxiety. I replied that this was probably due to the long hours, which only he and Drago had the power to convince the boss to reduce. He responded with a phrase that has become a mantra all over the world, signalling the naturalization of exploitation: 'this is the sector, this is hospitality'. And yes, most readers with experience of hospitality settings will recognize the above descriptions, in quality if not in intensity. How does migrancy impact the precise ways that hospitality is experienced, particularly for those migrants with secure residency status who *don't* face the debilitating effects of visa restrictions?

Simply put, La Dama relied on migrant workers because very few Scottish workers tolerated these conditions for these wages: *they had other options*. The workers of La Dama didn't, and this allowed the restaurant to continue reaping the profits from their intensified exploitation. The precarious contractual relation, as in other workplaces, functioned both as a management tool compelling workers to continually work harder, and as a filtering mechanism, allowing Drago to discard whoever didn't meet the very demanding standards that La Dama required to keep on operating as tightly as it did. Having come to Scotland through existing connections with Drago, most of the migrants' horizons were closed; indeed, many felt as if they owed him. This closure was exacerbated by the lack of English proficiency, the non-recognition of any qualifications they held, the sheer number of hours they had to work, their unfamiliarity with the wider labour landscape of Glasgow, and the non-existence of unions in, or anywhere near, the workplace or the communities of these workers. The effects of these primary barriers were deepened by their own temporary outlook, aiming to make as much money as possible and return to Albania, Greece, or wherever they desired and by the dual frame of reference, whereby they favourably compared the money they made in this intensely exploitative context with the conditions they left behind, where they would probably experience the same levels of intensity for a smaller remuneration. As with Kris in the radiator factory described in the previous chapter, they excelled in their jobs *in order to achieve the wider goals behind their migration*; yet this did not mean that they were not acutely, critically aware of the exploitation they faced.

After a month in La Dama, I decided to depart. My last conversation with John, mentioned in the previous chapter, illustrates the multiple barriers that migrant workers experience. In the small compartment next to the kitchen that we used to hang our street clothes and change into our aprons, I wished him luck and told him that I had just handed in my notice. After a firm handshake, his question mirrored his social position: 'alright man, but if you could find a better job, why were you here in the first place?'

For many, leaving is a privilege.

Informality and abuse

La Dama is exemplary of a wider landscape in the hospitality industry where migrant workers endure the informality and abuse that is enabled by precarious contractual relations. Almost all the workers I interviewed mentioned instances of humiliation and degradation. In these contexts, interpersonal relations assume an overwhelming importance, since they essentially *replace contractual security as well as guarantees to a dignified working life*.

Formality, informality and abuse interact with and condition one another. Each workplace's particular requirements and existing cultures play an important role in shaping workers' experiences. For example, rather than using agency workers as a pool of temporary, flexible labour, the radiator factory in the previous chapter used agencies to procure permanent workers: the initial contractual insecurity was simply a way for them to avoid committing themselves to someone who they didn't want in the long term. This company instrumentally cared about creating a positive working environment with those that they chose to keep on board – training was an investment that they couldn't endlessly undertake. For this reason, almost all interactions were respectful. On the other hand, my experience in the fish factory was exactly the opposite. While there was a degree of formality, since the labour was resourced by one of the largest existing global employment agencies, it was cold and demonstrably careless. Since a worker in the elementary positions could be trained in a matter of hours, there was no reason for them to invest in creating a more positive environment. They had a very high turnover rate due to the extremely unpleasant nature of the work, but there were always more workers willing to replace the ones that, like me, had left. Beyond these sectors, the complete nonexistence of any written contractual relation can be found on the lower rungs of the formality/informality ladder, and it is where many of my interview participants were located. Due to an extreme turnover rate – and the almost complete absence of unions that is associated with it – these conditions are highly prevalent in the various levels of the hospitality industry.

The ease with which one can access the hospitality industry attracts migrant workers, and everyone I interviewed had, at some point, passed through it. For example, Agnes, a Polish woman in her mid-20s, described working in a Glasgow city-centre cafe without a contract. She was one of three workers I interviewed who worked in that cafe, and all described a similar situation. It is important to note that, in this specific context, the employers used a narrative of 'family' and 'solidarity' to obscure the inequalities that manifested themselves throughout the employment relation. The cafe specialized in home-made sweets; its façade featured a cartoon character boasting a huge, welcoming smile, and every worker confirmed that during their first few shifts they felt as if they had finally found a healthy working environment. They quickly realized that this was not the case. The male boss was indifferent and detached, while his partner was openly abusive to staff even in front of customers. Her drunken outbursts and barefaced disregard for her employees' mental and physical health were superficially counterbalanced by gestures such as a monthly meal for the staff, paid through their accumulated tips.

These instances of bosses taking wide liberties with wages and ignoring the most basic dictums of human respect are not isolated; they cumulatively form a fabric of everyday experience that coexists with the fundamental precarity of the employment relation. This reduces workers' confidence, isolates them, and enforces the pressures to either individualistically survive or, if one has the requisite resources, leave the job. Informality can manifest itself even within and despite the contractual relation. Most zero-hours contracts are not, in themselves, a significantly stronger guarantee of contractual security than the verbal, non-written contract. While they do offer employees the opportunity to pursue and substantiate some claims – if they have the resources and the support to go to an Employment Tribunal – they can still be used punitively by employers. Hours can be reduced at short notice, leaving the worker in an immediate and unplanned state of economic insecurity.

> *Leila:* There was a lot of rivalry within the team. You would never hire guys for waitressing. The guys were always in the kitchen, in the floor it was always girls. They just had this horrible paranoia of trying to compete among each other, because basically if the boss doesn't like you that means that your life was going to be hell and that he wouldn't give you enough hours.
>
> *Q:* Were all the other girls also immigrants?
>
> *Leila:* Yes. The only one who wasn't was the manager. Who was a bitch! An absolute, the worst person I have ever met. And I am so gutted that I couldn't punish her. That my confidence was so low, that I could put up with her shit. She was just a terrible person. Because she was sleeping with this guy, she had so much power.

And she was, yeah. . . . Basically because I wasn't getting on with the girls, nor with the chefs, I started like, having less and less hours.
Q: How did this happen? Did he reduce your hours after disagreements?
Leila: Yeah! Literally. So basically, yeah, it was just like, you know, speaking my mind, and then my hours would be drastically cut.

Leila, Spanish/Tunisian woman, early 30s, hospitality

Formal disciplinary procedures can be completely replaced by unilateral actions from the managers or bosses, while at the same time the workers lack the confidence and resources to resist. These contexts are exemplary of the wider inequality that permeates capitalist relations; simply put, they offer a glimpse of the brute reality of capitalist labour relations as such, unveiling the real face of the system once it is shorn of anything that might make those relations seem more rational, more reasonable or more humane.[1] Power is no longer simply asymmetric; the foundational inequality that exists between every employee and their superiors is extremely aggravated by the almost complete absence of substantial workers' rights.

Emma worked in an Eastern European restaurant in Glasgow on such a contract. It was exclusively staffed by migrant workers. Front-of-house staff consisted of white, European workers, while back-of-house staff included some deeply precarious non-European workers without papers. The owner was himself a migrant, albeit a wealthy one. He used brute force in every aspect of the workplace's everyday life: holiday pay was routinely withheld and was a struggle to obtain, workers were constantly monitored by a network of security cameras which the boss was routinely checking, and he often penalized his workers' mistakes by docking their pay. Through this sustained threatening behaviour he had the confidence to try and avoid some fundamental employer responsibilities, including attempting to withhold wages.

It was like a threatening environment. I feel, like, in a busy environment it is very easy sometimes to make a mistake, or order, I don't know, instead of rice, tomatoes or whatever to the kitchen. And in this case, he would just start shouting at the workers. For example, once in the kitchen we mixed up the dishes for two different tables, because they were similar, and then the boss went to the guy that put it in the lift and just started shouting at him in front of everyone. And also, a girl that I was working with – she was my colleague, she was a bartender there – and she really needed a day off on Friday and he didn't give it to her, so that kind of started there, and she was like, 'I can't come because something really serious has happened' and then he didn't pay her for the whole week, but he made her work. He put her in the rota to work the next week, and he was like, 'if you come this other week then I will pay you', and she was like 'well, if I am not getting paid I'm not going to come'. But eventually her friends started sending him text messages being like 'OK, pay her or we are going to Citizens Advice Bureau', and then eventually he did pay her, but he also sent her very threatening text messages. And it's not the first time. In his community he already has this type of fame.

Emma, Lithuanian woman, early 20s, hospitality

Apart from the boss's blatant abuse of workers and his disregard for basic employment rights, here we see a glimmer of resistance. However, the intensity of the precarious relation means that such action is isolated and unable to substantially alter conditions. The workers' friends supported her, and threatened the boss with the only feasible course of action that was accessible to them. Citizens Advice Bureaus in the UK offer free advice on a variety of issues, including employment legislation; however, they do not support the worker beyond that, confining themselves at best – and depending on the mood of the case worker – to helping the claimant draft a letter to their employer or advising them whether they have a case in an Employment Tribunal. As we shall see in chapter 5, the Tribunal process – the main legal avenue for individual workers to pursue claims in the UK – is incredibly complex and usually requires weeks of sustained learning and effort, with no guaranteed victory. These are luxuries that most precarious workers simply lack the energy or the socioeconomic capital to pursue. In a legal context that enables the precarious relations that lead to such abuses, a strong union presence is the only feasible vehicle for directly challenging conditions. In their absence, resistance remains fragmentary – the individual worker may, drawing on every thread of supportive networks they have at their disposal, manage to win back some wages, and the existence of mechanisms such as Citizens Advice Bureaus allows governments to claim that they are, indeed, supporting workers; yet the desert of precarity proliferates.

Health and safety

One crucial aspect of the lives of precarious migrant workers that has not received adequate attention is the sheer, raw intensity of occupations that permeate everyday Western urban landscapes. These are jobs like the kitchen in La Dama, with conditions literally rendered invisible by its underground position, or those behind the closed doors of warehouses and hotel rooms that have just been vacated by their joyful, temporary residents. Incredibly important work has been written about the daily struggles and consequent health problems of some of the most acutely marginalized migrant groups in the West, such as Mexican fruit pickers in the United States (Holmes 2013) or undocumented Chinese workers in the UK (Pai 2008). Yet the occupations that are closer to us, and therefore less sensationalized, remain invisible, precisely due to their proximity. This lack of focus naturalizes both the conditions that underpin precarity as well as migrants' perceived suitability for these occupations. For example, Boswell and Geddes (2011: 86) write that migrant workers 'may also be ready to work on a casual or temporary basis, or with less comprehensive health and safety standards' than British workers, which they view as giving them an 'advantage' in securing employment. The two authors are strongly supportive of migrant rights; yet all language is social, and it reflects and reproduces underlying assumptions. These are assumptions that permeate the social body about migrants' allocations in the labour market. Destroying your body is not an 'advantage'. It is a necessity created, and continually reproduced, by *the lack of alternatives*.

A common theme emerging from my interviews is an overarching lack of respect for health and safety guidelines in workplaces, and the concurrent difficulty of challenging these conditions. Recall the fish factory at the start of the chapter, where health regulations were cursory and framed exclusively in terms of the damage that would be done to the employer if someone, for example, experienced an allergic reaction to their products. Meanwhile, workers were engaged in extremely difficult labour, in freezing conditions, for hours at a time without breaks. This wider lack of concern around workers' welfare was clearly illustrated by

Mateusz, a union organizer for the Bakers, Food and Allied Workers Union, when describing his experiences in a cake factory.

> *[Laughs]* Inside the factory? Health and safety was terrible. Basically, as I remember, there was no existing health and safety. You had cables on the floor, the floor was flooding, and on those floods was laying cables and stuff like that, the machine don't have any covers to protect your hands, sometimes we have to put, when we do the cakes, put plaster. Basically it's like a big tub with the holes in it, and you have to press the mix inside those holes, but the tumbler is constantly moving, so if you don't remove your hand quickly you gonna lose your finger. So... basically the treatment of the people, they used them for the maximum... if you have a job you have to work overtime, we don't have the right to say no or something. Our managers, we had Polish managers, but because they were on a position they treated us even worse than we should be treated. Our boss, he was basically racist and he discriminated people constantly, especially with migrant workers – which was 90 percent of staff – when he have a bad mood he coming over to you, 'you don't work any longer here'.
>
> *Mateusz, Polish male, mid-30s, union organizer with BFAWU.*
> *Here he is referring to his time in a cake factory.*

The individualization that precarity fosters can be mirrored in workers' perceptions of labour infringements. Not only are workers forced to develop personal traits of resilience to survive precarity, but the informality that is permitted by precarity makes the injustices they experience also appear personal. In both Mateusz's and Leila's testimonies, the source of their woes is described as a repugnant manager, rather than the structural inequality that gave these managers power at the same time as disempowering the workers beneath them. Even in the face of very clear asymmetries, since interpersonal relations replace contractual securities, the asymmetries themselves may be perceived as interpersonal.[2]

Once again, the contractual precarity that underpins migrant workers' labour is shown to be easily mobilized by employers in order to subjugate workers. The connection Mateusz drew between insufficient respect for health and safety and a rigid and arbitrary disciplinary system, with the constant, overhanging threat of instant dismissal, illustrates how difficult it is for workers in these conditions to claim even the most basic rights. Suzan's experience as a hotel room cleaner is exemplary of these complications. The uncompromising pace that she was required to maintain combined with the need to keep the job in order to feed her children had led to permanent bodily damage.

> *Suzan:* For one and a half, two years, I never had a weekend, never had time for myself, to say 'I have a free week!' I worked every Saturday, I didn't have a life anymore, my child. Nothing.
> *Q:* Earlier you said that they only gave you 4-hour shifts. . .
> *Suzan:* You never work more in the hotel. What they say are fairy tales. In the hotels the job is hard, and they tell you that you have 15 minutes per room. This is never true. You have 15 to 20 rooms to clean in the space of four hours, and you always go over, normally by about one hour. Which they pay you for, it's not like you work for free, but you don't have any energy to work more. They don't give you 8-hour shifts because you wouldn't be able to handle it.
>
> I have a problem. Two years before I came to the UK, I had an operation for a detached shoulder. My problem was healed, everything was good, but with two years of working in the hotel, it had returned. I go to the doctor and he says 'you have to be crazy to be doing what you are doing', and he gives me two months off. He asked me 'how long do you want to stay at home, from one to five months?' I respond, 'are you crazy? I'm going to go hungry!' He tells me that 'no, you will be paid, and if you were permanently employed, you could collect your pension!' I told him he shouldn't give me things like that, but he said 'woman, you must sit at home, or the day after tomorrow you will come to me again and I won't be able to help you. You must go through check-ups. We must see what happened to your arm.' It had started detaching itself during the night also. So, two or three times per day, and then again at night, I had many stories. Anyway. . .
> *Q:* And you were working? You were just popping it back in and. . .
> *Suzan:* Yes. Because if they found out they would say that I am not for them, they would have to pay me, so they would get rid of me as fast as possible. When I couldn't take it any longer, that's it, I left! I went to the doctor and he told me 'it can't go on any longer'. So I

took advantage of it, since it was summer. My shoulder popped out during work, and I just went and sat there with my shoulder hanging out. They called the ambulance and the supervisor came with me to the hospital. Everything was official. I went to the doctor and he told me 'what did I tell you?', and I thought, 'if you only knew how many times it has happened!' But now I wanted them to know because I wanted to go on holidays, and I said, 'let's see what happens. They will pay me and you'll see what happens.' So, I went to the doctor and all that. I go to the GP and he says, 'how much time do you want off?' I say 'two months', because I wanted to go back to Greece, to the doctor that performed my first operation. He told me to take the paper to my work and 'goodbye'. They told me to give them the GP's phone. I did. They call the doctor and he confirms it, he tells them 'she was here three months ago and I told her to stop then, but this woman is hungry and she couldn't stop working' and stuff like that. What do they want? But they told me that they think I am lying to them. The doctor told them, 'the woman didn't want to tell you about it because she has two children at home, and when she came here I told her I should give her five months off but she asked me not to, she told me "doctor please, don't do this because I won't have anything to give my children and I don't believe they will give me any money from this story and I don't have enough for the bills. I am a single woman with two children".' They shut up, they accepted it. And when I left for holidays. . .

Q: Did they pay you?

Suzan: No, they didn't pay the holidays, they didn't pay medical expenses, but when I came back, they pulled some papers out, some of their own stories, that supposedly I wasn't supposed to leave Glasgow, England, because they had to monitor me and that I had taken advantage of the doctor's orders in order to take holidays.

I told them that I don't care what they believe. I will sue them for this and this. . . I had found something online about having a workplace accident, and if you have witnesses, you could get some money, and stuff like that. I pick up the phone, the woman was trying, but she was fresh in the job. I tried to do something but I didn't manage to do anything, but I recorded and I probably have that recording somewhere. I thought that it might be useful in the courts. Anyway, I didn't manage to find a solution, and they basically forced me to quit. I was telling them that I wanted to go back to work. 'I am alright and tomorrow I want to begin working', but they were saying 'it's impossible, you have to sign this paper and you can't continue working with us.' 'No, I will not do it.' And in the end they fired me. The story ends there. I didn't know what else to do.

Suzan, Romanian woman, late 40s, hospitality and logistics [translation mine from Greek – Suzan had previously lived in Greece for more than a decade and, like me, had moved to Britain to avoid the consequences of the 2008 financial crisis]

Suzan does not have an 'advantage' in securing employment. Her example highlights the daily risks that workers subject themselves to due to the combined pressures of precarity, family responsibilities, employer lack of care and a paucity of information that is significantly worsened by one's unfamiliarity with the new country. It is exacerbated by the lack of appropriate institutional or community-based support networks for migrant workers. The need to make money overrides health concerns. Suzan needed her job, and her insecure employment status did not give her the confidence to consider pursuing some sort of resolution until it was too late.

For many workers, as Suzan's example demonstrates, the pressures created by the precarious contractual relation overlap with, and are significantly exacerbated by, their social experiences as women and mothers. Anderson (2013: 84) points out that the 'consequences of precariousness and its implications for time use, the balancing between work, family (reproductive labour) and leisure, are gendered and experienced differently at different points in life'. Of course, these pressures intensify workers' feelings of powerlessness and enforce a state of constant vigilance, further ensuring the reproduction of the precarious condition. They combine to position precarious workers in a parallel world, one in which taken-for-granted rights for secure workers are inaccessible luxuries. For her doctor, Suzan was crazy to *keep* on working. For Suzan, her doctor was crazy for telling her to *stop* working: 'I'm going to go hungry!'

Even after her shoulder popped out during work, her employers – a very large multinational hotel chain – used all the resources at their disposal to fire her as swiftly as possible without paying her any compensation. In the end, Suzan didn't know 'what else to do'. Legally, there were plenty of avenues that she could have pursued. But left to her own devices, with a significant language barrier, two young children, and no union or similar organization she could contact, she necessarily moved on. At the time of the interview, it was too late to bring this issue to an Employment Tribunal; this is something that is experienced by many migrant workers (Barnard et al. 2018). Her shoulder was still in a horrible state, but she had found another job. She had to keep working.

Alienation

Overworked, insecure, anxious to constantly overperform, physically and mentally exhausted, workers in precarious occupations have to choose between leaving their jobs – leading to further insecurity – or surviving through them. This precise choice to survive and the everyday experience of enduring exploitation leads to a deep internal rupture within the precarious subject, which in turn determines the ways that they respond to their precarity. Alienation, as analysed by Marx in the nineteenth century, is another major continuity between that era and today's reality.

The capacity to consciously – rather than instinctively – create is what, according to Marx, differentiates us from other animals. Despite the anachronistic nature of his anthropocentric conception, alienation is an extremely important theory for understanding how we experience labour under capitalism. According to Marx (1844), alienation involves '1) estrangement and fortuitous connection between labour and the subject who labours; 2) estrangement and fortuitous connection between labour and the object of labour; 3) that the worker's role is determined by social needs which, however, are alien to him and a compulsion to which he submits out of egoistic need and necessity, and which have for him only the significance of a means of satisfying his dire need, just as for them he exists only as a slave of their needs; 4) that to the worker the maintenance of his individual existence appears to be the *purpose* of his activity and what he actually does is regarded by him only as a means; that he carries on his life's activity in order to earn means of *subsistence*'.

Simply put, the hours wasted in meaningless, boring and tiring occupations for the sake of someone else's profit have far-reaching consequences; they are carried by the worker beyond the workplace, and produce a violent internal schism as the creative energy that organically emerges from every human is distorted, contorted and perverted to fit the stifling demands of someone else's profitability. This creative energy is our passion, our source of strength, our caress. Think about how fulfilling the *process* of cooking a breakfast for your lover is; then, think of the happiness that you experience as you see their smile, and the exhilaration you feel when they tell you that they like it. Every aspect of the labour process, as well as what comes after it, is experienced as art and completeness; you *put yourself* in that breakfast. Now compare this image with the experience of cooking a breakfast in La Dama, with burns on your fingers, stressing to meet the tight temporal demands to feed a person you couldn't care less about, to make money for someone else who is exploiting you. The breakfast is the same, and you are still putting yourself into creating it; however, instead of being empowering and life-affirming, this investment is now experienced as a deadly, suffocating *loss of self*. It becomes even more so precisely because this creative energy could be used for beauty – the perversity of our existence under capitalism is experienced continuously, until it becomes a thumping, dull pain and a self-propagating resignation. This is alienation, and its cumulative effects extend beyond the workplace, parasitically permeating every aspect of social and psychic life.

> *Lois:* I felt like a number there. They were treating us – not like dogs or something like that – but they were very snobbish and they had an attitude as if we were just numbers there, working. The agency workers were experiencing that much more than anyone else who was there with a contract. You could see that we were just doing our job and we weren't considered proper workers. That is how I felt.
> *Q:* So, you were not treated with respect.
> *Lois:* Exactly. Also, the conditions were very negative. Intense white lighting, which for me, I believe it is not healthy to stay under this light for long hours and miss out natural light. So, you would go early in the morning in the dark and leave in the afternoon. The only time you get to see the sun is during the break, which was of course a very small break. Also, the wage was minimum wage. There

was a lot of noise of the machines because it was a printing factory and the noise was creating anxiety in me. So, this, the light, and the way they were treating us with disrespect and also the precarity and feeling that 'I don't know how long I will be able to stay there' because I didn't have any contract, I was with a zero-hours contract by an agency, and they could sack me anytime, it was not a very nice situation.

Lois, Greek woman, late 20s, hospitality
[describing working in a print factory]

While the above statement resonates with most popular understandings of alienating, exploitative factory labour, the development of Western capitalism has meant that the compartmentalization of tasks has been extended to a wide range of occupations. The neoliberal imperative to squeeze costs has resulted in a proliferation of intensely alienating posts and increasing precarity even in occupations that wouldn't normally be associated with these characterizations. One such example involves the National Health Service's use of agency workers to fill short-term staff shortages. Here, the vocational quality characterizing popular perceptions of nurses and doctors is stunted and stifled, resulting, once again, in stressed, overworked and alienated workers.

Eleni: I have no ownership of what you do, you don't know what... So, like, I was taking blood, blood pressure. I don't know what to do with that, cause the only thing they told me, I don't have no connection to what happens after me. And the doctors can tell me like, jump in the hoop and you have to do it because they are doctors, and the nurse can tell me jump the hoop and I have to do it because she is a nurse, you know.

Q: So how was the experience there?

Eleni: It was shit! Yeah, it was shit because, first of all, I worked for the bank [flexible workers that are assigned to where they are needed], I didn't have a stable workplace. The ownership of the work I had was zero. You go there, they tell you 'what's your name, this is what you have to do today'. You don't know where, like, the storage is, you don't know who to speak to, you don't know anything, you are completely disposable basically. And that's fine for some people, but for me it was my only job basically and it really fucked me up. Because I could, I didn't have ownership of anything I did, they told me 'you have to do this', I was running from buzzer to buzzer to, like, you know, just provide personal care for people. That was it, that was my whole job.

Eleni, Greek woman, mid-20s, care sector

I shared these feelings in all the jobs I was involved in. While working, I was also completing my PhD, and I was struck by the difference between how people in those environments responded to the end of the workday when compared to the attitudes one finds in academic contexts. Undoubtedly, academia also contains high degrees of contractual precarity; but there is a significant qualitative difference in the content of this precarity, as academic labour usually involves a degree of creativity and personal control which is completely absent from factory, warehouse and kitchen settings. At the end of the working day, the University of Glasgow's sociology department is relaxed and content. One sees professors and PhD students casually leaving their offices, eager to stop and have a chat if you bump into them on the stairs. There is an abundance of activities throughout the day for which participation is voluntary, such as seminars and lectures. People attend these *even though they wouldn't be penalized if they didn't*: they attend them out of personal interest, out of a commitment to the wider structure of the work that they do. In contrast, precarious occupations create a deep, violent split between one's labour existence and one's personal existence: objectification is total. There is nothing voluntary, nothing fulfilling about this kind of labour. At the radiator factory described in the previous chapter, this was most overtly expressed by the only time that workers acted with passion: at the end of the day, when it was time to leave.

Despite the comparatively civilized labour conditions, everyone was in an anxious hurry to leave. They were lined up in front of the clocking-out devices 30 seconds before they became activated. They hurriedly clocked out and left, some of them almost jogging down the stairs. Once outside, people rushed into their cars and sped off. All the masks fell instantaneously. This is indicative of the level of experiential awareness of alienation. Nobody likes this job, even those who have comparatively good positions in the labour hierarchy. We are all caught, out of necessity, together in this environment, and we don't want to pretend, even for a minute, that there is anything fulfilling or satisfying in our predicament. As soon as we can, we drop everything and leave. We don't exchange lots of words outside. We walk fast. If it were socially acceptable, perhaps we would run. To make up for our lost time. To hug our partners and our children. To crash in front of the TV, not caring about anything for a few hours. (Fieldnotes, 24 October 2018)

Notwithstanding the wide differences within the precarious spectrum, every occupation in it induces a mentality of *survival* in the workforce. The overarching experience is one of anxiety, alienation, and an omnipresent but latent sense of competition with other workers and with one's own self, internalized as a compulsion to consistently overperform. The socialization of precarity is forged through the sweat, blood, smells, cramps, tension headaches, frustrations and anxieties that become fused with migrant workers' daily experiences of labour in the UK; while it consists of a range of mental dispositions, it emerges from the *material* world of exploitation. The everyday produces, and fortifies, the socialization of precarity.

3

The Socialization of Precarity

When Rudolf Rocker, one of the fundamental theorists of anarcho-syndicalism, began exploring working-class London at the turn of the twentieth century he witnessed 'an abyss of human suffering, an inferno of misery' (Rocker 2005: 25). Eager to get acquainted with the workers and the movements in his new city, he started going to the East End to attend meetings and socialize with fellow migrant socialists and anarchists. Many recent Jewish immigrants from Eastern Europe had congregated in the area, which was 'a slum district'. In his memoirs, Rocker recalls 'a church at the corner of Commercial Street, at the Spitalfields end, where at any time of the day you would see a crowd of dirty, lousy men and women, looking like scarecrows, in filthy rags, with dull hopeless faces, scratching themselves. That was why it was called Itchy Park.' The Jewish working-class Londoners who attended these meetings, primitive cells of what would soon become a powerful migrant trade union movement, 'looked sad and worn; they were sweatshop workers, badly paid, and half starved' (Rocker 2005: 26–7). The destitution Rocker saw in London led him to conclude that, contrary to widespread ideas of the time that located a revolutionary potential in worsening conditions, 'there is a pitch of material and spiritual degradation from which a man can no longer rise. Those who have been born into misery and never knew a better state are rarely able to resist and revolt' (2005: 25).

Social theorists and movements have long attempted to understand how material conditions are translated in the psyches of workers. Rocker's reticence is now firmly established: the pure fact of being aware of one's exploitation does not harmoniously translate into a revolutionary, politicized mindset. The conditions described in the previous chapter are but the tip of the iceberg; in other parts of the world they are markedly worse, both in quantity and quality. Indeed, the recognition of this fact is what underlies migrants' dual frame of reference. Yet the dual frame of reference does not mean that workers *like* these conditions; it is a mere appreciation of the fact that they are more favourable to those they left behind. One's experiential understanding of exploitation prevails. Yet what does this understanding translate to?

What encourages workers to *act* against their collective, and individual, interests? Beyond that, what encourages them to partake in the reproduction of the core ideas that underpin their disempowerment? These questions will likely prevail as long as acutely unequal relations permeate society. Marx famously wrote that the ruling ideas in society are those of the ruling class – the bourgeoisie, the owners of the means of production. In the first half of the twentieth century, attempting to understand the failures of the communist movements of his time and the triumph of fascism, Gramsci expanded on the concept of hegemony – the idea that, after material, economic relations, culture sculpts the ways that people perceive themselves as subjects within a social system and their political participation alters accordingly. The Frankfurt School fused psychoanalytical theory with Marxist materialist analysis to further develop these insights; through groundbreaking critiques of the Enlightenment, technological change and consumerism, they explored how workers in the West gradually incorporated the ideas of their oppressors. Foucault in turn contributed to this line of enquiry by studying the genealogy of the very categories that we use to understand ourselves as subjects, as patients, as model citizens, as lovers, as constant works-in-progress, believing that we act autonomously yet almost always thinking within a matrix created by power relations. More recently, authors such as Zygmunt Bauman (2012) and Mark Fisher (2009) have explored how the post-industrial socioeconomic turn in the West further isolates us and constrains our capacity to imagine alternative social structures. All these theories are invaluable, and without them a book like this could not have even been conceived. Yet, to understand the precise ways in which these theories actually relate to how exploited workers negotiate exploitation, and potentially come to reproduce its dictums, we must start from the shop floor.

Behind Amazon's smile

Amazon is one of the world's largest companies and is notorious for its working conditions; from demanding frenetic productivity to deaths on the shop floor and union busting, Amazon is at the forefront of some of the most worrying labour practices in the West.[1] Between 2018 and 2021, I worked two different stints in one of their 'Fulfilment Centres' in Glasgow – one of the smallest in the world – for a cumulative total of seven months. With its heavy dependence on precarious contracts, its ceaseless demands for productivity and flexibility, and its extensive reliance on surveillance technologies, Amazon warehouses could be considered as archetypal of the processes that collectively make up the phenomenon of precarity (Bloodworth 2019; Moore and Robinson 2016).

The hand-held scanner, a device that both monitors and directs workers, is the centre of the workers' individualized and constantly monitored universe. While in the hospitality industry exploitation is ensured through the close proximity and interpersonal relations that workers and superiors have with each other, Amazon represents the other end of the precarious spectrum. Whatever can be isolated, individualized and automated, will be. At the same time, conscious of its public image, Amazon invests energy into sculpting a façade of support and familiarity, which functions to occlude the fundamental inequalities that underpin every aspect of the labour experience. The use of language, once again, betrays a universe of perceptions: instead of being labelled as 'workers' or 'employees', everyone is an 'associate'. The message is subtle but clear: the company has no responsibilities towards you. However, if you desire any semblance of employment security, you must be fully committed towards your responsibilities to the company.

Like in other precarious occupations, one's accessing of labour security is an individualized struggle premised on one's capacity to consistently *over*perform; however, here some basic elements of labour life that are intimately connected with our experiences of human interaction *as such* have been mechanized. For example, in La Dama orders were coming from George or Drago; they had faces, they were humans – you could have a conversation with them, and you could, potentially, disagree. This fundamental aspect of autonomy (and, indeed, adulthood), one's capacity to voice an opinion and negotiate reality within a specific context, has not (yet) been erased. Similarly, even in intensely understaffed conditions, what is required from the workers fluctuates: in busy times demands rise, and in quiet periods they relax – it would be perceived as ludicrous for George to expect me to keep washing pans when there were no dirty pans in the sink. In contrast, Amazon has rigid minimum rates that workers are required to constantly meet: *there are no quiet times, only busier ones*. Even if no orders are coming through, there is a plethora of other duties to perform, all of which are monitored. This is all underpinned by an omnipresent fixation on the worker's individualized performance, which is the only avenue to accessing security.

The result is an experience that is entirely sterilized, atomized, intensely stressful, and, filtered through the panopticism of the hand-held machine that directs and measures your movements, resembles a dystopian virtual reality video game. In his famous analysis of Bentham's Panopticon, a tower positioned at the centre of a circular prison that ensured the total and uninterrupted visibility of every prisoner simultaneously, Foucault (2020: 201) wrote that its major effect was to 'induce in the inmate a state of conscious and permanent visibility that assures the automatic functioning of power'. A camera can be closed, but its dominance lies in the fact that it exists, and that those under its gaze know that it *could* be monitoring them; therefore, they act as if they are constantly monitored. Foucault continues: the effects of the Panopticon upon the inmates are *permanent*; 'the perfection of power should tend to render its actual exercise unnecessary', so that 'the inmates should be caught up in a power situation of which they are themselves the bearers'. Foucault also notes that this technique of ceaseless monitoring is transferable and could be productively applied in labour contexts. Moreover, he stresses the productive potential of panopticism to *train* those subjected to it: the issue becomes not one of constraining workers into a discipline that they are always trying to escape, but of moulding the worker's subjectivity so that 'he becomes the principle of his own subjection' (2020: 203). Technological developments and the proliferation of precarity have allowed the transition from the tower to the scanner – while Amazon still has human managers and supervisors, the scanner has removed even the slight possibility that one could momentarily evade the gaze of authority, or attempt to reason with it.

In an article written for *ROAR Magazine* (Theodoropoulos 2021), I argued that Amazon is at the forefront of the processes that aim to sculpt workers' subjectivities – their sense of self – in the twenty-first century: these subjectivities are defined by political and personal isolation, an incessant, internalized compulsion to perform, an acceptance and incorporation of continuous monitoring, and an overarching sense of personal responsibility that is, once again, internalized and starts to be experienced as a personal quest.

In essence, there is nothing new to this wish on the part of the ruling class; as Foucault has described, this atomization and internalization of discipline was the goal since at least the eighteenth century. However, there were almost insuperable barriers to its complete realization: the existence of strong working-class and community identities connected workers beyond the workplace, and these in turn created strong, community-based unions that prevented the disciplinary and individualizing forces of capitalism from completely permeating their psyche and labour experience. In contrast, in a context where proliferating labour market precarity is combined with the increased insecurity brought on by the incessant erosion of the welfare state, where impermanence is the only foreseeable permanence (Bauman 2012), without the existence of any form of collective bargaining or collective identity, and where the hand-held scanner mediates between the worker and the rest of the environment (including other workers and management), the conditions for the formation of the purely economistic, isolated, disciplined subject have never been better. In the same way that the production line could be considered as the emblematic tool of Fordist production relations, the hand-held scanner could be considered as the perfect symbol of the new constitution of labour subjectivities.

Working during the incredibly busy holiday period. The warehouse is extremely small, and mostly distributes groceries (ordered through Amazon Prime and sourced from Morrison's supermarket chain) or generally items that can fit into a grocery bag, from electronics to chocolate bars and books.

The process is simple: your hand-held scanner tells you the items that you need to pick and their corresponding location in the warehouse. You take a trolley. On the trolley you place the requisite amount of paper grocery bags (for example, if you have seven orders for seven separate clients, you place seven bags on the trolley). The scanner tells you where to go and what to pick from every location. You go to the location and scan its barcode, notifying the machine that you are in the correct place. Then, you scan the item's barcode, notifying the machine that you have the product in your hands. The machine informs you which bag you must place it in. After placing the item in the bag, you scan the bag's barcode, and the machine knows that the item has been picked – it also knows how long going to the location, finding the item, and placing it in the bag took you. The process continues, with you walking as fast as possible between the aisles until the end of your shift.

Labour is experienced through the scanner. It organizes almost everything and tells you where to go, what to do, and what to do after you have finished what it told you to do. In this warehouse, you are thrown into the deep end almost immediately and are supposed to figure things out yourself or get help, but if you get help you waste time – and your pick rate is recorded and monitored electronically by the machine.

You are an extension of your scanner and there is almost never enough time to exchange words with others. The breaks are completely atomized: you only get 15 minutes of break every four hours and you can take them whenever you want, essentially ensuring that people are kept separated. There are cameras everywhere except in the chiller – where food items such as meats and milk are kept – which enforces the perception that you are constantly watched. I found myself getting stressed about my performance without anybody having told me anything bad about it, and without even knowing what my pick-rate is (that is another factor that maintains the anxiety to perform: the rates are only visible to the managers. However, asking them betrays that you are not confident enough that you are meeting them). Even overtime is an individual, competitive struggle: the few overtime slots are released online at a specific day and time of the week, and workers are constantly refreshing their phones to manage to secure as many hours as they can.

Essentially, the system is perfected to the extent that it does not require coercion or mistreatment by the managers. You are already pushed into this position because of your class or migrant status, and you want to maintain a job which is in a clean environment, offers an above-minimum wage, and has comparatively fewer stressors than other similar occupations. The managers are always polite to you, the walls are covered with 'motivational' slogans such as 'Customer Obsession' or 'Never be afraid to ask'; however, you are compelled by the atomization, precarity, and strict mechanical regimentation to continually over-exert yourself. Of course, this leaves no time or energy to care about your co-workers. We have two objectives: to make as much money as possible, and to try to secure the job. (Compilation of fieldnotes)

THE SOCIALIZATION OF PRECARITY

NOMINATION

WHO ARE YOU NOMINATING? *(FULL NAME)* _____

NOMINATION FOR WHICH LEADERSHIP PRINCIPLE? *(Please tick only ONE below)*
- ○ Customer Obsession
- ○ Deliver Results
- ○ Bias for Action
- ○ Agile Associate

REASON FOR NOMINATION? *(Please provide explanation and give a specific example)*
_____
_____
_____
_____

YOUR NAME _____
YOUR ROLE *(PLEASE TICK ONE)*
- ○ Associate
- ○ Supervisor
- ○ Area Manager
- ○ Operations manager
- ○ Other _____

TODAYS DATE ___/___/___

At Amazon, workers are encouraged to nominate colleagues for excelling in the performance of the characteristics deemed most important in the job. It is one's consistent demonstration of these characteristics that might secure them a permanent contract.

Labouring bodies and exhausted, stressed brains fused with machines, in a frantic expulsion of energy that is entirely arbitrary, yet unquestionable, and compels the worker to consistently overextend themselves in pursuit of a security that is far from guaranteed. These mentalities are complemented by a profit-oriented collective scrutiny in which everyone is invited to 'rate', classify and supervise each other. The photograph above is a potent example.

I only observed people using this form twice; however, the extent of workers' participation in the classificatory game is largely beside the point. The strength of such practices lies precisely in the fact that they reinforce the constant idea that one is monitored in relation to their adherence to a set of predefined principles, the adequate performance of which might contribute to one's chances of accessing security. These forms directly demonstrate what Amazon expected from workers – regardless of whether people actively participated in this classificatory examination, the point was that nobody knew *who* was participating, but that everyone knew *what* was expected, and that others could *potentially* be participating. They were therefore exemplary of the extra, *performative* demand of labour performance: the scanner could verify that a worker was good at their job and whether they met the targets; however, their colleagues and superiors had no way of immediately knowing this, but could verify whether this worker *seemed* to be excelling at one of the 'leadership principles'. To the eye of the scanner is added the eye of the rest of the workforce. Sociability is not bypassed – through multiple cross-pollinating techniques, it is rather harnessed to enhance the pressures experienced by every worker to perform as an isolated individual.

These assessments directly impact one's job security. At any given time, most of the staff in the warehouse were temporary, agency workers (and were branded with the 'green badge'). Every few months, a select one or two would be promoted to receive the coveted 'blue badge', a permanent position accompanied with chances for further advancement and other benefits. These decisions would take into account the ratings of other workers and managers, as well as the individuals' pick rates and demonstrated commitment to the 'values' of Amazon such as 'customer obsession'.

Promotions would be announced in an impromptu break: workers would be instructed to set their scanner to the 'admin' setting, indicating that their temporary immobility has been decided by a superior, and enter the common area where we would be served snacks. Inside there, a small ceremony would ensue – sometimes accompanied by burgers and pizza to create a semblance of a 'festive' atmosphere – where managers proudly announced the workers that got promoted. The rest of us were expected to clap and cheer for them, while the managers would make a quick speech lauding the 'associate's' impeccable commitment to 'Amazon's values'. For example, a colleague was praised for his unwavering commitment to the 'customer obsession' principle, demonstrated through his vigilance in locating expired products and reporting them without hurting his pick rates. After a small, arduous celebration, we would resume work.

Despite their seemingly simple, supportive veneer, small rituals such as these have far-reaching foundations and consequences. Implicit in them was the idea that we could all become permanent if we sustained excellent performance over a long period of time while passionately performing our commitment to the company. Of course, absent any collective labour rights and with the limited number of permanent positions awarded each time, this was lived as an individualistic and competitive struggle to meet arbitrary numerical targets and demonstrate one's subjective suitability for a life spent picking and packing. Our cheering for those who had been promoted thereby emerges as a process that sanctified and reproduced the very premises of our disempowerment. These practices indicate that perhaps one of the most dangerous aspects of the ways that capitalist giants like Amazon mould sociability is that they do not seek to destroy it (as long as people work alongside each other, some sort of sociability will emerge); rather, it is meticulously controlled and directed towards individualist directions that affirm and favour the ideas, demands and priorities of capital. The objective is for the worker to subscribe, and reproduce, these demands – preferably, with Amazon's patented smile on their face.

The agency arena

Amazon is but one acute expression of the ways in which precarious conditions – and the anxiety, overexertion and mental and physical impacts they are associated with – are harnessed to *induce* specific traits in the workforce. Precarity is more productive than it is repressive; it is not simply about inducing fear in the worker, but inculcating a specific, deeply internalized mentality of overwork and vigilance. Various scholars (see, for example, Shubin and McCollum 2021; Forde et al. 2015; Holmes 2013; Sporton 2013; MacKenzie and Forde 2009) have argued that employers are acutely aware of the internalization that precarity produces; for example, in a study of the uses of agency labour MacKenzie and Forde (2009) found that employers consciously target marginalized groups, and are even liable to racialize them in terms of their work ethic, believing that migrants are somehow naturally 'better' workers. On the other side of the equation, always in the context of minimum wage employment and needing to save as much as possible, workers in this study welcomed the opportunity to work overtime, thereby themselves strengthening the structural connection between precarious labour and migrant workers.

Employers' awareness of how precarity can be used as a productive *management* tool was transparently demonstrated in the radiator factory when I notified the shop floor manager that I would be leaving.

With the days ticking by and nothing eventful happening, I decided to move on to a new job and notify the factory of my departure. This gave me the opportunity to make a few crucial observations. I went early in the morning and spoke to the manager, James. He told me that he was surprised; he wanted to keep me because I am a 'good worker'. He then proceeded to offer me a temporary, three-month contract directly with the company if I stayed, stating that he would bypass the agency they were employing me through. He said that 'the way I use agencies is that I take guys on and keep them if they are good. I already sent two or three guys home, but you are good and you work well within the existing team. There is a lot of work, and we were planning to keep you guys for some time.'

This illustrates how agencies act as organizing, distributive and socializing mechanisms for migrant workers in the labour market. James uses them to sort through migrant workers, as if they are mere objects, and keep the ones he wants, while the precarious contractual relation ensures that the migrant will do their best to be kept by James. The process of manufacturing the core part of a radiator is anything but unskilled: it requires patience, finesse, physical aptitude and concentration. It takes about two weeks of constant training to learn how to assemble a small radiator core, and at least a month until you can begin assembling a medium sized one. Turnover is not something that this company desires.

At the same time as he was offering me a contract, James had kept Viktor in an agency contract even though Viktor had been an exceptional worker for over three months. Viktor was visibly anxious about his future and regularly voiced concerns to me about whether he would get fired or not. Why did I get offered a direct contract? Because I told them I was leaving. This is the only reason. Otherwise, they would have been happy to keep me through the agency, like they did with Viktor who had been there longer than me and was a better worker than me. Our precarious status was maintained for as long as possible, and the prospect of security was like a carrot they dangled in front of us, making us compete for something we had already won. (Fieldnotes, 9 November 2018)

Agencies, alongside other precarious employers, utilize precarity as a filtering mechanism that enables them to sort through workers until they find, and keep, the individuals that conform to their 'good worker' standards (Forde et al. 2015). Usually, these involve personality traits that migrant workers are expected to perform, such as flexibility, docility and high productivity. In their attempts to gain stability and security, many migrants willingly perform these characteristics, a performance that frequently presupposes and involves indirect competition in relation to other workers (Lever and Milbourne 2017). This competitiveness is inscribed in the system of agency and precarious labour, as the pool of available workers is consistently larger than the available jobs. There is therefore an underlying, constant competition unfolding between workers as to who will excel at this required performance.

Moreover, as Lazzarato (2015: 186) notes, this competition is diffused throughout the social body and is also one held against one's own self: 'the permanent negotiation with oneself is the form of subjectivation and control specific to neoliberal societies. Just as in the Fordist system, the norm remains external, it is still produced by the socioeconomic system, but everything occurs as if the norm originated in the individual, as if it came solely from the individual.' Implicit in most zero-hours and agency work is the promise that through excellent work, the worker conquers a coveted job that now becomes unavailable to someone else. This is what I call the Agency Arena. While it most fittingly describes agency labour, it can also be a useful concept for analysing mentalities in other zero-hours contractual arrangements such as those found in hospitality. By not taking days off due to sickness or holidays, by tolerating infringements on labour rights, and by accepting all overtime that is requested, one might be laying the foundations for a permanent contract. These structural-turned-subjective mental projections secure everlasting, frenetic productivity on the part of the worker, while also guaranteeing profits for both the renting company and the agency. To put it in Marxian terms, these forms of precarious labour are therefore generative of an individualism on the part of workers which disempowers them in the face of the collectivism exercised by the owners of the means of production.

However, a worker's best efforts are frequently not enough to guarantee, or even approximate, security (Briken and Taylor 2018). This is especially true with agency labour. For example, my job in Amazon's warehouse was first accessed through an agency because they needed workers for the extremely busy Christmas and New Year period. At other times, for example in manufacturing, an employer might use agency labour to fulfil a particularly demanding order. The flexibility of the agency contract enables employers to use workers and then easily discard them when they are no longer required. While there is always a glimmer of hope that a minority of those workers might be seen favourably and offered permanent contracts, everybody operates with the knowledge that the overall volume of work is limited.

Workers are thereby caught in a seemingly irresolvable contradiction: in order to be perceived as a 'good worker', they need to be fast and efficient; this is the only way that they will be kept on the job and ensure that the company will not request a replacement. A positive review from the employer also signals to the agency that a worker is 'profitable', which then opens the path towards ascending the hierarchy of seniority and being offered more jobs in the future above other agency workers. However, in the proficient performance of the 'good worker', the worker progressively reduces the amount of work that they are required for; essentially, they are working towards their own redundancy. This paradoxical rationality is a requirement for the worker to be able to sustain their own precarious condition (the work supplied by the agency). The alternative would be unemployment, and a gruelling campaign of rising up the occupational hierarchy in a new precarious setting.

These requirements lead to the internalization of disciplinary control on the part of workers, ensuring the reproduction of the prerequisites for worker exploitation. One's attempts at surviving precarity therefore oil the wheels of the wider structures that foster and propagate precarity. I call this the Good Worker Paradox, in an attempt to encapsulate the constant vigilance and disorientation that is engendered by the precarious condition.

> *Lois:* Because they were operating with leaflets and cards, calendars, many calendars, we would produce so many calendars every day, but by that month we would need to sell a certain amount of calendars. So, we needed to work fast. Build up pallets of so many calendars. There was this dilemma therefore, that you either work

slow and you don't follow what they want you to follow, to be able to produce, to make all these calendars, and this would be a problem for you, or you work very fast, but you might end up not being necessary any more there.

Q: So you are progressively reducing your employers' requirements for your labour?

Lois: Yeah, in a way we knew that if this finishes, they might not give us so much shifts. Because when we were doing the calendars, they would ask for more and more workers there. Because there was a great need to work fast and efficiently. And at some point we realized 'Oh my god. When we finish these calendars, they might give us much less hours.' I remember I was discussing that a lot.

Lois, Greek woman, late 20s, hospitality
[speaking about her time working in a print factory]

The Good Worker Paradox may lead to some entirely contradictory and hopeless behaviours, as workers attempt to control whatever very limited aspects of their labour existence they are able to in order to avoid their obsolescence. For example, in contexts where a worker, like Lois, knows that they are working on a specific order – and they are being paid an hourly rate – they might try to slow down in order to extend their hours. However, this must be balanced with the requirement of showing that one is a good worker, and therefore worthy of either more hours, a reallocation to another duty once this one is finished, or at least a good word to the agency so that they choose them over other available workers for the next job. Furthermore, the interrelation of the various aspects of the labour process combined with the mechanization that is increasingly pervading precarious employment mean that even such doomed attempts at wresting some degree of control are frequently stifled upon conception – for example, the pace of a production line is set by the manager or the team leader, and if you cannot keep up, you are replaced. Nevertheless, precarious workers are constantly performing these calculations – these delicate balancing acts – which leads to further anxiety and a compulsion to self-regulate.

At its simplest and most powerful, precarity is associated with the constant insecurity of potential unemployment. This threat, the everyday and petrifying expression of class war, combines with the multiple anxieties triggered and maintained by the precarious condition to fundamentally disempower workers. These anxieties have both 'negative' and 'positive' aspects: knowing that they could be fired any second with no recourse to any form of representation or help, workers are compelled to foster high productivity levels and comply as fully as possible to company requirements; on the other hand, a successful performance of the 'good worker' might open the doors for more secure employment, and thereby afford them the wider stability that Suzan's doctor took for granted in chapter 2. Until workers reach that coveted status – which many never do – they are compelled to be constantly available, lest they are replaced in the agency arena. As Irene shows, this compulsion extends beyond the strict remit of agencies: the most fundamental aspect of the agency arena is workers' *replaceability* and their total lack of control relative to their employers' demands, irrespective of their formal contractual status.

> I couldn't plan my week; I couldn't plan my life. And they had a lot, they wanted to stay in control all the time. If it was an argument, he would tell me like, 'yeah, this is your job, it has to be like that'. And I was like, I'm thinking to myself, 'I have no contract, I have no rota, they treating me like, not as equal, whatever'. And yeah, they pay me money, everything is fine with that, but at the same time I am not happy how everything is working. And I don't like the control they are having on my life. And at some point, they give me less than 20 hours a week or something like that, sometime they give me 30, sometimes 40, sometimes 50 even. It's fine if I want to work more, but without rota, everything is. . . you can't control it.
>
> *Irene, Lithuanian woman, mid-20s, hospitality*

The socialization of precarity

While every labour regime aims to inculcate certain traits in their workforces, the extent to which they are successful is far from guaranteed. The conversion from a precarious, exploited worker to one that fully subscribes to, and reproduces, the mental and behavioural traits required of them is not automatic. Yet, through the combination of precarious employment conditions, an absence of inspiring alternative narratives in the workers' environments, and subjective traits associated with the migrant condition – such as an initial temporary motivation focused on making money to establish oneself in the host country, language and cultural differences, and disorientation – a specific form of socialization may be produced that I term the 'socialization of precarity'. It involves a behavioural and subjective set of learned dispositions that allow us to encapsulate how migrant workers in precarious occupations relate to, and perceive, their identity and positionality in work. I argue that this term is useful for understanding precarious migrant labour because it provides a conceptual framework for interpreting the complex ways in which structurally-generated experiences can impact workers' subjectivities and behaviours; furthermore, it provides a framework through which to view exercises of agency, as well as illuminating some of the barriers towards collective action.

The socialization of precarity can be conceived of as consisting of various stages. Initially, it can simply be used to refer to the loosening of social bonds within precarious workplaces: workers do not invest time in getting to know one another, knowing that they are there temporarily. A subsequent phase could be considered to be the internalization of the demands to overperform on the part of the worker, or self-exploitation (think of Lazzarato's 'competition with the self'; see also Kukreja 2021). Finally, confronted with the intersecting pressures induced by migration and precarity, migrant workers may internalize the conditions they face and reconstitute them into proud aspects of their identity: the fatigue, stress and scars that result from their precarity become badges of honour and ability rather than signs of an exploitative situation that must be overcome. This individual survivalism further isolates workers. Perversely, precisely in attempting to wrest some degree of agency, autonomy and individuality from a social context that disempowers, marginalizes and exploits, the subject might actually be reinforcing the foundations of their precarity.

This also entails important complications in relation to the issue of collective action and organization. This is because the shared experiences of exploitation that are instrumental in the creation of a unified political subjectivity are instead interpreted as difficulties that one's ability to overcome them *by surviving through them* is the *measure of one's self-worth and dignity*. One's identity as a worker is therefore constructed precisely through their capacity to survive conditions, rather than changing them.

This does not mean that workers are unaware of the exploitation that underpins their employment; it does, however, mean that, absent alternatives, they might naturalize the situation in order to best adapt to it.

> *Nicole:* These zero-hour contract I think is, how could I say, it's not very fair for people. It's not natural. If you hire someone, you need to give them something, to be more secure, in his life and his income so he knows what to do. It's not something normal, not something that supposed to be. You can make a day contract or whatever, but not zero hour. It's not a contract basically. In my opinion. In a matter of human rights, I don't think it is something that should exist, zero hours contract. If you need someone, hire him! Hire him for a time, give him that time, so he knows what he is earning more or less.
>
> *Q:* I completely agree with you. Why do you think that a lot of people accept these contracts?
>
> *Nicole:* Why they accept it? I think. . . oh, gosh. They need it. They need it. They are forced to accept it. The circumstances are horrible, their life forces them to accept this. And they said, 'oh my God, it's better than nothing, at least I am there and maybe, hopefully, they will call me and put me on the rota'. And 'maybe they will see how good worker I am and they will change', yeah *[laughs].*
>
> Nicole, Romanian woman, mid-40s, hospitality

Nicos Trimikliniotis et al. (2016: 1038) provide an important first step towards conceptualizing precarity as an aspect of a wider socialization when they write that, for workers, 'various embodied experiences of precarity constitute the primary terrain on which value creation takes place; simultaneously they are all confronted with the structural insecurity imposed by the system of a nationally organized compromise of normal wage labor (that is, full time, long term wage labor). The system of wage labor and the corresponding welfare system produced a space-fixated work subjectivity (i.e. normal, full-time, wage employment) measured according to work time. Precarious labor implodes this subjectivity on various levels: it is not space-fixated, the precarious worker works in a multiplicity of locales; his/her work cannot be quantified and remunerated according to the system of wage labor measurement; finally, the experiences of precarious workers cannot be accommodated in the unified subjectivity germane to the national social compromise of normal employment.' They go on to state that, 'precarious labor exists only in the plural, as a multiplicity of experiences variously positioned, exploited, and lived in the system of embodied capitalism, and not as a unified subjectivity or "precariat"' (2016: 227). This means that, precisely because of the way that precarious contractual relations and labour markets result in transient, disconnected and differentially positioned precarious workers, speaking of precarious workers as a unified class that is associated with unified perspectives is impossible; what connects precarious workers is precisely their disconnection.

The multiplicity of experiences and positionalities impedes all attempts at defining a universally applicable 'subjectivity'; this is the basis of Hardt and Negri's (2017) argument that the modern revolutionary subject is to be found in the 'Multitude' rather than in a strict, bounded conception of a class that is basically a reworking of the ideas that were attributed to Western industrial working classes. However, I argue that precisely this volatility, this insecurity, this constant motion under conditions of intense exploitation can contribute to the production of a specific, very real, form of socialization. This argument follows and expands the conclusions drawn from the theoretical foundations of Berardi (2017), Hardt and Negri (2017), Bauman (2012) and Fisher (2009).

Bauman (2012) argues that, under conditions of neoliberalism, the only remaining guarantee is that of liquidity, transformation and instability, engendered by the deepening ruptures of social bonds and the onslaught of individualization and responsibilization as replacements to collective engagements and understandings. According to him, precarity is internalized particularly by those caught in precarious occupations: 'they know that they are disposable, and so they see little point in developing attachment or commitment to their jobs or entering lasting associations with their workmates. To avoid imminent frustrations, they tend to be wary of any loyalty to the workplace or inscribing their own life purposes into its projected future. This is a natural reaction to the "flexibility" of the labour market, which when translated into the individual life experience means that long-term security is the last thing one is likely to learn to associate with the job currently performed' (2012: 152).

These individualizing and isolating circumstances are situated in a wider social context of insecurity in which Fisher's 'capitalist realism', a 'kind of invisible barrier constraining thought and action' (2009: 15), reigns supreme. The limits of what is possible are therefore strictly confined to what already exists. One is isolated and insecure, and the only way of resolving this insecurity is *through excelling in isolation*.

The socialization of precarity thus can be described as stemming from the combination of four distinct, overlapping and mutually reinforcing elements, all of which may be exacerbated by migrancy: awareness of precarity and the associated stress of insecurity, isolation and individualization; naturalization of the above as unchangeable realities; and a resulting self-exploitation. This self-exploitation pervades all aspects of one's labour existence; for example, Lois talks about how people are afraid to risk claiming very basic rights, resulting in them working for ten or twelve hours without breaks:

> *Lois:* So on a 12 hour shift, you get one hour break, and they don't take it. They don't have time to eat, they don't have time to drink. It's ridiculous. No one is there to replace them. For example, this guy at the reception, he often comes and asks me to give him crisps from the bar. And I am like 'why are you eating crisps, eat something from the things we have for lunch', and he's like 'I don't have time to go get food, I don't get breaks at all'. And I am like 'why do you accept this', and he's like, 'there is no one to replace me'. Or another problem is that they might be overwhelmed by the hours they have per week, but they still accept working ridiculous amount of hours just because it's work.
>
> *Q:* Are they afraid that if they don't accept it something will happen?
>
> *Lois:* Yeah, it's basically fear being completely normalized and accepting the most extreme situation just because you are afraid to risk, to claim your rights as a person. And I see that very often.
>
> *Lois, Greek woman, late 20s, hospitality*

Dimitris Papadopoulos et al. (2008: 233) write that these forms of self-exploitation occur 'when someone tries to anticipate and explore the future through its dissemination into the present and to intensify their own efforts to ensure that they remain competitive in the future. This post-contractual form of dependency is twofold: it is a dependency on the employer, who offers limited contracts, as well as a dependency on oneself to increase one's own capacity to get such contracts in the future.' Simply put, since the worker cannot control the contracts they receive, they attempt to control the only aspect of their existence that they can: their performance. These instances of self-exploitation saturated the every day of every workplace I entered. For example, in the radiator factory, announcements of available overtime were greeted with cheers, while in Amazon workers were competing for the limited number of overtime slots available and would proudly proclaim that this week they managed to secure 'fifty hours'. Of course, this willingness for overtime must be seen within the context of low-waged, insecure employment: you had to make as much money as you could, while you still could. However, it also entailed a performative aspect: you were *seen* to be a good worker.

Examples such as those described by Lois were extremely frequent; indeed, it would be surprising to find a worker that *wasn't* overexerting themselves. Crucially, the fact that these behaviours have been normalized means that new workers are socialized into also accepting them, as not doing so would disrupt the entire flow of the workplace. For example, in La Dama, breaks were only taken when the workflow permitted them (of course, if there were more employed workers, there would be more opportunities for achieving a better balance – but this would mean paying extra wages). This resulted in me regularly working more than ten hours without a single break; however, if I did take my break, this would result in someone else from the already understaffed kitchen having to pick up my work. This would in turn further disrupt everything, alienate me from my colleagues, and possibly lead to my being fired as a disruptive member of the workforce.

> *As I am rushing to complete my tasks, I am conscious, once again, of capitalism's cruelty. I have had one break in 10 hours. My feet are pulsing and aching from the sole to the calf; I have been working with a cramp for more than an hour, adapting my movements in order to keep working with minimum pain. This is fully counterproductive, as it makes me work slower on the one hand, while worsening the pain on the other; however, taking a break right now is out of the question. (Fieldnotes, 20 July 2019)*

When a subject is immersed in oppressive social and economic conditions, Bourdieu (2010) argues that the operations and reconfigurations of habitus turn *necessity into virtue*. This transformation is critical for appreciating the final stage of the socialization of precarity. Habitus refers to the complex of dispositions, movements and thoughts that are inculcated by the social structure one finds oneself in and which, through constant repetition, fuse with one's identity to the extent that they become second nature. Workers know that they are positioned in an objectively unequal economic environment, that they are at a disadvantage vis-a-vis employers and in a constant latent state of competition with their colleagues. This awareness operates alongside the hidden, but impactful, nonexistence of alternative social narratives – such as those provided by strong unions or social movements – that would impede the normalization and acceptance of working conditions. They work inside these parameters, incorporating the overexertion, stress, fatigue and physical pain as aspects of their existence. Absent an alternative narrative, workers may accept that this *is* their reality; the goal therefore becomes one of excelling within the confines they find themselves in. The signs of their exploitation are thus converted into signs of their capacity to survive, into symbols of their 'good worker' credentials, into proud aspects of how they perceive themselves. This is the conversion of necessity into virtue as manifested in precarious workplaces.

This transformation has been noted by other researchers examining migrant workers. For example, Datta and Brickell (2009) find a process of self-essentialization occurring in the subjectivity of Polish workers, who use their perceptions of 'superiority' vis-a-vis British workers in order to negotiate their disadvantaged position in the labour market. Similar conclusions are drawn by Ruth Gomberg-Muñoz (2010) in her study of Mexican undocumented workers in the US, who argues that they actively cultivated an identity of hard work in order to both survive in the labour market and enforce their sense of dignity. These mental processes nurture the socialization of precarity as they enable the subject to rationalize their disadvantaged position through a narrative that turns this disadvantage into favourable self-representation that emphasizes skill, durability and perseverance. This narrative, borne of concrete social conditions, is thereby owned by the worker, who then proceeds to proudly reproduce it in the context of their labour performance and their relationships with other workers. One cannot simply refuse to work hard; this would immediately be met with ridicule. Beyond the ridicule of others, it would be an admittance of defeat, a rupture of the very architecture one has created to sustain one's sense of dignity.

> *I understand by now that you cannot complain about the difficulty of the job; it is part of the prevalent habitus to 'pucker up' and pretend like everything is cool. Later on, I hear George tell another worker, in a loud voice intended for everyone else to hear, to 'never let it be seen that you are not in control. You might be panicking inside, but on the outside you should always look like you are in control.' However, there were times when my facial expressions were betraying me.*
>
> *At one point, after hours of working in pain, Afrim came up to me and asked me how I was. I told him that I am beginning to struggle and that, in busy periods, this job requires at least two people. I gestured at the dirty pots, cutlery, and plates that had piled up. In a loud voice, he replied that 'this is a job for three people, Panos. But you have to have the ass for the job! The ass! The ass! You know what the ass is?'*
>
> *In this case, it is true that virtue is made of necessity: the soul-destroying labour conditions, whereby the company chooses to save money from the employment of an extra worker by imposing an extremely heavy workload on the existing workers, are completely taken for granted as unalterable and therefore not worthy of discussion. The focus shifts on the personal qualities of the worker, who must have the 'ass' for working in gruelling conditions for minimum wage. His capacity to persevere and keep up is a measure of his worth and his ranking in the 'good worker' hierarchy, a notion that everyone in the kitchen has internalized. This is something that unions and other social movements will have to contend with, as a large group of people have elevated their suffering into a form of righteous struggle that they identify with. (Fieldnotes, 10 July 2019)*

The socialization of precarity interacts with the agency arena and may result in the almost total normalization and acceptance of precarious working conditions. This does not mean that migrant workers are incapable of resisting; it does mean, however, that the more precarity is perceived as a 'natural' part of labouring life, the more it becomes entrenched and accepted. As has been repeatedly noted, employers of precarious occupations are looking for specific subjective characteristics in their workforces: these can summarized as a willingness to accept the arbitrariness and instability of one's personal working conditions, combined with a demonstrable and effective desire to perform the employment obligations. Their daily operations and entire structure intimately depend on workers' acceptance, or at least begrudging fulfilment, of these requirements. The internalization, reconceptualization and eventual reproduction of precarity, encapsulated in the concept of the socialization of precarity, therefore further fortify the conditions that position migrant workers in the most precarious, insecure and stigmatized occupations. When oppression is accepted as just the way things are, alternatives are pushed beyond the realm of imagination.

> *At one point, cognisant of the fact that this is one of my last observation sessions, I remember that I haven't ever seen Jonathan since the first time I came in for the trial shift. I ask Marcin what happened to him and he replies, 'he was fired, he worked too slow'. I am taken aback at this terse proclamation divorced of any empathy, so I ask Marcin whether he thought it was deserved. He just replies, 'I don't know, but he was very slow, and they fired him'.*
>
> *Drago comes up next to me, and I take the opportunity to ask him what happened. He replies that 'he wasn't good at his job. He was here for four weeks and we kept on having to show him how to do everything. We showed him how to close the washing machine three times, and he still left it open two times and went home.' I said that it's a shame because he was a good guy. 'Yes, but being a good guy is not enough in a kitchen like this. You have to be up for the job. Plus, then you showed up, so we had another reason to get rid of him.' This realization hits me like a wall of bricks. I respond that I never wanted to take anybody's job, and he responds by saying 'Yeah well, life is unfair. That is just the way it is.' Once again, this is evidence of the almost complete acceptance of capitalist realism, without any capacity or desire to imagine alternatives or to even critically engage with the situation. (Fieldnotes, 24 June 2019)*

You swim or you drown. Despite the overarching awareness of the unfairness of the labour regime, it is accepted that your survival depends on you. And, if you do not manage to effectively perform the traits required of you, your termination is guaranteed; 'that's just the way it is'. Nobody will bat an eyelid; it is the fate that they themselves are trying to escape from. The most important aspect of this quote though, is what was not said: it involves a process where in-groups and out-groups are drawn, boundaries are defined, and those who can swim are elevated above those that cannot. As Drago said, 'being a good guy is not enough in a kitchen *like this*'. Despite the exploitation, despite the pain, despite the stress, those who remain in the job have a common source of pride in that they have managed to endure, and potentially thrive, in these conditions.

Isolation, competition and conflict

The socialization of precarity in turn impacts the formation of solidarities. In conditions that carve precarious subjectivities, *contractual precarity can result in interrelational precarity*, as people rarely invest in the development of strong bonds with others who probably will not be there in a few months. The language barrier in workplaces that employ different groups of migrant workers further exacerbates this tension. Finally, the organization of labour is another barrier to workers' communication: the strict compartmentalization of tasks prevalent in many workplaces prevents close association between workers. In some jobs this is further enforced by managers preventing workers from speaking to each other in the name of 'productivity', as was reported to me in interviews with Suzan and Lois. Everyone has a specific task to do, and usually this task must be done within a very strict timeframe. This pressure is combined with the overhanging threat of dismissal to compel workers to overexert themselves as much as possible, thereby foreclosing all avenues towards any interactions not strictly related to getting the job done.

This is most evident in warehouse work. As I mentioned above, the radiator factory had a relatively supportive culture, premised on the non-replaceability of the workforce due to the skillset required to excel at the job; nevertheless, every worker was positioned in a specific sector of the production process that was spatially distant from other workers. In the canteen, which provided the only real opportunities for communication, the socialization of precarity was still operative: most of the time, everyone was focused on their phones, quietly eating without saying much to each other, the TV constantly blasting inane talk shows. The smoking shelter was not much better: while there was some conversation, it was mostly between older Glaswegian workers who had been there for years, with migrant workers either listening idly or, more frequently, checking their phones. Based on my experiences, I would say that this is a relatively positive environment compared with most factory settings. By contrast, the fish factory presented some of the most alienating conditions I encountered:

> *There are signs everywhere about 'productivity' and 'keeping custumers happy'. Some simple mistakes, such as momentarily placing a crate on the floor, can lead to instant dismissal. In general, many things could lead to instant dismissal. I was placed on a production line in the packing area, working with the finished product (salmon fillets). The socialization of precarity is omnipresent – in more than eight hours of work, I never saw people communicate more than a few words to each other. (Fieldnotes, 28 November 2018)*

While the wider organization of labour in warehouse settings results in very specific, identifiable barriers to workers' socializing with one another, the hospitality industry presents a different facet of the socialization of precarity. Here, workers are necessarily near one another, and have to collaborate and communicate in order to perform their duties. Despite this, the intensity of the jobs combined with the precarious contractual relation results in the constant turnover of a considerable section of the workforce. Either workers are fired for underperforming or they leave by themselves once the first opportunity presents itself. Those that remain either rise up the occupational hierarchy and assume some degree of authority over the newcomers, or they accept the current labour regime in the hopes that they eventually *will* rise up the ladder.

In La Dama, the comfort arising from their intimate knowledge of each other resulted in a more inclusive and less alienating workplace; however, our contractual precarity was always a barrier between us. Furthermore, the shared mentality of valorizing overwork *as a condition of sustaining a precarious job* and internalizing the 'good worker' discourse seemed to unite long-timers on the basis of their suffering, not on the basis of their collective bonds and power to overcome this suffering: here as in the warehouses, sociability takes an individualized form. This was most clearly expressed in my last day at that workplace:

> *This was my last day in work, another 14.5-hour shift. One of the most striking elements of the day was that there was barely any reference made to the fact that this would be probably the last time they saw me. It is just a part of life to see someone leave. There is a specific culture amongst the people who have been here a long time. This culture is one of the survivor who has incorporated the habitus of overwork to the fullest in their personality* – *references made to people being 'one of us' or 'this is La Dama, get used to it', or semi-sarcastic comments along the lines of 'aaah, I love La Dama, this would only happen here', attest to habitus being virtue made of necessity, and to a shared affinity to the workplace forged through the necessity of working there but also through the reality of having found a stable, relatively secure job and then having internalized and analysed its difficulties as unavoidable. Therefore, when they found out that I was leaving, there was almost no reaction other than the acknowledgment of my action as a rational act by a worker looking to improve his situation. We might be in this together; but we are nevertheless isolated, economic actors.* (Fieldnotes, 28 July 2019)

The socialization of precarity is mostly directed inwards, towards the subject, gradually sculpting comportments, attitudes and behaviours. Yet it can also present itself outwardly in eruptions of pent-up frustration. The anxiety and competitive strain are difficult to contain under conditions of stress, giving rise to conflicts where the objective conditions of disempowerment call for solidarity. Primo Levi's (1988) concept of the Grey Zone, written in relation to his time in the Auschwitz concentration camp, is a useful conceptual tool to understand these conflicts. Obviously, one cannot fathom comparing a precarious workplace to the Nazi concentration camps; however, his analysis is relevant insofar as it describes a situation where 'survival imperatives overcome human decency as inmates jockey desperately for a shred of advantage within camp hierarchies, striving to live just a little bit longer' (Bourgeois and Schonberg 2009: 19).

The Grey Zone is one where morality and solidarities are eroded due to the immediacy of survival in a structure which is designed to foster and exacerbate their mutual destruction. This is the case with precarious occupations, although to a much lesser extent: competition is indirect, but it is nevertheless constant. One's personal survival is consistently juxtaposed to the collective interests of the group they are a part of. Every single worker knows that there are two possible outcomes for the months ahead: either they will be made permanent, or they will be fired. This pressure is made worse by the knowledge that their sacking does not necessarily have to stem from unsatisfactory productivity: they could simply be made redundant due to having completed the work they were required for. Rather than investing in developing bonds of trust with one's co-workers, it seems wiser to simply work as hard as possible and strive for a permanent contract, which then enables a firm grounding in the labour hierarchy. One's subjectivity in work is thereby fully individualized.

Concurrently with these overarching pressures towards individualization, workers must also face the contradictory fact of the interdependence of their labour functions. Contractual precarity results in labour regimes that are set up in such a way that a worker's personal aspirations directly contradict the interests of workers in general. Excluding intensely atomizing jobs such as courier driving, most occupations require some form of coordination between workers. This fact has been extensively drawn upon by revolutionary theories of working-class emancipation such as Marxism and anarcho-syndicalism that heavily invested in the belief that workers' proximity and interdependence can lead to feelings of mutuality, solidarity and common struggle. However, in the modern workplace, absent of collective agreements and with intensely precarious contractual relations, this interdependence clashes with the fact that workers are assessed and managed as separate units, their labour security constantly hanging by a thread. For example, in Amazon, we were assessed individually based on how many items we picked per minute or how many we stacked on the shelves for others to later pick. One very efficient way of increasing our pick rate was to stack the shelves as quickly as possible, without really caring about placing everything in the correct location – after all, someone else would have to find the items. However, this created enormous problems for that 'someone else', because they would have to significantly damage their pick rate by searching for items incorrectly positioned by another worker.

THE SOCIALIZATION OF PRECARITY

A similar contradiction was observed in hospitality: the precarious waiters of La Dama were in a hurry to serve customers. Their anxiety resulted in them carelessly throwing all the leftovers, together with dirty plates and cutlery, on a tray and shipping it down to the kitchen where I was supposed to put everything in the washing machine. However, I couldn't simply throw everything in the machine because it would jam and the kitchen would flood. I had to carefully separate the plates from the big chunks of leftover food and separate the cutlery from everything else because they were washed separately. In busy periods these tasks significantly slowed me down, with the frenetic fear of underperforming leading to deep cuts, burns and bruises.

To make matters worse, this situation would have a domino effect over the entire kitchen, since I was not only responsible for washing plates but also pots, pans and other cooking utensils that the chefs required. These were left in a different sink, and I would have to run between sinks to complete everything; if I didn't find time to wash a necessary pot or pan, the chef would be late in cooking the food, which would then also reflect badly on the waiter. Sometimes the entire labour process would come to a standstill and would damage everybody's prospects of job security, simply because some individuals felt compelled to put their short-term security over our collective interests. Of course, all this would have been easily avoided had the boss employed more workers; however, the socialization of precarity was key to directing our energies towards personal competition and overexertion instead of towards finding collective solutions to our problems.

These ceaseless, overlapping and cross-pollinating pressures may erupt in moments of overt hostility towards other workers. My interview participants spoke of several instances of conflict with other workers, all underpinned by the environment fostered by the employment relation. These conflicts are of a highly variable nature and also naturally depend on workers' personalities, positions in the hierarchy, etc. However, the impact of precarity is central: for example, Agnes spoke of a worker from Bangladesh who, due to her intensely precarious position as a deportable worker, often sided with the boss and developed what she termed 'Stockholm syndrome', leading to her experiencing resentment and isolation from other workers; Felix, a sous-chef in a hotel in Sterling, was constantly aggrieved by his relationships with his co-workers, who he felt were disrespectful and benefited from preferential treatment; and the Angry Workers (2020) write about the lack of trust and blame-game taking place between groups of migrant workers in precarious warehouses in London. These incidents further suggest that, in the Grey Zone of precarious employment, the shared experience of migration on its own is not enough to counteract the ensemble of structural and subjective pressures that stifle solidarity and alienate workers from each other.

> I had unimaginable, unimaginable difficulties in the hotel. Looking back, I wonder how I survived, since I now have psychological problems. I was there for a long time, many months, and I found girls that were looking for jobs and I was helping them get the job through a connection. It was bad luck. They were three girls. After a month they were all against me and they were betraying me to the manager *[Suzan was trying to get holidays to fix her detached shoulder]*. They were Romanian. And they started causing trouble [. . .] so at some point when this story was happening she came to me and said: 'look, you are my friend' – this is a small girl, 10 years difference between us – she told me 'I admire you, I like how you work and all that, but I want to tell you that this and this is happening. You try to help them but you know how people are, you know how Romanians are, you know what happens and this is what is happening, and you are lucky that I love you and I appreciate you, but you should not do these things and you could lose your job.' I was shocked. How is it possible? But I knew that she was not lying, because she was telling me things that I had myself said. So that is how a war began.
>
> Suzan, Romanian woman, late 40s, hospitality and logistics
> *[translation mine from Greek]*

Resisting alone

Without the possibility of collective struggles to improve conditions, mobility emerges as one of the few avenues of resistance. Berntsen (2016), Wu and Liu (2014) and Alberti (2014) have all examined migrant workers' use of their contractual precarity to switch jobs when confronted with problematic employment conditions. Reversing discussions that posit migrant workers' precarity as a source of weakness, Alberti (2014) argues that migrant workers can use their precarious labour status as a means of resistance. Migrants' awareness of the temporariness of a specific job, combined with a wider subjective temporariness, fosters a sense of detachment which in turn could make them 'more prepared to leave their insecure job and dis-identify with it' (2014: 874). Similarly, Lisa Berntsen (2016: 482) argues that, for migrant workers in the construction sector, 'the common pragmatic response to exploitative terms of employment is to change jobs instead of trying to get an employer to change the conditions'. Mobility between precarious jobs therefore appears as one of the main ways migrant workers attempt to address labour conditions that they view as intensely oppressive or exploitative.

While the workers in La Dama, for example, were essentially tied to their job due to their lack of cultural capital in Scotland and their limited, insular networks, many of the other migrant workers I interviewed were much more comfortable with switching jobs. Of course, this was dependent on their proficiency in English, as well other factors; taking the risk to change jobs is much harder for a single mother with caring responsibilities such as Suzan than it is for a single, younger woman that is fluent in English. Without discounting these differences, for many workers switching jobs was presented as the only conceivable way of improving their labour conditions. Strikingly, it was much more common for workers to leave jobs by themselves than it was for them to be fired. Migrant workers have a clear consciousness of how the employment relation depends on their exploitation; they therefore have an equally clear understanding of how deeply their bosses depend on their labour. The confidence with which they switch jobs attests to this knowledge: particularly in big cities, they know that other jobs are available and hiring. This is especially true for migrants who have lived in the UK for a longer period of time and have therefore developed some familiarity with the labour market. For example:

> I don't have limit. No. I can't speak about my colleagues. But if you ask me, I have no limit. I am not scared *[of speaking out]*. This is the thing. You have a limit when you have something to lose. I have nothing to lose, so I have no limit. If I lose my job, so what? I find another one like that *[snaps fingers]*.
>
> *Nicole, Romanian woman, mid-40s, hospitality*

This availability in Glasgow was confirmed during my research. Between September 2018 and January 2019, I worked for three different companies in their warehouses. Similarly, between June and August 2019 I accessed the kitchens of three different restaurants as a kitchen porter, eventually opting to remain in La Dama. The first stint was accessed through multiple labour agencies, who swiftly found precarious occupations that needed workers. The second stint in hospitality was accessed by simply walking around Glasgow and handing in CVs. In most cases, I secured the job within hours; the maximum period that I had to wait was three days. Finally, at the end of my PhD research, I seamlessly moved back to my old job in Amazon; since I was already considered a 'good worker', there were no barriers in my return.

Despite the ease with which some workers can switch jobs, it remains a relatively privileged choice that many can't afford. Even for those workers that are confident of finding new work, switching jobs means exposing themselves to high levels of stress and anxiety. In her exploration of low-wage employment in the US, Barbara Ehrenreich (2021 [2001]: 205) speaks of 'the general reluctance to exchange the devil you know for the one that you don't know', and this is worsened by poverty: simply put, the poorer you are, the more constrained your mobility is.

These pressures are even stronger for migrant workers: for example, those whose right to remain in the UK is tied to their sponsorship by specific employers are extremely constrained in their mobility (Anderson 2013; Interview with Arjun). Anderson (2013: 89) therefore writes that 'compliant migrants can feel unable to challenge employers, and in some instances, employers have taken advantage of immigration status as a means of exercising control over work permit holders'. Since 2021, this has now been extended to all new arrivals from the EU, vastly expanding the pool of super-exploitable workers. Similarly, workers with caring responsibilities, children and debts are much less likely to risk a protracted period of unemployment for the sake of switching jobs – in some cases, stability can be more important than comfort. Finally, one's ability to navigate the labour market is closely connected to one's possession of various forms of embodied and cultural capital (Bauder 2006). While Nicole believed that she could find another job at the snap of a finger (beyond the availability of other similar jobs, this comfort was also intimately connected to her perception of herself as a good worker), the workers in La Dama were tethered to the workplace through an intricate network of family responsibilities and feelings of being indebted to Drago, combined with a relative lack of English language skills and familiarity with the Glasgow labour market. One must possess a range of tools to view mobility as a solution.

> So I told the boss, 'these are my duties, and if they gonna change you need to inform me earlier and I need to say yes or no. And if I say no, you still need to give me one week notice to change job.' And she was like, 'you are not going to leave now, we are so busy' and I'm like, 'yeah, every place is so busy, so finding a new job right now is a few hours'. So, she was nice to me because she knew that I am made from hard stuff.
>
> *Agnes, Polish woman, mid-20s, hospitality*

'I am made from hard stuff': this is the socialization of precarity expressed as personal resilience. While highlighting such exercises of agency is important in counteracting sensationalized perspectives that reify the disempowerment of migrant workers, I concur with the Angry Workers collective (2020) that these individualized forms of resistance are by themselves not enough to substantially alter the unequal relations that lie at the root of migrant workers' exploitation. The same conclusion is reached by Lisa Berntsen (2016: 476), who writes that 'the impact of individual job jumping on changing conditions of exploitation, unless collectively performed, is generally minimal'. Recall the salmon processing factory in the previous chapter, and the purely procedural way in which the onboarding was conducted. The pool of available workers competing for these jobs is sufficiently large that, once an individual worker leaves them in search of something 'better', a replacement is immediately found. As such, employers have no incentive to improve conditions, and workers' transience – also spurred by their own, perfectly rational desires to find better occupations – helps to maintain precarity because the bonds of solidarity that could be established through remaining in a single site are never formed. Switching jobs could therefore be seen as an expression of limited power – a constrained manoeuvre – in conditions of powerlessness; essentially, as the only form of power that the socialization of precarity allows, itself a manifestation of that socialization. Migrant workers operate within the confines of the structures they find themselves, and they act upon the limited opportunities introduced by these structures. However, the overall framework that conditions their available choices is far from liberatory, especially when it directs workers to select individualized avenues for the rectification of the injustices they experience.

Nivedita Majumdar (2017) argues that 'choosing between two options that have been generated by an oppressive social structure is not resistance – it is acquiescence to that order'. Workers' glorification of their opportunities to switch between precarious jobs can therefore ultimately be seen as a glorification, or at least an acceptance, of the structurally-induced 'flexibility' and 'fluidity' that underpins workers' insecurity and exploitation in precarious occupations. Without powerful collective responses targeting the foundations of socioeconomic precarity, migrant (and all) workers are condemned to a continuous, Sisyphean search for a 'dream job', that, for many, will most likely remain a dream.

Workers are not passive objects that merely conform to external economic calculations: people's acceptance of precarious conditions is nuanced and conditioned by a variety of factors such as wishes of progression up the job hierarchy or the need to make quick money to support children. However, as the short-term interests of migrant workers coalesce with both the short- and long-term interests of employers, those workers undergo a process of socialization. The combined effects of the pressures of precarity result in behaviours such as workers distancing themselves from each other, overexerting themselves, and internalizing the characteristics required of them; gradually, they may come to identify with the precarious condition as a proud aspect of their identity as workers.

Although the precise manifestations of the socialization of precarity change according to the labour context in question, its basic characteristics remain constant. The workings of the national economic structure (legislative impositions such as the permittance of zero-hours contracts, the setting of the minimum wage, etc.) thus combine with employer demands and subjective features of migrant workers to create, and reproduce, a complex of social and economic relations that, ultimately, reinforces its own neoliberal foundations.

4
The Precarious Migrant Subject

Our society conditions the ways that we view ourselves. Like trying to visualize an alien civilization, imagining something that completely escapes the limits of our social reality is almost impossible. The ways of seeing that have been honed through our everyday interactions with our environments limit our vision, and what we imagine ends up looking dishearteningly similar to what we already know. Our identities are thus constructed by drawing upon the resources of the very same environment that we may be wishing to oppose.

This is the insidiousness of the socialization of precarity: even when people attempt to resist precarity, they usually end up reproducing its fundamental qualities. The workers at La Dama had all naturalized overwork and had forged their *proud* identities as workers in relation to the demands of the kitchen; the 'associates' at Amazon run through the aisles, hoping that *this* month they will be granted the coveted permanent contract that they are all competing for. Agnes believes herself to be made of 'hard stuff', the results of a long migratory journey where she consistently demonstrated resilience and managed to survive. Now, she feels confident challenging her boss because she knows she can find another job; indeed, as Nicole said, she can find it at the snap of a finger. In the atrophied, individualist landscape of neoliberalism, people enact resistance by mobilizing the contestational resources that are available to them; very frequently, as is exemplified by the tendency to view changing jobs as a source of strength, these are themselves ideological components of neoliberalism.

While migrant workers operate within the confines of the dominant structures and ideas, their interpretations of these constraints, and of themselves as actors within them, are highly nuanced and complex. In his seminal study of migrant labour, American economist Michael Piore (1979) labelled the migrant worker as the quintessential '*Homo economicus*' – he wrote that migrants are defined by a short-term, economistic outlook, aiming to secure as much money as possible and return home to their countries. While that may have been largely true in the West of the late twentieth century, this is only partially applicable to most migrants today. Initially positioned in precarious occupations due to the workings of the national and international socioeconomic environment, many view these jobs instrumentally not in order to amass money and return to their countries, but in order to progress to better jobs and establish a secure life for themselves in *this* country. This desire to 'move on' may take different forms, always conditioned by an individual's class, race, gender and priorities; some may be satisfied with rising up the occupational hierarchy in a specific workplace, for example by becoming managers; others might want to make some money in order to invest in further education; while others simply want to secure themselves in the host society before making other moves. For everybody I interviewed, the desire was to attain security, to settle. To varying degrees, migrants are therefore invested participants in the society they choose to remain in. The subjectivities and identities of migrants emerge as constantly changing outcomes of the dialectic between social structures and the individuals operating within them (Topak 2021).

How does being a migrant influence the ways that workers perceive, negotiate and resist their precarity? The initial disorientation of the migratory experience may eventually give way to more knowledge, confidence, and a critical – perhaps even oppositional – stance towards one's labour conditions. The extent to which migrants have access to oppositional narratives, whether through contacts with radical social movements in the host country or whether they are 'carried' with them from their countries of origin, significantly shapes their proclivity to engage in collective resistances and their potential to rupture the stranglehold of the socialization of precarity.

'Just a foreigner': migration and the dual frame of reference

One of the key factors that differentiates migrant workers from other members of the precarious workforce is the multitude of additional subjective and objective elements that are connected to one's migration. To understand how migrant workers interpret their position and experience *as workers*, we must therefore examine how their everyday experience in work is filtered through their migration.

When I met Manu I was involved in the early stages of setting up the – now defunct – Migrant Workers Network with the Industrial Workers of the World (IWW) in Glasgow. A vibrant yet soft-spoken young man in his mid-20s, he had moved to Scotland a few months earlier from his home in a working-class area of a rural city in Spain. Following the route of many Spaniards in the UK, he had secured a job while still in his hometown through an agency that he found on Facebook, which sent him to a small hotel in rural Scotland. Armed with only a suitcase, some rudimentary knowledge of English he had picked up in school, and a goal to escape the economic crisis that was ravaging Spain, he found himself in the Scottish Highlands and quickly became acquainted with the abuse that festers in so many small, secluded establishments. His introductory experience in Scotland was that of wage theft. His testimony encapsulates many of the difficulties that migrants face in their initial steps.

> *Manu:* The problem was that in these kind of jobs that I can find on Facebook, were jobs that they offer you a room and food. You only work, receive all your money, and you don't spend anything. Then when I arrived there, the boss told me that I must pay £200 for my room, and not all the food was included. And after that, they told me that they cannot make me the contract, and it was crazy, it was not 40 hours per week, it was 'if I need you today three hours, then you will work three hours', like a zero-hours contract. And after all, when I came back, he pays me lower than that. It was like £1100 more or less, and he paid me £600, a little more. Discounting £200 for the room, £100 for this, some more for that. . . difficult.
>
> *Q:* Can you describe the conditions there?
>
> *Manu:* They were treating me with respect almost every time. But when they give the food for the employees like me, they were little of racism, I think. Because they were big recipe with the food for the people who were at work at that moment, and then you take your plate and get your food, so each time that I get food for me the chef look at me and tell me 'no, you have taken too much, you must put away food from your plate'. And it happened a lot of times.
>
> *Q:* And the chef was Scottish?
>
> *Manu:* Yeah.

Q: What were the other demographics? You were many immigrants or just a few?

Manu: Almost half the staff were Spanish, like me.

Q: OK, what were the positions that they were doing?

Manu: All the Spanish were like me. Me, I was kitchen porter, one other Spanish was waiter, another was receptionist, and another one, two more were housekeepers.

Q: So it was just the lower positions.

Manu: Exactly.

Q: OK. Did you discuss your conditions there with the other Spanish people?

Manu: Yeah, and they told me that it was normal, there is no problem, and the boss is a good person so he will pay me once I work. But at the end it wasn't like that.

Q: The boss didn't pay you almost half of your wage. What did you do?

Manu: The problem was that one day I got very angry about that kind of problems, taking my food. And then the boss told me 'you have taken too much', with no respect. Like 'huuuh, you are taking too much' *[mimics angry boss voice]*. And I was very, very angry because it was, I don't know, the seventh time that happened, so I decided to talk with him. And when I was going to talk with him I walked through the kitchen and I saw that, the bowl where all the staff take the food, there was food. So all the people eat, and there was food that were going to the bin. So I was more angry. Then, when I found him and I told him that I want to talk, he told me that now he was doing other things, we will speak tomorrow. And the next day again, when I came to the kitchen, again problems, and then the chef told me that the boss wasn't going to talk with me directly. I was going to talk with the chef about that problem. And the chef was angry with me because I was taking food again, and there was a little discussion about 'there is some problems, bla bla bla, and you are fired'.

Q: Just like that?

Manu: Yeah. The problem was that when I was there, I didn't have any contact with any union, I didn't know. I know that it was illegal, but I didn't know how to fight against that. How can I demonstrate that I have been working there, and how much I have been working there. It was problematic. And finally I decided to not do anything, I am not really sure about taking some measures in the future. You were asking me if I know my rights. I know my rights, but it was difficult for me in that moment to defend myself.

Q: Of course. So what was the situation like? You got fired, but you are living in a hotel in the middle of nowhere.

Manu: The situation was like 'yeah, you must go away'. I look for travel by bus to Glasgow and it was two days after that problem. And I think that I should stay there until they pay me, because then I can act, I can defend myself. But I didn't do that and it was a mistake.

Q: But it makes sense because you were alone in a very hostile environment.

Manu: I didn't want to stay there more.

Q: Of course. So then he paid you about £500 less than what you were owed. Did you talk to him?

Manu: Yeah. I answered him telling him that it wasn't enough. And I told him that I was, I had worked 132 hours or something like that, so I told him that I was going to contact a union, and if he don't pay me my money he will have a problem. And then he answered me that he will send me my payslip by post. And yeah, another thing, one of the first days when I was there I took two or three beers without telling that to anyone. I just wanted to take some beer. So one of my colleagues, Spanish colleagues, saw me doing that, told that to the boss, and then the boss, when he answered me to that message, after paying me less than I deserve, he told me that he has paid me enough because I was a stealer.

Manu, Spanish man, mid-20s, hospitality

Manu was already familiar with the anarchist and trade union movement in his native Spain, and therefore was aware that resistance through unions is one of the few ways for workers to claim their rights in the face of employers' abuse of authority. When the interview finished, I represented him in claiming his money back, which was one of the easiest labour victories that I have ever participated in. All it took for the boss to return the full amount of stolen wages was a phone call and a twenty-minute process to lodge a claim in Scotland's Small Claims Court. This ease is testament to how employers consciously abuse migrants' initial disorientation and lack of awareness of remedial procedures (during the interview, it also emerged that the boss had withheld all of Manu's accrued holiday pay – another very common occurrence in hospitality).

Manu's story is also emblematic of the ways that migration constrains oppositional action, inevitably leading to individualist avenues for survival: Manu knew that he could reach out to a union, but being in a new country, he simply did not know which to contact, or how. Critically, operating based on his knowledge of employment rights in Spain, he was not aware that in the UK there is a cut-off period of three months for lodging most claims in Employment Tribunals.

We are brought back to the story that Suzan recounted in chapter 2, where she was unable to access support after permanently damaging her shoulder: this lack of awareness of British employment law feeds a cycle of disempowerment, as workers are not equipped to challenge their employers should the need arise. The conditions that maintain precarity are thus oiled by employers' *awareness* of the difficulties of the migrant condition, migrants' *lack of awareness* of avenues for resistance, and the overarching *nonexistence* of unions from most precarious workplaces.

Raquel and Charles, a mother and son who were working together in a hotel in Stirling, add another critical component to the understanding of how this ensemble operates.

> *Charles:* I never knew my rights.
> *Q:* OK. I don't want to be annoying, but why? Why did you not try to find out?
> *Raquel:* Right. . .
> *Charles:* I never had a reason to find my rights. And I never had some like big problems, so yeah.
> *Raquel:* And we are always so tired, that when is a day off you go to sleep, you just want to rest. And that's it, you know.
> Raquel and Charles. Both are Portuguese. Charles is a male in his early 20s. Raquel, his mother, is in her mid-40s. Both work in hospitality.

Sometimes, the outright physical and mental exhaustion that are inseparable aspects of the daily life of such occupations can be enough to prevent a worker from pursuing further knowledge. This is combined with the prioritization of making money and with the initial disorientation experienced in the new society. Together with the isolation that is an almost constant feature of precarious jobs, these conditions may result in a wider sense of resignation. This resignation may in turn contribute to naturalizing precarity. All this is in line with Bridget Anderson's summary of Piore's theories (2013: 82), arguing that 'the imagined temporariness of new migrants' stay means that at the earlier stages of a migrant's immigration career, perhaps when he or she has lower subjective expectations, less language, and more limited understanding of the labour market, he or she is more likely to view work purely instrumentally'. This instrumentality is also a reason that some migrant workers will not waste time and energy on fighting for their rights. It can potentially combine itself with the resignation resulting from the socialization of precarity to direct workers' aspirations simply towards securing enough capital to be able to move on to a different job.

> I think when I came here, I was a bit in shock. I think, for me, doing the job was really soul destroying. In the sense that, I really wanted to separate my identity from it. So, I didn't want to consider that I was doing any more than just working. Which I can realize now, after being here for two years, how non-beneficial it was to me, but back then I was like, 'I want to do a job, I want to finish this job, and leave, and never think about it again.' Because it really fucked me up, basically.
>
> *Eleni, Greek woman, mid-20s, care work*

The dual frame of reference – the comparison between the conditions currently experienced and those left behind, in what many migrant workers described as a 'crisis', 'mess' and 'hell' – invariably influences one's perception of their labour situation. Manu put it very clearly: 'you need to work. If they exploit you, that is better than not working. And anyway, *the situation is better than in Spain*. In Spain, everyone is getting exploited. That is the usual way of working [italics mine].' This exploitation that 'everyone' experiences in Spain is accompanied by wages that are significantly lower than even the minimum wage one may earn in the UK.

Manu continues: 'so, when I came here and I started to earn that money, I was happy, "finally!" – but then I noticed that we were getting a lower wage than the normal people, the Scottish people'. Challenging underpayment is an attitude that emerges from an ethical or political opposition to the conditions that make underpayment possible in the first place. However, for someone who has just arrived from an objectively worse labour situation such as crisis-ravaged Spain, even the minimum remuneration in the UK is at first experienced as an ascent and as an initial *victory* in the migratory struggle that has been embarked upon. In this context, precarity is made tolerable.

As we saw in the first chapter, the socialization of precarity may even have begun to be fostered *prior* to migration, through an acceptance of the conditions one was confronted with in the country of origin. Within the limits of precarious jobs and the universe of accepted – deemed as unchangeable – conditions that forge people's subjectivities as workers, a relative improvement in wages or conditions is accepted as precisely that: an *improvement*, valuable in and of itself. Eleni describes fighting for improved conditions as a *mindset* that must be developed, contrasting it from simply having a political awareness of inequality. The dual frame of reference involves using a mindset that was developed in response to past conditions as a filter through which to perceive one's present. Changing it takes time, because it involves not only the process of acclimatizing oneself to the new context, but also reworking nuclear perceptions that may have been inculcated from much earlier periods in one's life.

> Coming here two years ago, I could barely speak the language, you know, I was like 'I don't know anything'. And coming from Greece, I do have the mindset that tells me 'you are not entitled to holidays'; 35 hours a week is a very good condition because in Greece, would be 40 or 50. So I definitely have the mindset and I understand it a lot now, being here, that I do have this mindset of a Greek worker that, like, works for three euros an hour. I think it's a mindset, it's not just 'happening'. It's a mindset you have, and you try to get rid of. Because I think the less privileged place you come from in the country of origin you are, the less you expect, you know. I was doing lots of shitty jobs while I was studying and I never knew about contracts, working rights,

I never even thought about these things, even though I considered myself politically active. But the workplace is something different I believe. And coming here, I definitely have this mindset of like, 'oh shit, I can't really ask for holidays' because I don't know, I can't really ask. I do it now, but it takes time, I think.

Eleni, Greek woman, mid-20s, care work

Importantly, both Manu and Eleni make direct connections between their class backgrounds in their countries of origin and their expectations of, and responses to, their labour conditions in Scotland. These accounts develop the classic Piorean ideas of migrant subjectivities by including the deep ways in which our origins influence the dual frame of reference. Arguably, a migrant worker from a wealthier background, carrying a different socialization regarding what is acceptable and what isn't, would be inclined to demand more from their employers. However, a wealthier migrant would normally not be positioned in these precarious workplaces to begin with – at worst, they would find themselves in these workplaces temporarily before they moved on to occupations more befitting of their class background and accumulated cultural and economic capital.

Ettore Recchi and Anna Triandafyllidou (2010) argue that many migrants perform a trade-off where they temporarily accept a reduction in class status in exchange for opportunities post-migration – in this way, a middle-class person might use their resources to study in the UK and work at a precarious job to make ends meet while aspiring towards working in a completely different environment once they finish their studies. Eleni adds further nuance to this understanding by explaining that how the trade-off itself is subjectively experienced is heavily dependent on class origins. For those that left the working class of a crisis-ridden Spain or Greece in order to enter the ranks of the precarious migrant working class of the UK, 'opportunity' may simply mean an improved remuneration or the chance to enjoy rights that locals take for granted, such as holidays.

While the dual frame of reference can contribute to a degree of acquiescence and acceptance of current conditions, it is important to note that it does not exclusively operate as such. Beyond class origins and the myths of migration that may proliferate in a given country, legacies of politicization may also play an important role in shaping migrants' perceptions of their labour. This is confirmed by a range of academic studies: for example, Beltrán Roca and Emma Martín-Díaz (2017) examine Spanish migrant workers' radical organizations in the UK and allude to the existence of already politicized and active migrant sections among their ranks. Similarly, when examining the trade union activity of Latin American workers organized in the Latin American Workers' Association (LAWAS) in London, Gabriella Alberti and Davide Però (2018: 702) write that 'the founders all had a history of union militancy in their countries of origin and their migration was connected to that. Their political background and identity had played a very strong role in their participation in LAWAS and indeed its creation.' This is also true in various examples of migrant workers' organizing in the United States (Milkman 2011).

It could thus be argued that contrary to Piore's (1979) rigid analysis, the dual frame of reference may, in specific cases, *foster* political action and act as a buffer against the most insidious manifestations of the socialization of precarity. For example, Manu became involved with the Clydeside IWW Migrant Workers' Network after only two months in Scotland, whereas other migrants I interviewed never challenged their employment conditions even years after their initial migration. Unfortunately, Manu was the exception, and most migrant workers' experiences of being foreign were usually experienced as a barrier to resistance in the workplace.

> *Irene:* Before I came here, I didn't know nothing. And I was trusting a person, in this case my sister *[who had migrated some years before Irene]*: that she knows more, that she can provide me this, that she can help me, and then I found out that she is in the same situation, she knows nothing. She can't help with this. So then I started thinking what is best for myself. So is also difficult just in relation to, she is my relative and I trust her, I feel like it must be a good shot, and then it is like OK, she also gets mistreated and maybe even more, because she is here longer, and just because I am here new, I can notice it faster. And if I can't deal with it, I will say, 'OK, I will go back to my country' because it is just a few months. Even like this, it's different, because if you live here longer, and you are getting this, treated like this all the time, I think you can just get

used to it. Like, 'I am just a foreigner here, an immigrant, so who cares?'

Q: Is that something you feel? That you are 'just' a foreigner?

Irene: Yeah, at this point, a little bit! Because I was thinking 'OK, I have education, I could do it better', but then my confidence. . . it's like, I don't know, I am not sure. . . I am losing it or maybe I didn't have it at all when I come here. . . so I had confidence to make a move forward, but I find myself in this place and it's not the best place to be in, you know?

Irene, Lithuanian woman, mid-20s, hospitality

Apart from illuminating the complex ways that structural constraints interact with subjective traits stemming from the migrant condition, this excerpt is also important because it develops the understandings of migrant subjectivities in the works of Anderson (2013) and Piore (1979). They argue that migrants' initial feelings of powerlessness and disorientation tend to dissipate as they become more embedded in their communities and gain confidence. This was, indeed, often the trajectory that was recounted to me in the interviews. However, Irene inserts a crucial caveat that disrupts this neat linearity: when one is 'treated like this all the time, I think you just get used to it'. She argues that a worker may reach such deep levels of resignation, combined with an uncritical adoption of the essentializing discourses directed towards them by mainstream society, that they are likely to uncritically accept their exploitation as a quasi-natural by-product of their 'foreignness'. This realization further supports the assertion that agency labour constitutes a form of migrant worker socialization in the new country's labour regime (Forde et al. 2015); it is a socialization which, for some, may reach deep into the recesses of subjectivity. Inequality is naturalized as intense levels of exploitation are fused with the wider experience of migration: as John Berger and Jean Mohr (2010: 115) write in their classic photographic study of migrant workers in Europe, 'tragedy is more real than explanations'.

With her EU citizenship conferring her pre-settled status – she moved to the UK before the 2021 Brexit cut-off point – Irene could be considered a fortunate migrant. For many others, the perils of 'foreignness' are significantly more arduous. Migration regimes perform a critical function alongside labour environments in socializing workers (Anderson

2013, 2010; Bauder 2006). Following Mezzadra and Neilson's idea of 'differential inclusion', it becomes possible to see borders and bordering as a process that produces particular types of workers – a process that extends to subjectivities, too. Anderson et al. (2011: 6) argue that 'national borders are better analysed as moulds, as attempts to create certain types of subjects and subjectivities'. For workers from outside the EU or those arriving after 2021, all the characteristics outlined above are exacerbated by the migration controls they are subjected to. These include their being dependent on an employer to guarantee their right to remain in the country and their exclusion from most sources of public funds. This dependency and insecurity thereby condition how their migration is experienced and assume an overwhelming weight in the definition of workers' priorities.

> Most of the people who are migrants, they are concerned about the payments. Their main concern is that. If they lost their job, it would be a big problem for them. Like, a person like me. I am still not settled. I do not get any benefits. What I earn is what I eat. Majority of the people who are like me, I will do all things to save my job rather than to move to another job. That is the main reason, financial insecurity.
>
> *Arjun, Indian male, late 40s, care sector*

'Foreignness' therefore means different things for different groups of migrants. In contrast to the liberatory 'foreignness' of tourism, in precarious occupations it is lived through a continuum of constraints that range from an exclusionary perception of one's distance from the realm of claims making (Irene's 'I am just a foreigner') to a much more debilitating spectre of deportation and destitution (Arjun's 'what I earn is what I eat'). Despite the differences in migration status, it would not be an overgeneralization to state that these multiple manifestations of physical, juridical and cultural borders are experienced as sources of disadvantage and restrictions on action. That is, indeed, their purpose.

Perceiving difference

Experiencing oneself as a foreigner is not just a result of internal, subjective feelings that result from the act of migration. It is also a relational outcome of one's interactions with the wider social context and other people within it. Migrant workers enter a context where they are already constructed as different and potentially dangerous, unwanted, abject; in the UK, these ideas played a fundamental role in the politics around Brexit and continue to shape everyday politics and culture. Working alongside these wider narratives, embodied codes play a crucial role in widening the disconnection between migrant and local workers.

Bauder (2006: 48) writes that 'immigrants who enter an unfamiliar habitual terrain will be denied full and equal participation in the social and economic game until they either assimilate and learn the rules or the rules are re-written'. These rules involve a multiplicity of actions and comportments such as accents, terminology, tone of voice and even body posture. For example, in the radiator factory I was caught by another Scottish worker resting with my hands on my hips, a common action for men in Greece; he promptly informed me that, in Glasgow, this posture is considered a marker of femininity and that I needed to 'lose it' if I were to be accepted in this hyper-masculine setting. All these markers significantly impact the ways that migrant workers navigate a socioeconomic environment in which they have already been marginalized and essentialized; they illustrate the ways that borders are expressed in the social body, and deeply impact the ways in which migrants perceive their positionalities.

> *Eleni:* Healthcare assistants, usually, the moment I open my mouth, I'm Polish and I'm there to take their job. And they ask me shit like, 'where are you from, is your family here, do you claim benefits?'
>
> *Q:* They asked you things like that?
>
> *Eleni:* Yeah of course, of course they ask you things like that. The moment I say that I am Greek, it's a bit better because, like, people go for a wee holiday in Greece. A good example of this is when I was working with two 50-plus-old people from Paisley, Glasgow. And we were talking, and I said, 'I live in Ibrox'. And I said, 'I want to move out but I still want to stay in Cessnock', and they said, 'No, no, don't stay in Cessnock.' And I said, 'why not', and they said, 'you know, it's not really safe there'. And I was like, 'you talk about Rangers *[football fans, a subsection of which is notorious for supporting racist views]*, right?', and they are like 'no, no, there is lots of ethnic people there'. And I'm like. . . You do understand I am 'ethnic'? I

am not Scottish, and you know, I'll never be Scottish. And they're like, 'no, you're European and you're from Greece, so you are not the same'. And for me that really hurt me, because I don't know, at the same time they accepted me, but in a really weird way.

Q: In a really exclusionary way. . .

A: Yeah, like, what should I say? And that happens all the time. I was in the NHS, and I speak, they see my badge, and they are like 'what's your name', I say my name, and 'where are you from', and I'm like, 'I'm from Greece', 'AH! Alright! I thought you're Polish and I don't want to work with Polish people.'

Eleni, Greek woman, mid-20s, care sector

Eleni recalls being immediately targeted with popularized stereotypes and fears relating to locals' perception of migrants as competitors over benefits and jobs. This fits squarely with Robert Miles's (1982) argument that these perceptions are operative in sustaining working-class racism. Fox et al. (2012: 686) write that 'although East European migration to the UK is a relatively recent phenomenon, the tabloids' reporting on it makes use of extant cultural tropes and racialized plotlines from previous migrations', building on existing racist and discriminatory cultural foundations and adapting them to the present. In this complex process of essentialization, white European migrants' shared whiteness is further qualified by characteristics extrinsically ascribed to specific groups of migrants, with some being perceived as more desirable than others (Anderson 2013; Fox et al. 2012). Eleni experienced this first-hand: initially the victim of aggression because of her perceived Polishness, she was then brought back into a category of 'acceptable whiteness' through her Greekness, established in stark contrast to the non-European 'ethnic people'. Indeed, Anderson (2013: 45) writes that 'the whiteness of Eastern European is racialized: it is not a simple marker of privilege but revealed as contested and unstable, unsettling and subject to internal hierarchies'. The extent to which the exclusion of certain groups has become part of everyday life and common parlance is exhibited by the ease with which Eleni's co-workers said that they 'don't want to work with Polish people'.

These mentalities are so deep that some workers prefer to hide their true origin in order to avoid discrimination from their colleagues:

Eva: I was just thinking, it also depends what kind of immigrant you are. Because, for example, I have noticed that if you are Italian, you know, I was born in Moldova and I was raised in Italy and I speak Italian. . . Moldova isn't really my country, so when they ask me, 'where are you from?', I just say 'Italy' in general. And of course, there is a difference. If you are from Italy, they will treat you much, much better. Just because it is a country that, you know, they like and, whereas if I said 'Moldova', or 'East of Europe', Poland for example, no. Don't say that. It is better to say Italy. And I know it is a bit bad to not recognize my country, but I was just trying to say Italy, just because I know that Moldova is not an advantage. I have to do it, because yeah. . . *[laughs]*

Q: Have you ever had the experience of saying you are Moldovan and seeing a negative reaction? Or is it just instinct?

Eva: People don't even know where the country is! So, they are like 'wow, where is that?' That is just the reaction I get. If you say you are from Italy, they will probably love you! *[laughs]* Italian, pizza, pasta, whatever *[laughs]*. Very stupid. They don't know what Italy really is. For example, they asked me 'why did you leave the country?' They have no idea what is going on in that country, they just think that is food and beaches, they don't know that there is an economic crisis. I think this is why they don't really discriminate Italians, because they don't realize that Italians are coming here because their country is. . . is poor.

Q: So, you think that if they realized it, it would be different? They would be negative towards Italians?

Eva: Yeah, because the kind of stereotype they have when they think about Italy is about a very rich country. If they knew that it isn't, um, yeah. They will probably be like, 'you are coming here to steal our jobs'. They think that we are coming here as tourists, basically, to get more experience, to travel, etc.

Eva, Moldovan woman, early 20s, hospitality

The most important aspect of this vignette is that Eva is fully aware of the hegemonic narratives that prevail in British society. She encapsulates the previous arguments quite succinctly: if a migrant worker is thinking about identifying themselves as Eastern European, 'Don't say that. It is better to say Italy.' She is also firmly aware of the importance that conceptions of competition play in fostering hostility against migrant groups. Furthermore, exhibiting a nuanced understanding of cultural perceptions in the UK, she understands discrimination as having the potential to extend beyond the ethnicities that are at any given point vilified in the popular media, to include all those who are perceived as economic competitors. Eva draws on her understanding of popular conceptions of migration to manoeuvre and organize the way that she expresses her own migrant background. One's understanding of oneself as a migrant and one's perception of what foreignness means is never independent of the dominant social narratives that saturate our everyday; in the case of migrant workers, they are constructed through, and in relation to, a wider environment of hostility, suspicion and competition.

Contradictions of the 'Good Migrant'

Whenever we embark on a study of the subjectivities of a group as heterogeneous as migrants, we must be prepared for contradictions. Migrant workers occupy multiple positions in society while simultaneously being excluded or included in accordance with the political demands of the day. Whether by rejecting the underlying premises of this conditional inclusion or by enthusiastically partaking in constructing the dominant narratives that underpin it, they nevertheless are fully active social agents – albeit not in conditions of their choosing. In an economy that is structurally reliant on artificially devalued, precarious migrant labour, where overlapping economic and cultural forces combine to create and maintain migrant marginalization, it is important to understand how migrant workers themselves perceive their migration and their status *as migrants*.

One of the main contradictions that I encountered was that many people were conforming to, and reproducing, an exclusive narrative that is essentially an evolved internalization of the good worker paradox; yet, at the same time, they remained conscious of their exploitation *as migrants*. It was not uncommon to hear migrants demeaning other groups of migrants who were perceived as 'lazy' or racialized as inferior, while foregrounding their own credentials as 'good migrants'. The oppressed are not immune from upholding xenophobia, racism and discrimination

(Balani 2023); if anything, one could argue that precisely due to the competition that exists at the lower rungs of the national labour ladder, enmity between different groups may be accentuated.

Bridget Anderson's (2013) ideas on how national 'communities of value' arise may help explain such apparently contradictory positions. For Anderson, 'communities of value' are formed through the collectively accepted binary categories between what are considered characteristics of 'good' and 'bad' citizens. In these collective representations, 'the Good Citizen is the liberal sovereign self: rational, self-owning, and independent [. . .] firmly anchored in liberal ideas about the individual, autonomy, freedom, belonging, and property' (2013: 2). It is not difficult to imagine how these attributes may connect with the socialization of precarity: in order to access the status of a 'Good Citizen', migrant workers in precarious occupations must first excel in the characteristics required of them as Good Workers – thus the demonstration of flexibility, capacity to overwork and individualism, beyond just offering a potential for job security, also opens the door to wider social acceptance.

In contrast to 'Good Citizens', 'failed citizens' are those who are seen as not conforming to these characteristics. Anderson (2013: 6) writes that 'migrants and their supporters are usually eager to differentiate themselves from failed citizens with whom they are often associated. Assertions that refugees are not criminals, or that migrants do not claim benefits, are attempts to counter these associations by affirming the community of value. Migrants and refugees are fit to belong because they have the right kinds of values, unlike criminals and benefit scroungers. [. . .] Contingent acceptance turns tolerated citizens, who must often struggle for acceptance into the community of value, into the guardians of good citizenship.'

These cultural processes reproduce hegemonic ideas about which groups and individuals are 'worthy', thereby masking deep structural processes of inequality. Importantly, they do so *within* and *through* the processes by which people contest and negotiate their own structural and symbolic marginalization. For example, a migrant worker performing the 'good worker' stereotype while simultaneously not accepting benefits will be applauded as a model migrant. This applause will mask the fact that this worker is structurally and culturally compelled to perform the 'good worker' stereotype in order to keep their precarious job (Gomberg-Muñoz 2010) in an unequal economy that is based on differential inclusion (Mezzadra and Neilson 2013). Crucially, migrants' reproduction of these discourses further fortifies the wider structure that produces their exploitability.

For example, Agnes had an acute awareness of how employers use migrant workers in ways that exploit their vulnerabilities and disorientation. She also had a class-conscious approach to work. Nevertheless, once asked about how she thinks that Brexit might impact her, she reproduced a 'good migrant' discourse:

> Right now, I feel secure. For the next two years, I feel really, really secure because basically I'm untouchable. If they touch me, other European countries are going to touch their citizens, and they are not that stupid. I have clean tax history, I have no record, I have never taken benefits or anything, so for that country, for that economy, I am a 'good immigrant'. And because I am staying there, I make money here and I spend money here, so the balance is the same, I'm not sending my money abroad like a lot of other immigrants do. I am not saying that it's bad, but I am making money here and spending money here so for them is the best situation. I'm really secure. The only thing is that after Brexit I have to remember to book my flights on my passport instead of booking my national identity card.
>
> *Agnes, Polish woman, mid-20s, hospitality*

This is not in itself problematic, as she is rightfully proud of her individual accomplishments in the face of adverse socioeconomic conditions. However, it is an indication precisely of the individualizing socialization that migrants experience, as well as of people's desire to be included in the 'community of value'; furthermore, Agnes's account demonstrates the hierarchization that exists within migrant groups with different levels of access to security on account of their migrant status. As a 'good migrant' who has secure status due to the timing of her arrival in the UK, Agnes can afford to be confident and optimistic: for her, the biggest annoyance caused by Brexit is simply the fact that she will have to remember to book travel tickets using her passport rather than her identity card. For every migrant – whether from the EU or not – arriving after the 31 December 2020, remaining in the UK is much more difficult.

Nicole, on the other hand, displays a more complex understanding of her role as a migrant and her connections with other migrant workers. She views herself as a strong woman who has gone through many precarious occupations, has proudly fought her share of battles, and has a critical understanding of how the migrant status of workers is used by employers in exploitative ways. She interprets her precarity through the prism of her resilience, despite her understanding of the unfairness that underlies it. Her statements are an example that one's migrant identity does not immediately equate with solidarity towards all migrants; Nicole seems to form relations of affinity with those conforming to the 'community of value', since she herself proudly reproduces these characteristics. At the same time, she is fully aware of the contradictory positions that are engendered by one's status as a migrant.

> *Nicole:* So, I am saying, there are too many immigrants in terms of other countries. And we know that some of them, immigrants, are building a life here, whatever they are doing, some of us we are paying our taxes, and some don't pay but stay on benefits or whatever. And I understand that UK citizen, maybe they feel insecure with the jobs, which is not true *[laughs]*. They don't wanna work, they don't wanna do that jobs, they only want to do from supervisor and above. So, we don't take any jobs. And it's true without us, without immigrants, nothing would work here and most of the company would be closed down. So yeah, they need us, but in the other point, I said there are too many. I said so because Angela Merkel, when ask the British government to take more immigrants, because from here everything started, when they said that UK have to take, I don't know what number of immigrants. . .
>
> *Q:* It was 20,000, it was not that much. . .
>
> *Nicole:* In Romania they say, 'you have to take this number of immigrants'. What the hell, you know! Why? Not me, because I am not living there of course. . . well I am still paying taxes because I have my house there, I have my family there – why my family has to pay to support these ones? But then I turned, and I was like 'hmmm, I am one of them, hello!' It's a tricky thing. But I understand both positions. I need to be honest, you know.
>
> *Nicole, Romanian woman, mid-40s, hospitality*

In the above quote a range of characteristics relative to migrant subjectivities can be observed. Primarily, there is a clear understanding that the UK economy structurally depends on immigration, as well as an identification with the immigrant category ('without *us*, without immigrants, nothing would work here'). However, Nicole also understands why British citizens might be against migration. This is partially connected to her Romanian nationality and is evidence of the reproduction of a hostility towards migration that is well established in Romania, an importation which uneasily coexists with her new status as a migrant. Consequently, she says that she understands why her family should not have to pay taxes to support refugees; at the same time, she understands that in her daily life as a migrant in the UK she benefits from a tolerance similar to that which her family rejects. Nicole seemed to have resolved this contradiction by developing an identity as an empowered woman who is an excellent worker. Once again, this is a manifestation of the individualizing effects of the socialization of precarity, as well as an indication of her belief that she is a member of the British 'community of value'.

These inclinations towards positioning oneself firmly within the 'community of value' can lead to migrant workers adopting and reproducing explicitly racist narratives regarding other groups. As Anderson (2013) argues, 'the community of value' is most closely policed by those on its outer borders; disregarded, marginalized and exploited, migrant workers may internalize the competition inherent in capitalism and proceed to externalize it in the form of racism towards other groups who are firmly positioned outside the 'community'.

> *I had a brief conversation with Afrim in the kitchen. He asked me where I live, and I responded that I live close to Victoria Road. His eyes widened; his voice rose in surprise: 'you live in Victoria Road? Lots of Roma there! Drugs, dirty, selling children, I never go there.' This is a further depiction of the racism and the divisions within migrant groups. The interesting thing is that Albanians in Greece and Macedonia (where he is from) are racialized in almost the same way that Roma people are racialized in Scotland. They are considered essentially dirty, unworthy, untrustworthy, primitive. This experience of marginalization however is clearly not enough to foster understanding and solidarity towards other members of marginalized communities. It would be more accurate to argue that the*

marginalized may, in the absence of political projects aiming at unity and common struggle, seek incorporation within the mainstream community of value by partaking in the demonization of those collectively defined as beneath them. (Fieldnotes, La Dama, 21 July 2019)

In contrast to dominant narratives that frame them as passive recipients of xenophobia, exploitation and racism, migrant workers are fully involved in participating and reproducing the discourses that compose the 'community of value' in diverse and contradictory ways. Anderson (2013) writes that 'the Migrant (hardworking, legal, and a taxpayer) must distance herself from the Illegal Immigrant, and her impressive "work ethic" (disciplined by deportability and the figure of the illegal) is a reproach to the lazy and lacklustre benefit dependant' (2013: 6). However, I would argue that it is more than simply a 'reproach'; in line with Gomberg-Muñoz (2010), I suggest that it is also an almost necessary subjective manoeuvre in order to maintain their tenuous, precarious balance in the social and labour hierarchy. Absent a viable, trustworthy, alternative collective narrative, in the desert of individualism and the socialization of precarity, one's aspirations for inclusion in the 'community of value' seem like a one-way street.

These cultural narratives may assume deep subjective authority, interacting with other traits such as the good worker paradox or the tendency to participate in one's own essentialization as a migrant to ultimately produce subjects that are inadvertently firm supporters of society's existing boundaries. In a similar fashion to how precarious migrants might reproduce the underlying premises that make precarity possible, they also participate in the reproduction of the narratives that collectively function to disempower migrants *as migrants*. These two processes – the reproduction of the underlying ideas of neoliberalism and the reproduction of the community of value – are not separate: *they are rather mutually constitutive*, one category existing and becoming legitimized through the other. A migrant worker cannot be a 'good' migrant and a bad worker; indeed, the dominant culture is one where migrants are judged by *reference* to their contributions as workers: a 'good' migrant is almost by definition a Good Worker, and their own subscription and reproduction of these ideas further solidify their potency in the collective culture. Filtered through the wider neoliberal imaginary, the quest for achieving acceptance in both of these categories is simultaneously individualized: a 'good' migrant means a good worker means a 'good' migrant, and you have achieved this status through your own individual performance of the characteristics associated with each category, through your *own* capacity to survive.

This might contribute towards explaining the difficulty in establishing lasting, organizational solidarities between different oppressed groups. Without these solidarities, establishing a unified identity as a collective political project is impossible, and the individualism and isolation fostered by the precarious condition become further naturalized. Being accepted as a 'good' migrant worker is the reward given for the invested performance of the traits that underpin our continued disempowerment.

Becoming a migrant worker

How migrant workers perceive their status as migrants, and by extension their power as subjects in a foreign society, directly influences their choices and behaviours. Perceptions of difference and powerlessness function to constrain migrants' opposition to labour injustices. I wanted to find out how people's perception of their status *specifically as migrants* contributed to shaping their understandings about what they could or couldn't do *as workers*, and therefore the degrees to which they participated in reproducing the various traits associated with the socialization of precarity. The case of EU citizens, who at the time of the interviews were not subjected to such strict immigration controls as people from outside the EU, is particularly enlightening in this respect since their relative privilege offers a glimpse of migrant subjectivities unconstrained by the debilitating, overhanging spectre of imminent deportation.

I met Felix on a quick trip to Stirling. The historic city is a one of Scotland's most lucrative tourist attractions, its picturesque castle overlooking an idyllic scenery upon which sits a monument commemorating the famous Battle of Stirling Bridge. In the shadow of these imposing landmarks, an army of migrant workers staffs the expensive restaurants, posh hotels and cosy pubs that line the streets. A tall and confident man in his early 30s, he had moved to Scotland to accompany his sister in her migratory journey. Already having graduated from university in Canada, he had found a job in Stirling as a KP and was proud to have been promoted to the position of a chef in 'only six months'. After leaving that job, he was now employed in the restaurant of a large hotel serving the tourists that descend on Stirling. Having trained for what he termed 'four-star standards', he experienced the deskilling that many migrants face and was currently working as a runner. Apart from the unfair advantages he felt were conferred on the Scottish labour force, he explicitly connected the demeaning treatment he was experiencing to his migrant background; this migrant background was also experienced as preventing him from having the confidence to pursue action.

> *Felix:* I am a European citizen, but, in my job, I feel like an immigrant. Yeah. When I was chef, it was different. I was feeling like a European citizen, my chef was British but he really enjoyed everything about French food, French culture, so he really wanted to just, change the menu, just to make me happy. But, no. The other place, they just want to feel like you are an immigrant because they give some privilege to kids and not for you. You are more skilled than anyone and, yeah, you feel like a fucking immigrant. I was talking with some people from Peru who was working in the kitchen, and sometimes we speak in Spanish, and each time some people came, some Scottish people, not my friend but they are friendly with me, and all the time say 'yeah, what do you say?', and I say 'yeah, I am just' (I will be a little bit rude, but) 'I am like in the 17th century in South Virginia, I am like a fucking black slave on a plantation.'
> *Q:* You feel like that?
> *Felix:* Yeah, yeah. I feel like a fucking slave. I say, you know what, I know slavery existing there, in India. Is not in there. It's in Scotland. In that job, I feel like an immigrant.
> *Q:* One very interesting thing is how you equate feeling like an immigrant to not being respected. Being an 'immigrant' in your words basically means that you don't feel respected. And that shouldn't be the case; even if you are an immigrant, you should be respected. Do you feel that the word 'immigrant' right now, in our times, has assumed a negative connotation?
> *A:* Yeah, yeah. They make that.
> *Felix, Guadeloupean (French) male, early 30s, hospitality*

The most glaring aspect of this excerpt is that Felix, a black male from Guadeloupe, compares his situation in Scotland to slavery in the United States. The first layer of this feeling concerns his experience of sustained disrespect by management, which he attributes to his being an immigrant and to the management's practice of privileging local Scottish 'kids'. However, I believe that there are further factors that have to do with deskilling and alienation. Felix has notable experience in hospitality in France, and he was initially hired in the hotel with promises of a rapid rise up the labour hierarchy. He contrasts his experience in this hotel to his previous experience with a British chef, in a context where he did not feel 'like an immigrant' because the chef appreciated his skills and gave him free reign to utilize them *creatively*. Instead of this creativity, he was now confined to menial duties well below his promised contractual status, which has left him feeling disrespected and undervalued. He compares his situation to that of slavery because *he attributes all of this to his status as an immigrant, as someone perceived as different*; the injustice that he faces *is founded on his difference* from the local and more privileged members of the workforce. The fact that he is a black male potentially enhances the discriminatory practices that he is subject to daily. Contrary to white European immigrants in Scotland, in this case the discrimination he faces is founded on ethnicity, class *and* race.

Mirroring the dominant narratives that follow the colonial organization of the world, Felix contrasts feeling like a 'European citizen' to feeling like an 'immigrant'. Being an immigrant is equated with exploitation, poverty and mistreatment, whereas being a 'European citizen' is associated with respect, prestige and opportunity. In David Roediger's (2007) analysis of how white workers in the United States became complicit in systemic racism and slavery, he argues whiteness became associated with liberty and autonomy, whereas blackness became connected with subjection and exploitation. As has been repeatedly stated, the characteristics of the jobs that groups of people perform, over time, become correlated with the social group performing them. These theoretical analyses offer reasons as to why Felix would reproduce the rhetoric that connects 'immigration' with exploitation and vulnerability: according to this schema, a rich French banker working in the City of London would be classed as a 'European citizen', whereas a working-class French hospitality worker would be considered an 'immigrant'. Crucially, Felix notes that 'they make that': the emergence of such perceptions is not an organic process, but an outcome of specific policies enacted by employers that result in the devaluation of migrants as workers.

Over time, the migrant condition is naturalized as one that intrinsically involves exploitation and precarity. The socialization of precarity works together with the existing cultures and narratives around migration to exacerbate migrant workers' feelings of powerlessness and disorientation: at worst, the conditions they encounter are a debilitating shock; at best, they are merely a daunting confirmation of their prior expectations, nurtured even before the act of migration.

How do these feelings impact workers' confidence to resist labour abuses? Felix offers an indication when he describes an incident that occurred in the hotel. When the managers decided that everybody's tips would go in a common pot and be used to celebrate another manager's birthday, Felix wanted to respond. However, he felt that his position as an immigrant in his workplace did not afford him the requisite authority to confidently speak out. Even though he eventually did, and his action of resistance was successful in that everybody else also refused to give up their tips, he nevertheless expresses his discomfort at asking Scottish workers to follow his lead.

> *Felix:* The assistant manager, she asked 'we want to donate the tips'. I just look at her and say 'you know what, last weekend you stole my money, this weekend, even for one penny, I take my tips. I don't care. I will take all my money tonight.' That's it. And finally, at the end, because I was the first one to say that, everyone took their money. Everyone took.
>
> *Q:* So, nobody liked this, but nobody spoke up. You were the only one.
>
> *Felix:* Yeah, yeah. And I say sometimes you just need a first call, and then people just follow you. And in my mind, I was thinking, 'yeah, that's how team leaders work'. So, you say something, people follow you, some will not, just that. Who wants to follow you? 'We Scottish, we wanna follow a French guy?' Eeeeeh. . . *[makes a hand gesture symbolizing how strange an idea this appears to be]*
>
> *Q:* So, you have felt a little also like. . .
>
> *Felix:* Yeah!

Q: OK. Can you talk about this a bit more?
Felix: What to say. . . *[laughs resignedly]*
Q: Do you feel something close to raw, hardcore racism, or do you feel something closer to, you know, slight instances of discrimination?
Felix: It's small discrimination, you know. . . I can call that, like, day-to-day racism. Yeah. . .

Felix, Guadeloupean (French) male, early 30s, hospitality

This dimension of the 'everyday' is crucial in the long-term establishment and perpetuation of all the aforementioned subjective traits. In his discussion of how the everyday informs wider systemic racist and racializing realities, Smith (2016: 6) suggests that racism 'is enacted in and through everyday situations including, of course, the "backstages" of formally public contexts such as workplaces and political institutions'; the comparatively insignificant and mundane behaviours, comments, fleeting glimpses, that collectively form our experience of daily life play as much of a role in reproducing the wider structure as the structure plays in producing them. The 'everyday' is the glue that connects the spheres of structure and subjectivity to produce intelligible totalities – it is where structural elements such as precarity and exploitation and sociocultural factors such as hostile media and discrimination connect with the 'dual frame of reference' or with migrants' disorientation to collectively produce subjective characteristics such as the socialization of precarity or the negative connotations associated with being a migrant. Felix's account is indicative of the cumulative effects that discrimination, overwork and disrespect can have on migrant workers' understandings of themselves, their condition and migration/migrant work as wider social phenomena. In many cases, these experiences can further feelings of disempowerment in the workplace that are intimately connected to one's self-perception as a migrant.

Nevertheless, migration is not *necessarily* connected with disempowerment. In the same way that the dominant narratives of society combine with concrete actions by employers to 'make' – in Felix's terms – one's migrant status a source of oppression, migrants themselves can intervene and forge a powerful identity from it. This is a process that has been repeated throughout modern history, with oppressed people mobilizing on the basis of their shared experiences of oppression to challenge inequality. Such movements, like Black Power in the Anglosphere or the East End Jewish workers in London at the turn of the twentieth century, connected their oppression to their status as 'outsiders' and proceeded to take direct action (Ramdin 2017; Virdee 2014; Rocker 2005; Sivanandan 1983). Recognizing that racialization and marginalization were crucial components of their exploitability, itself an inseparable requirement of the wider economic structure, these groups connected their grievances as outsiders with their grievances as workers, joining or forming trade unions and powerfully intervening in the wider labour and social struggles of their eras. The forging of these politicized identities, or, as Sivanandan put it, 'communities of resistance' (1990), is an inescapable prerequisite to organizing such movements. The first step of this process is identifying as a migrant and connecting this identity with the prevalent forms of one's exploitation.

> I think I would definitely say I am a migrant here, and I think that is identified by other people, not me. Because of the jobs I've done, so I would say, because I am in an environment, since I've been here, with, like, Glaswegian working class, people working in care, yes, I am a migrant. Because to them, it doesn't matter where I am from. Before they meet, some of them they don't give a fuck if I am Greek or Polish or whatever. And I think I would say I am a migrant because I don't really have the same rights! I mean, I don't know, I have to give more papers to prove myself. For example, I am trying to recognize my degree, and I cannot recognize it because I don't meet the requirements of the Scottish services, so I can't practise. I have to give, like, a reflective account of everything I have done in the UK to prove I belong here and I can do skilled labour. A Scottish person that studied exactly the same thing as me never has to do that. And the fact that I have studied a field that is more social focused, social-science focused, not, like, not program developing or whatever, it's even worse because I have to be part of, like, this culture, and this culture 'others' me. And this culture, the moment they see my name, my accent, I'm not the same. So, I guess I could not be a 'migrant' if I came here and I didn't have to interact a lot, or I decided, you know, I could just go back and forth on vacation, but I am a migrant because other people identify me as a migrant.
>
> *Eleni, Greek woman, mid-20s, care work*

In this excerpt, Eleni is connecting various threads that have been analysed previously. The identity of a 'migrant' is a relational one: it is extrinsically imposed on migrants on the basis of what they are not (i.e. Scottish or British), and it is then used by migrants to conceptualize the totality of conditions they find themselves in. Eleni recognizes the various structural and cultural barriers that create and sustain her 'otherness': initially she refers to how she is being treated by Scottish people, but she goes on to cite deskilling, in this case the non-recognition of qualifications, as an integral component of this process. Then, she focuses on the practical effects of her structural and cultural othering: 'I am a migrant because I don't really have the same rights.' These overlapping categories that create and sustain difference and marginality mean that 'the moment they see my name, my accent, I'm not the same'. Eleni adds a class dimension to this understanding: she recognizes that if she were a tourist, if she didn't need to work and live in this country as a precarious migrant worker, she probably wouldn't feel like a 'migrant'. However, the combination of her everyday experiences in labour and society has coalesced into a strong identification as a 'migrant'.

In contrast with Felix's quote above, in Eleni's case this is not a purely negative identity: it seems more like a reflexive realization of the results produced by the intersection of migration, economics, state policies and culture. Manu goes one step further, explicitly speaking about the political potential of mobilizing as members of a migrant working class.

> *Q:* Is 'migrant' a political identification for you?
> *Manu:* Now, yes.
> *Q:* Many migrants don't connect their migration to politics. What made you experience it as a political identification?
> *Manu:* I started to have that identification when I noticed that I have a lot of things in common with other people from other countries that came to Scotland to work. I know that before, but I didn't think a lot about that before I came here. When I came here, I considered myself, 'I am Spanish in Scotland, so they are exploiting Spanish people.' But then, it doesn't matter if you are Spanish, you are Italian: you are migrant. That is the reason they exploit you. That is the reason I identify with the word 'migrant'. Because the reason is, you are a migrant. Is not just because you are Spanish.

Q: Fair enough. And do you think that this identity can be a basis for organizing?

Manu: Yeah, of course. It is very important actually. If the people are not conscious about that, then it is more difficult to build a. . . net of people, of support, of people in the same situation. They need to be identificated with the same ideas to work together.

Manu, Spanish man, mid-20s, hospitality

Like Felix and Eleni, Manu notices that the nature of his exploitation is founded on his difference. However, in this excerpt he expresses a more complex politicized analysis: he connects his experience as a migrant worker to that of other migrant workers in precarious occupations. He recognizes that 'it doesn't matter if you are Spanish, you are Italian. You are a migrant.' In doing so, he directly alludes to the entirety of social relations that sustain migrant exploitability. Furthermore, he argues that identifying as a migrant is a crucial component of empowerment, in order to create a 'net of people in the same situation'.

A crucial caveat is warranted here: acknowledging the role of migrancy in the specific way that precarity is experienced, and thus identifying with 'being a migrant', does not mean reifying the migrant identity above other social positions, or struggling exclusively on the axis of migration. The formation of a political subject – a collective that identifies with each other and pursues shared political goals – can only proceed based on a common understanding of oppression. Far from enforcing dominant conceptions of 'the migrant', this process of developing collective bonds departs from a shared understanding of the forces that perpetuate the real, material ways that oppression is experienced in everyday life and labour. In drawing these connections, oppressed groups are empowered to directly confront both symbolic and structural sources of their oppression, rallying around 'the unifying power of a word' (Bourdieu 2010: 483). Manu's reclamation of the migrant identity is therefore not a decision that perpetuates the dominant narratives around migrant workers; rather, it is viewed as a fundamental first step in overturning the social relations that underpin them. It is a recognition that, in order to work towards the empowerment of migrant workers, they need to struggle *both* as workers and as migrants (Alberti et al. 2013).

Despite their awareness of the role migration played in the specific forms of exploitation they faced, few of the people I interviewed expressed a politicized migrant identity. This adds a second crucial caveat to the aforementioned discussions: *everyone who strongly identified with the 'migrant' identity had existing histories of political participation.* Some became politicized through the Occupy movements of the early 2010s; others were, and are, active trade unionists; and others had long trajectories in autonomous, grassroots projects, both in the UK and in their countries of origin. This resonates with Smith's (2016: 6) assertion that 'the ways people make sense of their lives are necessarily shaped, not just by context, but by the availability or otherwise of intellectual, cultural and political resources'. This does not necessarily mean that the other interview participants consciously decided *not* to adopt a politicized migrant identity; rather, it is more an indication of the relative absence of a widely disseminated oppositional political narrative in the communities and workplaces they inhabit, an absence which reinforces the solidarity-destroying and atomizing tendencies fostered by the socialization of precarity. Indeed, as will be discussed in the next chapter, everybody who was asked whether they would support a trade union or similar organization led by migrant workers, for migrant workers, replied affirmatively.

Class

In contrast to the complexity surrounding how migrant workers negotiated their status as migrants, everyone demonstrated a developed awareness of class inequality and of their disadvantaged position *as workers*. This can perhaps be attributed to the very direct way that class is experienced in precarious occupations; beyond being an identity or an extrinsically imposed classification, it permeates all other social positions one may occupy (Young 1990). Hierarchical injustices, working in unsafe conditions, informality, abuse, low pay and alienation all coalesce in producing clear, unambiguous feelings of class inequality. Another key component must therefore be underlined in our understanding of the socialization of precarity.

In contrast to popularized theories that claim that the identity of being a worker is dead (see, for example, the influential and otherwise brilliant

2017 essay by Byung-Chul Han, *Psychopolitics*), the contemporary individualist and hypercompetitive environment does not inescapably result in workers *rejecting, ignoring, forgetting* or *disassociating from* their working-class status; it does mean, however, that in the absence of convincing alternatives they are compelled to negotiate its effects individualistically. Regardless of how those I interviewed rationalized class inequality or their position within the wider social structure, everyone I spoke with firmly referred to it as a key source of injustice.

> I was completely exploited. I was doing the job of a manager getting paid at that time, it wasn't even £7, it was £6.25. Imagine working 35 hours and after taxes earning less than eight fucking hundred quid per month. That was it, you know. Poor, constantly a poor worker. A full-time, a poor full-time employee.
> *Leila, Spanish (Tunisian) woman, early 30s, hospitality*

Every word that Leila uses is important and specific. She calls exploitation for what it is (the surplus profits gained from paying workers less than the value of what they produce), and she connects her poverty to this exploitation. Implicit in her exasperated interview is a clear recognition that the demands and promises of neoliberalism, whereby one is supposed to tolerate overwork, flexibility and low payment in the hopes of an improvement in conditions, falter when confronted with the realities of the precarious economic landscape. Clearly, work on its own is not enough to guarantee security, and earning less than £800 a month is dismissed when it is associated with the labour hours and pain that have gone into earning it. While the dominant 'management-speak' that is currently burgeoning everywhere from shop floors to social media attempts to convince workers that they are 'associates' or 'partners', Leila firmly positions herself as an exploited, poor worker.

> The boss always saying to us that we are not employees and boss, we are friends. But in my opinion, you can't be friends with your boss. The only thing that you can be friends in a business is when you are business partners and you are in the same position. And you can be friends because, anyway, you gonna make the same amount of money, and your friend can't sack you. You have the same power. And it's

even better to be a friend with your business partner because you can make more money together, being friends. But is no friendship with your employer as boss, they are already in the hierarchy; they are higher than you and she can sack you.

Agnes, Polish woman, mid-20s, hospitality

'You can't be friends with your boss': without any previous experience of political or class-based organizing, Agnes vocalizes a central argument that radical unions and other social justice movements have been trying to disseminate for centuries. To be sure, this position is more class-conscious than that propagated by most of the big unions in the West! Agnes proceeds to lucidly explain the foundational disparities of class: 'they are already in the hierarchy; they are higher than you and she can sack you'. Her experiential awareness of injustice organically nurtures class consciousness.

This is consistent with Bin Wu and Hong Liu's (2014: 1404) analysis of Chinese migrant workers in the UK, who argue that 'there is no doubt that ethnic and social connection, which is based upon kinship, place of origin, family and dialects, remains an important element in linking Chinese migrant workers abroad. [. . .] However, as time evolves, shared sentiments among workers, including class consciousness, are increasingly becoming a demarcation in the social and cultural lives in the migrant communities.' Even though migrant workers may be argued to represent a distinct class fraction (Miles 1982) due to the particularities associated with being migrants, they nevertheless have a developed class consciousness as *workers*.

This was also repeatedly confirmed during my incursions in workplaces. For example, in almost every workplace I was in, other workers initially helped me learn how to perform my duties in what were faint manifestations of solidarity based upon a common awareness of the constantly overhanging threat of our dismissal. They did not want to let someone get exposed in their first few days. As was made evident from Jonathan's firing in La Dama, however, this assistance was by no means unconditional; after a few days, you were expected to be able to pull your weight. This was not entirely altruistic either, as it was founded on a sharp awareness of the interconnectedness of the labour process: as we've seen, if one link in the chain broke, everyone would look bad. Yet this precise awareness attests to everyone's joint consciousness of the precarity of our class position.

I also witnessed multiple instances of what Lisa Berntsen (2016) terms 're-working', or subtle acts of resistance that do not directly challenge the foundations of the employment relation but nevertheless are evidence of workers' attempts to navigate its inequality. For example, in La Dama our contract strictly stated that unauthorized use of a phone would result in instant dismissal. However, I was quickly informed by other workers that the kitchen is a separate world, with its own rules and contingent solidarities; even though there were two cameras constantly observing us, workers had located their blind spots and we could all use them to check our phones without fear of reprisals. Similarly, in Amazon we had realized that for a brief time the cameras in the chiller were not working, and it was there that workers 'stole' some minutes to speak to one another, make a few jokes, or simply momentarily rest their legs before dashing out again. In this hidden space, workers found a crevice that allowed a passing escape. Simply put, even in the most precarious and individualizing circumstances, and even in cases where workers had largely adopted the mask of the 'good worker', any opportunities that arose to wrest some agency from the overarching experience of alienation were seized.

Indeed, class awareness permeated almost every interaction, every utterance. This could be seen as the flipside of the socialization of precarity; in order to develop – and perhaps eventually adopt and reproduce – the comportments required by the precarious structure in your attempt to achieve some semblance of security, you must first be conscious of the precipice of unemployment, the abyss into which you are precariously peering. Paradoxically, the socialization of precarity *cannot* proceed without an awareness of class, for if you were secure, why would you tolerate these conditions? Recall Afrim's exclamation from the previous chapter: 'this is a job for three people, but you must have the ass!' The onus is placed on the individual worker to develop the capacities to work with the strength of three humans: yet this demand is premised on an understanding of how ridiculous the proposition itself is!

The absurdity of class, the contradiction between promise and reality, effort and remuneration, struggle and reward, was regularly voiced in the form of sarcastic remarks in all the workplaces I entered. For example, when the management left sweets out for us in the radiator factory, Kris told me, 'Here, take one. This is what they pay us for our work.' Management was always perceived as incompetent, distant, self-serving – and, indeed, everything proceeded much more smoothly when they were otherwise occupied; the unrealistic and entitled expectations of clients were ridiculed, our collective frustration forming bonds of affinity amidst our precarity and perhaps also triggering a few laughs; faulty equipment was directly attributed to the bosses' carelessness and attacked with a menace that was a sublimation of the anger felt at the job *as such*; although conflict was not overt, and was definitely not expressed politically, it saturated every single moment.

Despite the proliferation of the socialization of precarity, it is therefore entirely myopic to assume that class identities are no longer relevant or are no longer experienced as such. For migrant workers in particular, it could be argued that the ways that they connect their exploitation to their difference may, in fact, make the underlying exploitative nature of their labour relations more apparent to them than it may be for 'local' workers, whose investment in other dominant constructs and narratives (such as national belonging or whiteness) may obscure or dilute this awareness. Like all workers, they are reflexively aware of the socioeconomic landscape they inhabit; their actions, and in-actions, are results of personal decisions made in accordance with the context that surrounds them and the resources, or lack thereof, that are available.

The *content* of how one interprets class is related to their personal degrees of *political* consciousness. Unsurprisingly, migrant workers who were involved in political projects expressed more nuanced, politicized perspectives on class relations and conflict. For example, Eleni and Lois had both participated in the autonomist and anarchist movements of Greece; their fluency in political terminology allowed them to be very specific in articulating the nature of the exploitation they experienced. In contrast, other migrant workers expressed their dissatisfaction using less precise language, but without eschewing specific references to class or hierarchies. I would argue that it is possible to bridge the two poles: in the next chapter we will look at the story of Mateusz, a Polish worker in his mid-40s who, despite not having any previous engagement with political activities, contacted a union in his sector to resist his manager's abuses of authority in his factory. After a successful union campaign, he proceeded to become a paid official and is currently engaged in helping precarious workers organize themselves all over the UK.

Workers with class consciousness but without collective affinities, citing migration both as a source of abuse and of strength, acutely aware of disempowerment but simultaneously fostering strong, resilient individual identities: the ways that migrant workers relate to their status as migrants, workers, and as *migrant workers* are extremely heterogeneous and, sometimes, contradictory. As Agnes and Nicole demonstrated, they may adopt a strong class analysis but nevertheless be fully invested participants in the narratives that make up Britain's conception of the 'community of value', thereby accepting and reproducing the mystification of the conditions that enable that exploitation. Some might try to empower themselves by investing in the development of strong personal traits; others feel that their status as migrants fundamentally disempowers them relative to their peers. Some might feel both simultaneously. All understandings are mediated by the available contestational resources in migrants' workplaces and communities, their everyday experiences playing a foundational formative role in the construction of their identities as migrants.

It is no surprise, then, that in the absence of strong and socially embedded migrant workers' movements, the only migrant workers expressing a politicized migrant identity are those already politicized and active in such movements. Nevertheless, the socialization of precarity, although tending to naturalize inequality, *cannot* erase one's awareness of it: departing from the visceral, corporal realities of exploitation, a degree of class consciousness, despite the pressures to erase it, survives.

5
Solidarities and Resistances

In the face of deepening exploitation and worsening inequalities, collective struggles remain the only sustainable way for oppressed groups to claim improved conditions. The fantasy of the post-Cold War capitalist system that victoriously assured my generation and those after it that we would grow up in a democratic world governed by a flexible yet benevolent market swiftly proved itself to be a nightmare. In the 'developed' world, the rapidly expanding levels of wealth for the few have been accompanied by precarity, anxiety, burnout, drug epidemics and a permanent stratum of marginalized, incarcerated and 'surplus' human beings; in the 'developing' world, it brought almost complete market dysregulation, poverty, genocides and environmental catastrophes.[1] As the interrelated forces of globalization, neoliberalism and technological improvements change the patterns, speeds, methods, outputs, circuits and wider relations of production globally, the need for cheap, exploitable labour remains constant. These precise geopolitical vibrations trigger and sustain a steady supply of migrant workers to wherever they are needed to ensure profitability (Castles 2000). Border controls create precarious workers (Anderson 2010), with governments, employers, think tanks and transnational entities collaborating to fortify the disempowerment of the disempowered. As saviours in the form of 'progressive' political parties constantly prove incapable and unwilling to improve the lives of the many, the latent power that is held by those who keep the productive and reproductive functions of society operative remains the only resource that they – we – can harness to improve our lives. There is no way around the necessity of collective struggles.

Historical movements by oppressed groups have understood this, and migrant workers – despite their disadvantages in every society that could be used as an example – have been central actors in emancipatory processes. In the UK and the US, their organization has been premised on the understanding that, owing precisely to their marginalization, they had to organize autonomously. In the UK the Colonial Seamen's Movement and the Jewish workers' struggles of the early 1900s, and the Indian Workers' Association and the Black Power movements of the mid to late twentieth century, are examples of potency that should not merely be relegated to history.[2] In the process of fighting for themselves, these workers also developed bonds of solidarity with, and supported the struggles of, the local working class. Their autonomy was a source of strength, helping communities establish themselves and develop strong institutions and political identities.

This was made possible through a combination of three crucial realizations: one, that they had to rely on themselves, since most unions were invested in the various processes that maintained their relative disempowerment; two, that their oppression was based on their migration, race *and* class status, that therefore these categories were not abstract theoretical jargon but co-constitutive foundations of their oppression, and hence *battlegrounds*; and three, that solidarity could not just be built on the shop floor: it required sustained involvement in the community, a process that lifted people above the anxiety and alienation of their daily labour and allowed them to imagine alternative modes of life.

The conditions of our contemporary world are vastly different to those that birthed these movements. Perhaps the most significant development in terms of collective organizing has been the weakening of class-based *collective* identifications. As the previous chapters have argued, this does not mean that (migrant) workers are unconscious of their class status; it means that this consciousness is individualized, no longer a source of connection but a constant reminder of powerlessness and of the necessity to wage one's own solitary struggle in the hopes of accessing an ever-elusive promise of security. Identity politics, initially an empowering development that challenged precisely the tendency of established movements to reduce everything to questions of economics and class while neglecting the roles of gender, race, sexuality and migration in determining social relations, could be argued to now act as forces that further erode our awareness of how class permeates all other social positions. These identities, as isolated points of struggle, do not offer solutions for overcoming precarity (Balani 2023). In contrast to the societies of the historical migrant movements mentioned above, we are now living in a moment where almost all social narratives – even progressive ones – insinuate the irrelevance of class as a perspective through which to develop radical, emancipatory collective action.

However, the lack of collective class consciousness in the midst of overwhelming and expanding inequality is not enough to explain the socialization of precarity; it itself must be explained. The previous chapters attempted to do so by looking at how work and migration are experienced on the shop floor, in the mangled and twisted interactions between structural forces, daily labour experiences, and workers' own dreams, backgrounds and senses of self. I argued that even though the socialization of precarity is pervasive and obstructs the formation of solidarities, it lacks the potency to completely erase workers' experiential awareness of class-based injustice. The suffering brains and bodies that precarity produces do not allow workers to forget that they are still *workers*, and the injustices that are understood to stem from their migrant background are constant reminders that they are *migrant workers*. To understand the barriers to migrant worker organization, we must again look at how solidarities, community relations and resistances are experienced and enacted through the daily lives of precarious migrant workers.

Hierarchies and precarious solidarities

If migrant workers understand that the precise content of their exploitation is significantly premised on their migrancy, it makes sense to look to this position as a foundation for emergent solidarities. We saw in the previous chapter that the formation of politicized migrant identities is disrupted by the multiple contradictory ideas that migrants carry about themselves and their position as migrants and workers; however, beyond subjective factors, the reality of precarious labour and the hierarchies that develop within such hypercompetitive contexts are additional barriers to the development of sustained bonds of solidarity, even within the same communities. It must be remembered that the societies from which migrants migrate are themselves class-based societies, and these differences could become accentuated, rather than diminished, following migration. Simply put, as Satnam Virdee and Keith Grint (1994) argued in an influential article on Black self-organization in trade unions, the inter-ethnic class differences that exist between and within minority groups mean that ethnicity-based solidarities cannot substitute class-based organizing. This was repeatedly confirmed in my explorations of precarious workplaces, with La Dama offering an illustrative example of how ethnic affiliations can foster exploitation just as easily as they could potentially encourage solidarity.

Despite the many barriers to personal advancement and security in precarious occupations, some migrant workers rise up the ranks and become managers, supervisors and team leaders. In order to do so, these individuals usually have to demonstrate their long-term commitment to the values that comprise the 'good worker' schema: they have to be flexible, eager to accept the roles they are allocated to, and *perform* their willingness to engage in hard work. Although their privilege relative to other migrant workers is frequently not enough to secure substantial power and control over their labour experience, it is sufficient to exert various levels of coercion on those immediately below them. These migrant workers thereby perform a 'buffering role' in the labour hierarchy (Vasey 2017), standing between the mass of the workers and the levels of the upper management.

In environments thoroughly saturated by competitiveness and individualization, these minor increases in the authority of individual migrant workers are more likely to lead to a fortification of the existing labour regime's dominance, rather than to enhanced power in the hands of the migrant workforce. Alongside Virdee and Grint, this conclusion is also repeated by the Angry Workers collective (2020) in their discussion of organic leaders. In an influential book that explores strategies for organizing precarious workers, Jane McAlevey (2016) asserts that unions need to locate, train and work through organic leaders (activists coming from within the community that can inspire and mobilize others) in workplaces in order to achieve substantial union participation. However, the Angry Workers collective, drawing on their six-year trajectory of organizing in London warehouses, write that 'these people tend to be the ones that are bought off by management and the sex/race/class hierarchies tend to be reproduced in their elevated role as shop-floor union organizer' (2020: 111). This does not mean that individuals with relatively more resources will exclusively function against the interests of other migrant workers. It does however mean that the assumption of authority in precarious contexts gives rise to complex and contradictory actions and interests.

The relationships between the Albanians working in La Dama illustrate this uneasy symbiosis of support and exploitation. As discussed in chapter 2, every Albanian worker in La Dama had accessed this job through extended familial connections with Drago, who was something between a patron, a boss and a friend, towering over almost every aspect of their lives in Glasgow. His power was founded both on his paternal role and on the absolute mastery with which he managed the kitchens of the restaurant's chain; in short, he commanded an authority that was nearly impossible to not respect.

> *This is perhaps the only full shift that I will work alongside Drago – he has come in as an emergency measure because we are even busier than usual. I pay close attention to the interactions that unfold. The first thing I notice is that he runs a tight ship, but with compassion and a desire to make everything easier and more efficient. For example, he is the only head chef I have ever seen who drops to his knees to clean the floor. When he isn't working, he cleans around him to improve the working environment. Amidst the chaos, he will politely approach me – a friendly touch on the shoulder, followed by a 'please, Panos, can you brush here, can you mop here when you get a minute', but always with respect and never as an order. Note the 'when you get a minute' part, which encloses a myriad of hidden meanings: having risen himself through the dregs of the kitchen hierarchy, he makes a point to show that he understands our position; this compassion, however, is contingent on the fact that we also respect him for offering it – the insinuation is that we must prove our worth to be treated in this way. The underlying notions of hard work that underpin the regimes of respect in this workplace are omnipresent. I notice that John, another Albanian who is already an extremely fast worker, works even harder and faster when he is around Drago. This could either stem from a desire to impress him so he benefits from preferential treatment regarding his aspirations of upward mobility, a real sense of respect towards him, a sense of fear that he has to perform for his 'benefactor', a competitive/performative depiction of the 'good worker', or a combination of all these. Whatever it is, the reality is that the kitchen **does** work better with Drago than with anyone else. Indeed, the workday becomes borderline enjoyable, even though it is by all accounts one of the busiest in recent memory. Everything is smooth, there is no stress, and we all do our best. I even find myself working harder and*

trying to impress him, simply out of respect that he partakes so many of the kitchen's activities when he could have a completely different attitude. (Fieldnotes, 24 July 2019)

Having risen up the labour hierarchy through hard work, Drago was fully invested in his idea of himself as a 'good worker' and respected those who he thought also conformed to these standards. With the other Albanians he had deeper and more intimate relations than with the rest of us; as explained above, these were premised on his role as their main source of support in the new country. However, this support was not unidirectional: these migrant workers, who often spoke very little English, were largely dependent on him in various ways and repaid this indebtedness whenever it was required. For example, after working a particularly gruelling eight-hour shift, Manos, a young Greek-Albanian worker, told me that he was going to Drago's house to help him paint the walls for free. This would be understandable amongst friends, but the relationship seemed more transactional; I asked him why he was doing it. He was shocked that I even asked – 'because it's Drago, of course you would. In any case, what else would I do with my day?'

These workers, faithful to their ethnic ties and thankful for Drago's support, reciprocated by working fourteen-and-a-half and, occasionally, even sixteen-hour shifts and making themselves available to Drago for everything he required. Essentially, despite his good intentions – or, perhaps, through them – Drago had succeeded in using his authority to create a highly dependent, precarious and loyal workforce for the profits of La Dama. Towards the end of a shift where I was alone with George, the Scottish head chef, he told me that he was concerned about the Albanian workers (the same workers who he regularly used racist language to deride and mock). 'The guys are indebted to him for getting them the job, and he exploits them.'

The very last conversation that I had before leaving La Dama sheds further light on the complexity between the relationships of paternalism, solidarity and exploitation that may emerge between migrant workers of different hierarchical positions in precarious occupations. While helping migrant workers in various, extremely important ways, Drago was ultimately the main beneficiary of these relationships; far from simply aiding his position in the hierarchy, it emerges that his privileges directly depend on the disempowerment of his co-ethnic inferiors. What follows was revealed to me by George, who was probably only comfortable in opening up in this manner because he knew that I would never enter the kitchen again.

> *There is a box where all the workers' amalgamated tips are kept. This box includes tips from other restaurants owned by the same owner (around five or six just in Glasgow). These are meant to be shared amongst everyone in the business, according to how the managers choose to distribute them (which is problematic in itself because this decision can be completely arbitrary: for example, I get £10–15 of tips a week whereas the waiters get a lot more, so we once again have indications of preferential treatment). Every worker immediately pays (loses) £1.5 a day for the food that they consume in the business, which I was not notified of. Indeed, many times I didn't eat anything due to the work and the stress. Had I known that I was paying for it, I would have made a point to eat. This amount is taken from our tips.*
>
> *However, the situation gets much worse. When we were discussing all these infractions that are commonplace in hospitality, I told George that he could make the situation better if he brought his union in (he is a member of one of the largest unions for chefs in the UK). Despite being high in the hierarchy of La Dama, he also experiences the difficulties of the labour-intensive job: for example, he was always complaining about back pains. George was completely honest with me, and he told me, 'look, for the KPs and the kitchen staff the situation is bad, but for me and Drago it is very good. The boss pays us half our wage in the bank, and half of it in an envelope. The cash from this envelope comes out of your tips!' It was difficult for me to hide my disgust, to which he responded affirmatively, foregrounding his own complicity in the system that exploits us. The reasons for which he chose to make such a confession remain unknown to me; in hindsight, perhaps I should have asked him. In any case, this means that our hard-earned tips are used as an untaxed, under-the-table payment to the two head chefs, allowing them to make hundreds of extra pounds a month.*
>
> *This is extremely exploitative for many reasons, but what is most striking is that the business wins over the people that are the top in the hierarchy by creating a division between them and the other workers through the provision of such an immense privilege. The chefs are constantly aware that*

their privilege depends on appropriating the hard-earned tips of all the other workers in the business. This is a prime example of how divisions are created and manipulated by bosses and the management to further workers' exploitation while shoring up their own privileges. Most importantly, Drago, the great benefactor of his fellow Albanians, is complicit in this! It begins to look more like a pyramid scheme than any type of normal relationship. It is in his direct interest to bring in workers who are loyal to him and will not leave, because this guarantees more tips which then come to his pocket in the form of untaxed wages. This obviously has grave implications for solidarity, and is more akin to a dystopian pecking order, a human centipede of the kitchens, where each superior exploits their inferiors ad infinitum. (Fieldnotes, 28 July 2019)

Not every workplace has a Drago, and not every workplace will exhibit these precise characteristics. However, this complex continuum of interpersonal support and exploitation in the restaurant exemplifies the problems of establishing solidarity across unequal class and authority positions. Regardless of the differences between workplaces, it is possible to argue that solidarity between migrant workers is by no means guaranteed. This does not mean that migration can never be the basis of some sort of mutual aid; but it does mean that the role of class and authority can never be overlooked, even when there is a shared migratory background. In the Grey Zone of precarious employment, interpersonal relationships may be impossible to define in a definitive way: rather than being supportive, hostile or dispassionate, they are more accurately conceived of as themselves precarious, with all the fluidity that this entails.

Precarious solidarities

And yet, despite the forceful pressures towards individualization outlined in these chapters, mutual aid has not been completely erased from precarious workplaces. This is testament to the fact that the socialization of precarity and the entirety of the socioeconomic and cultural structures that nurture and reproduce our exploitation are not able to completely eradicate our modest, yet momentous, propensity to care for each other. Nevertheless, in the absence of a wider collective process these actions remain generally atomized. They are confined to the interpersonal realm as exchanges between individuals and do not, in themselves, represent a movement towards more politicized activity. This does not mean that they can *never* be the fuel of such a process; it does, however, mean that we have not yet established the conditions under which such a development may be realized.

For example, Eva recounts a special connection with one of her managers who is also a migrant. Amidst an environment that essentializes, patronizes and generally disregards her as a human and as a worker, she thinks that their shared experiences of migration and exclusion in that specific workplace function as a bridge of support and understanding. Of course, even this affinity is qualified by Eva's work performance – the determining factor of securing the manager's solidarity seems to primarily stem from her satisfaction with Eva's productivity, with migration being a secondary, albeit important, contributor.

> *Eva:* She is from Lithuania. And in fact, I think this is why me and her have a good relationship. Because she is not very liked in my workplace. So I think she needs someone to be friends with. And she likes the fact that I am very hard working.
> *Q:* OK. So you have a good relationship with her, and you think this is because you are from countries that are close to each other?
> *Eva:* Yeaaah. . .
> *Q:* Or because you are also immigrants? There is a small difference.
> *Eva:* I think because I'm immigrant. . . is because I am hard-working, but I suppose we are both immigrant.
>
> *Eva, Moldovan woman, early 20s, hospitality*

Instances of mutual aid emerging from the crevices left uncontaminated by precarity were daily occurrences in every workplace I accessed; they were also mentioned by multiple migrant workers that I interviewed. The only workplace in which I felt completely isolated and helpless was in the fish factory. By contrast, in the radiator factory I was consistently assisted by the other migrant workers (all of whom were Polish). It is important to not overstate the extent or the meaning of this assistance – it was usually confined to small tasks, the performance of which did not jeopardize their ability to meet their workloads; if anything, by demonstrating that they could engage with more work, they further foregrounded their 'good worker' credentials. Yet, beyond any cynical interpretation of these actions, it is important to also not *understate* them. It is precisely the fact that these forms of aid find a way to break through the barbed wires of precarity, individualization and hypercompetitiveness that allows us to imagine a different future.

> *Despite the lack of any union presence, there is a certain conditional, contingent solidarity. Today I noticed Kris struggle with constructing a particularly large radiator core. After hours of work, every thrust of the tube inside the metal interior necessitated ever more effort, and he was noticeably straining; beads of sweat had formed on his brow, and the grace of movement that I was accustomed to seeing was disrupted by a visible discomfort stemming from his shoulder. Eager to repay him for his mentorship over the previous days, and enthusiastic to demonstrate that I had indeed sharpened my skills, I offered to help him. He immediately refused, without even considering the option. 'No, you are new so you have more risk if you fuck it up; I will do it.' He does not want someone else to experience the cruelty of precarity and dismissal, especially if he can help avoid it using his comparative privilege. He prefers to use the very limited space of seniority that he has carved to protect a fellow worker, even if it means that his body will not thank him for this choice the next morning. (Fieldnotes, radiator factory, 25 October 2018)*

This form of assistance is particularly pronounced in the initial stages of one's employment: conscious of the interdependence of our labour functions, workers have a direct interest in properly training new arrivals in order for the entire process to be smooth and efficient. As I discussed above, one's chances of being considered a 'good worker' largely depend on the performance of one's peers. However, help can go beyond raw instrumentalism: despite the socialization of precarity, coexisting in a common predicament, in specific conditions, can foster genuine feelings of mutuality and care.

> *Manos (always greeting me warmly and full of friendliness) is supposed to finish his shift when I arrive, but he stays for a bit and does odd jobs to help (moving this plate there, carrying this bucket here, wiping down some surfaces). I ask him why he stays even though he does not get paid for*

this time; I tell him that the boss won't reward him for his commitment. He flashes his characteristic, radiant smile, and responds that 'it's not for the boss mate, I don't give a shit for the boss. It's for you, to help all of you.' This is another example of selfless support. Earlier, he had told me that all the Albanians had gone to a club recently and had taken drugs together. This represents a significant difference from the other workplaces I have done observation in, since here, the socialization of precarity is less violently atomizing. There is a conditional camaraderie, bolstered by: 1) pre-existing ethnic and familial networks between the Albanians, which are translated into the workplace, and 2) the proximity, cooperation and communication fostered by the tight workplace environment where we all work together and necessarily help each other. The absence of a manager directly monitoring us – George and Drago are the highest authorities and can hire and fire, but the main restaurant manager is literally above us, in the main restaurant – further enhances the opportunities for the development of some very fragile social bonds through banter and discussion. The separation that is observed in other places doesn't exist here, and presumably these bonds have the potential to translate to actual united labour action. Of course, this camaraderie does not exist independently of the overarching 'good worker' schema – it is a camaraderie afforded to those who have managed to survive and remain in La Dama. Nevertheless, it is not insignificant. (Fieldnotes, La Dama, 15 July 2019)

This is consistent with Ruth Gomberg-Muñoz's (2010) study of Mexican migrant workers in the Chicago hospitality sector. She notices that there is an acute awareness amongst workers of the interconnectedness of their labour, and that they develop instincts of support and coordination to make sure no one is left behind. In a workplace where people are sufficiently coordinated and have respect towards each other, this initially instrumental manifestation of support may be a foundation towards the development of genuine connections of affinity. However, this support depends on each worker in the circuit being able to pull their weight: as analysed above, one 'bad', 'careless' or overly individualistic worker is objectively harmful to the job prospects of every other worker in the circuit.

The clearest illustration of how quickly manifestations of aid give way to the socialization of precarity was observed in La Dama when they fired Jonathan, a black man, for underperforming (see chapter 3). According to Drago, his firing was made easier by the fact that I turned up – Jonathan was swiftly replaced, and I had no idea until, towards the end of my tenure in La Dama, I asked about him. When I spoke to my colleagues about his firing, I was met with detached shrugs – such is the industry, and he was perceived to be underperforming. This is testament to how, even in supposedly supportive environments, in the absence of unions and strong foundations of workers' power, the ultimate determinant of people's interactions remains individualist survival. This is further mediated by existing networks of affinity; the workplace's informality, in the same measure that it can foster instances of support, is also a factor that can objectively disempower workers when one's position is not guaranteed through the fostering of strong interpersonal ties with those in authority.

Some notes on the issue of Jonathan's firing. First of all, it highlights the intense precarity of this workplace. Under the veneer of a primitive solidarity, under the helpfulness and the jokes, hides the dark reality of working in entirely insecure conditions in a cut-throat capitalist environment that is centred on quick service of the hungry, demanding customers and also on a performance of this urgency to be perceived as 'good workers'. Jonathan had no rights in that place. As long as we were there for less than two years, and we couldn't prove that we had been overtly discriminated against, labour legislation in the UK holds that it is perfectly legitimate to dismiss us immediately. As soon as someone came who worked 'better' than Jonathan, they found their chance to get rid of him. However, blackness and age (he is in his 40s or 50s) might have played a role – my identity as a white straight male from the Balkans could have been perceived to be better suited for the kitchen dynamics than Jonathan's, and this privilege might also have been the reason that I could get off with some mistakes that in Jonathan's case were potentially detrimental (I also left the washing machine open after my first shift). All in all, the bottom line is that an African black man lost his job to a young white man in an environment where hiring and firing is decided by a white, Albanian chef. He was not given a chance to rectify the perceived problems with his performance and was, of course, not given the opportunity to be represented by a union or a friend. As I understand it, there wasn't even a disciplinary. Everything was entirely informal. The fact that the rest of the kitchen workers simply shrugged their shoulders at this injustice is further testament to the precariousness of this solidarity. (Fieldnotes, 24 July 2018)

In precarious workplaces, the socialization of precarity permeates almost all interactions workers have with each other, significantly disrupting the potentialities for the formation of substantial bonds of trust and solidarity. The stress that saturates the everyday and the overhanging threat of instant dismissal induce anxiety and competition amongst workers. Their interdependence and coexistence, instead of being tools of solidarity as envisaged by classic Marxism, can instead be a source of added pressure that distances workers from each other.

It therefore emerges that the socialization of precarity, and the additional pressures emanating from the hierarchical divisions within migrant communities and discriminatory attitudes from without, act as powerful barriers to solidarity. Unsurprisingly, relationships fostered in conditions of precarity tend to also be precarious – the threat of dismissal seems to be much stronger than individual workers' desires to collaborate. Yet, as was demonstrated above, instincts of care and the impulse to support one another *do* exist; the question, then, if we are concerned with social justice, becomes one of harnessing them towards a direction that would allow them to reach their full, empowered, solidaric potential.

Collective resistances

The crushing combination of the structural and subjective effects outlined above can seem daunting and insuperable. This has led Lisa Berntsen (2016: 485) to cynically argue that migrant workers 'are reluctant to challenge the boundaries of the system. This implies that if regulators, enforcement authorities and trade unions want to protect these workers from the deteriorating effects of cross-border recruitment and market competition, they need to take a more proactive stance, as the initiative for change on a broader level is unlikely to come from the workers themselves.' While it is true that trade unions need to take a more proactive stance (as will be discussed below), it is also true that such statements partake in the naturalization of migrant workers' supposed vulnerability, ultimately reinforcing their oppression. In contrast, migrant workers have historically been on the frontlines of social struggles. Moreover, migrant workers are currently engaged in a plethora of autonomous groups and trade unions, directly refuting such sweeping generalizations. While collective resistances remain generally small and localized, they are nevertheless important in that many migrant workers recognize their power, and that, despite the socialization of precarity, many use it.

An episode from Suzan's employment in a warehouse that cleaned the laundry of large hotel chains, nursing homes and other such establishments exemplifies the dormant power that migrant workers possess. After consistently working above and beyond their production targets, Suzan and her group of Romanian friends and relatives felt empowered, drawing on the dependency upon their labour that their own overexertion had created, to demand better wages and conditions from their employer.

> *Suzan:* After three or five weeks of working there, we had the chance to receive a permanent contract. We were very good at our job: we were a team of five Romanians and we worked the machines, and we had lifted the production targets to the roof, which no one had done. So, since they saw that we are good, they offered us a permanent contract. We said that we accept a permanent contract, but we were not willing to work weekends, and if we worked six days, we would never work Sundays since you don't pay us double. And what else? Oh! We also asked for more money. Because if nobody meets the target, and we are hitting it at 200%, it means that you can fire someone else, because I am working for two people. You are happy and I am happy, and I can keep this rhythm up. Because they told us, 'fine, if I pay you more money, can you keep this target up?' And we said, 'we will keep up the target as long as we make more money.'
>
> *Suzan, Romanian woman, late 40s, hospitality and logistics [translation mine from Greek]*

This account is particularly illuminating because Suzan and her group of Romanian friends basically engaged in collective bargaining without the input of a union or any other social movement. Most discussions of workers' power in the literature emanating both from academia and social movements tend to proceed based on a strict binary opposition:

they either see individual actions such as workers' use of their precarity to change jobs (see, for example, Alberti 2014) or they focus on grander collective actions organized through formal institutions such as unions (for example, Lagnado 2015). However, the power contained in existing ethnic networks, groups of friends and wider 'spaces between unions' (Sullivan 2010) is left unscrutinized; this is particularly problematic when it is precisely such networks that might be best equipped to challenge the atomization of the socialization of precarity. I don't want to disproportionately glorify this story; however, it is an important reminder of the power and solidarity that are contained within people's already existing human bonds with one another. Perhaps these existing bonds can be a starting point for organizing against the cumulative effects of the socialization of precarity.

As has previously been discussed, such confidence to bargain collectively can only arise after a certain amount of security in various aspects of life has been achieved (Però 2014); from that point on, workers can issue demands to their employers, especially when they have become indispensable components of the labour process. Here, it is important to repeat a word of caution issued by the Angry Workers collective (2020): when separated from larger collective narratives, such exercises of agency may ultimately lead to further hierarchical demarcations between the working class, as power is contained within specific groups instead of being collectivized. This can be seen in the above story, where Suzan mentions her group suggesting that other workers be fired so that they could receive higher wages for their productivity. Nevertheless, this demand must be viewed in the context of the agency arena (see chapter 3), where competition between workers is already an established and widely acknowledged fact and forms a foundational component of the socialization of precarity. Workers' demands pivot precisely on their ability to lay claim to, and exemplify, the status of the 'good worker': it is precisely *as* good workers that they make their claim. Despite the political and theoretical problems, Suzan's account remains an important example of the power that migrant workers can wield, a power that is frequently disregarded in academic and movement literature. One is compelled to ask: what would Suzan's demands have looked like had there been a wider structure of support and a narrative of solidarity connecting the workers of that workplace?

Mateusz's story represents another instance of collective power. In this case, existing ethnic networks interacted with a formal union structure to directly challenge, and eventually alter, labour conditions. Once Mateusz got settled in his new job and community, he contacted a powerful union active in hospitality to address issues of discrimination and disrespect, particularly expressed through the behaviour of an aggressive manager. This led to a strong union structure in the factory and to his subsequent activity as a community organizer. Mateusz mentions a qualitative shift in attitudes amongst the workforce: from accepting an alienating social order that sacrifices life for the sake of survival, to an outlook that fights for dignity. What is visible in the interview quoted below is the gradual formation of narratives that question, oppose and propose alternatives to the overarching socialization of precarity. It is presented as fully as space allows in order to show the consistent effort that such initiatives require, but also to allow space for the pride associated with this victory to emerge through Mateusz's words.

> *Mateusz:* So basically, our colleague said, 'I know a guy who is in the union. I'm in the union.' So, people said, 'we understand what a union is because in Poland we have Solidarnosc[3] and stuff', but a lot of people think that it is not for us. They thought that it is only allowed for Scottish people or citizens of the UK. So, some people think that. . . Even I thought that I am not allowed to be in a union at that point. So, we have a meeting with our colleague from the union, he explained for us everything, and we slowly, slowly start to sign members to the union. In the start, that was like, a slow process. But my story was that I had enough of this situation with my boss. And I said, 'I'm going to join the union and I'm going to do something about it.' So, basically, I put a grievance with another guy, but because the bank was on administration of our company, they couldn't do nothing.[4] When the company take over our company, they said, 'look that's the past, we can't deal with that'. But in the meantime, we have started shaping the union, bringing more people. Accidentally, people come to me and start speaking to me.
>
> *Q:* How did people get interested in the union? You started the union. . .

Mateusz: No, it was different. Because we were on administration, we don't know what is going to be happening with us. We need to find some protection. So, when our colleague tells us, 'there is a union, they can help us, just in case', we start chatting. We don't have the money to hire the solicitors, or we don't have any ability, we don't know the law. We don't know how everything works or what are our rights. So, we start chatting and we have a meeting with *[a union official]* and people start joining. But when I was in a position, I put my case in the union, I was at a stage that I was in my nervous breakdown and I have enough. So, the biggest change was when I challenge my manager. He attacked me on production, he was shouting, humiliating, aggressive, red face, 20 centimetres from me, shouting in my face. I was like, 'I have enough, I need to go out because I could do something wrong and I don't want that.' So, I left the production, but for his bad luck, he followed me. So, when I stop in the corridor, I look around, nobody there when he approached me, I jumped to him, and I be exactly the same as he was. I told him that if he came to me again, I'm gonna break his leg, I'm gonna fucking rip his head off, I'm gonna find him in house and I'm gonna burn his house. I know it doesn't sound good, but at that stage, in my head, that was the only way. Nine months of abuse, every day. I just have enough. The guy said, 'oh oh, don't be nervous, don't be nervous', and he ran. And when I see that he is just a coward, I change. So, everything change in my head. Because I was 100 percent sure that he would do a disciplinary, because I was giving him life threats, but he didn't. Never. So, after this situation he never showed up for one week when I was on a shift. So, when I spot this, that he is just a coward and that he is easy to challenge, I start challenge him. When he attacked anyone, I started speaking out. Because of that, people see that I not afraid of him and they started coming to me. That is how I became the guy who start to create the union, I convince people to join the union and then we go for the recognition.

Q: Specifically, I am interested in the period between the other workers knowing that the union exists, and them actually joining. What happened between those points?

Mateusz: I approached them. I told them 'look, no matter what you think, if we don't protect ourselves we will not have any chance to win with them'. And I think that two things was in our favour. One, is the money, the wages they owed us. So, I said, 'look, you allowed someone to take from you nearly £800'. One month living. 'You allow someone to steal the money from you.' People said, 'no, is not fair'. Because they have a family, they have mortgages and stuff like that. £800 for some people that work on a daily basis is a lot of money. And second thing is, a simple question: what they have to lose? Did they want to be treated like shit constantly? Did they want to be treated worse than a dog, or did they want to come over for eight hours, do the shift, and after the shift go back home? Because that is the way it should be. We live for work, we not work for live. So, that was two ways I spoke with them. I know them. I see how they are treated. Why you allow for something like that? At that time, we don't have any rights. If they want to remove you from the company, there was no investigation. There was no proper processing. And second, the most important thing was that you don't have ability to have representation. Even the colleague can't be with you in any disciplinary. So it's you, manager, and supervisor. So, what kind of chance do you have against two managers? Nothing!

[. . .]

Q: So, slowly things got better?

Mateusz: On the start, you know, that's a big learning curve. Sometimes people have too many expectations. They want everything in one day. Some things you are not going to be able to change right away. But some things changed. The general manager was put in a lower position, without access to the people. We start slowly changing health and safety. The company had a priority with the safety. Then other changes. It's a long process. One of the things that the union official promised the people was that he would remove this guy who was harassing them. It's going to take a while, but he will be removed. And a year later he been removed, but in the same way how he removed the people. He was throw from the door like a dog. They don't allow him to speak with anyone, only to take the key to the car, not to speak to anyone. Karma come back.

Mateusz, Polish male, mid-30s, union organizer; speaking about his experiences in a cake factory

Suzan and Mateusz's experiences of collective action represent two exceptional cases of workers recognizing their power and organizing themselves to directly improve their working conditions. While such cases are rare when compared to the wider socioeconomic landscape, they nevertheless strongly suggest that migrant workers are not weak. And, while the ground may not yet be adequately fertile for a generalization of such grandiose oppositional activities, smaller but nevertheless significant acts of resistance still occur.

For example, Lois – already politicized from her time in the Greek anarchist movement prior to her migration, and a member of the Industrial Workers of the World in Glasgow – contacted the IWW when she was unfairly suspended for challenging her boss's disrespectful attitudes in a cafe largely staffed by migrant workers. This is the same cafe discussed by Agnes and Irene in chapter 2 with the drunken owner who, while claiming that the owners and the workers were 'family', did not hesitate to regularly abuse her staff in front of customers. By accessing union support for her disciplinary process, Lois managed to be paid for all the hours she lost due to being suspended, and secured enough money to carry her over until she found a new job. This victory is significant in itself; however, its most important aspect in terms of migrant worker unionization is to be found in the impression it left upon her colleagues – one of whom was Irene –who previously had never encountered a union.

> *Q:* In your jobs, have you ever come into contact with a union or another social movement fighting for better rights?
> *Irene:* See, that's the thing, I didn't have any experience, I didn't know anything about it, until the café.
> *Q:* So, you had no experience. . .
> *Irene:* That situation, I seen one of my colleagues using the service.
> *Q:* And, without talking too much about that other situation because it involves somebody else, could you describe briefly what you saw, how you perceived it?
> *Irene:* What I've noticed is that. . . when the union was involved, the worker was treated differently and she was, she was taken seriously. But again. . . she, I'm not sure if she got fired or she just quitted. Either way, it was a difference in the reaction of how bosses treated.

Q: What changed?

Irene: So, what happened after she left, the boss changed the management, all the structure, the system changed. So instead of paying weekly, she started paying monthly, she started doing payslips, she says that we will get payslips after each month. So, this is what I am expecting.

Q: Was there any change in the way that she was treating workers?

Irene: So, the thing is, the manager changed and there is a new manager, and she is treating everyone nice and she is behaving nice in front of the manager. So now the atmosphere changed.

Irene, Lithuanian woman, early 20s, hospitality

These examples of collective action, beyond simply demonstrating the power migrant workers possess, indicate something deeper: they illustrate the extent to which employers in precarious occupations intimately depend on the artificially produced disempowerment of migrant workers. As has been discussed previously, bosses rely on migrant workers' lack of knowledge; for example, the fact that some workers don't know if they were entitled to holiday pay makes it easy for employers to simply avoid payment. Many migrants that I encountered throughout my employment history were not even aware that they *could* join unions as foreigners; this was also mentioned by Mateusz in his account above. The daily abuse that is frequently enabled by the combination of workplace informality and migrant workers' disorientation relies on those migrant workers' lack of access to tools of empowerment. Conversely, this abuse can come to be challenged when workers are able to draw on such resources, whether through the mobilization of ethnic networks (as in Suzan's case) or through unions (as was described by Mateusz and Lois). In an influential contribution to the discussion of migrant labour, Manuel Castells (1975: 52) wrote that 'the utility of immigrant labour to capital derives primarily from the fact that it can act towards it *as though the labour movement did not exist* [emphasis mine]'. This section attests to the possibility that the scales can tilt. And to the fact that sometimes, this tilt might not be as incredibly difficult as it initially seems.

Workers' experiences with mainstream unions

The above testimonies demonstrate that migrant workers are rarely simply resigned or fatalistic. Yet, as we have seen, their political agency is inhibited by a whole range of experiential and structural factors, including that combination of factors that I have described as the socialization of precarity. There is, moreover, another issue that needs to be considered here, which relates to their relationship with established trade union organizations. While unions are largely non-existent in most precarious occupations, three of the people I spoke to recounted experiences that are illustrative of the difficulties migrant workers experience in accessing and acting alongside mainstream unions. I use the term 'mainstream' loosely to refer to the three biggest unions in the UK: Unite, Unison and GMB (Connolly and Sellers 2017). While they have at times been involved in a variety of initiatives aiming at establishing connections with migrant and other workers experiencing precarity (see, for example, Holgate 2021), they remain for the most part strictly hierarchical and controlling of their initiatives, with Connolly and Sellers (2017: 240) writing that they are 'cautious about working outside their own structures and have been actively opposed to organizations setting up "alternative" worker initiatives for migrants'.

Reflecting on their experiences of multiple labour struggles in London, the Angry Workers (2020: 13) go further and report that 'the union framework is built to stifle initiatives on a rank-and-file level'. While some localized initiatives aiming to organize migrant workers have at times taken place in the UK, there does not seem to be a specific overarching strategy, or outstanding desire, to organize migrant workers in precarious occupations (Connolly and Sellers 2017). The initiatives that do occur seem confined to attracting migrant members by providing learning opportunities or through exploiting 'hot shop' situations where migrants themselves initiate organizing drives, but do not generally extend towards a tactic of substantial empowerment and inclusion of precarious workers.

The few contacts that the participants I interviewed had with these unions were overwhelmingly negative and exemplify some of the aforementioned criticisms of them. For example, Lois encountered one of the three big unions in her time as an agency worker in a printing factory;

according to her, absolutely no attempts were made by the union to establish connections between the local, unionized workers and the non-unionized agency migrant workers.

> *Lois:* What I learnt was that the contract workers in *[company name]* were unionized with *[union]*, and that was it basically. But even when I asked them, 'OK, did you ever feel that want to use your rights against your employers, defend yourself as a worker', they said that they haven't faced any problems.
> *Q:* Did the union make any attempt to organize the agency workers?
> *Lois:* No, not as far as I know.
> *Q:* Do you know who the rep was at that place?
> *Lois:* No.
> *Q:* They didn't make any contact?
> *Lois:* No. The agency workers were in the worst situation. They didn't have any clue.
> *Q:* But there must have been a rep in that workplace, or for that region, and you were working there for weeks. . .
> *Lois:* We didn't learn it though.
> *Lois, Greek woman, late 20s, hospitality/ freelance journalist [speaking about a print factory]*

This account fits with one of the main criticisms made by the Angry Workers collective (2020) of unions, in that they tend to respect and reproduce a strict split between agency and permanent workers. The former are frequently seen as 'unorganizable' due to the temporary, transient nature of their contractual status (Alberti et al. 2013); and the Angry Workers collective has reported multiple instances of unions shutting temporary workers out of meetings that were of concern to them, or even sabotaging temporary workers' efforts to self-organize outside their structures. This exclusionary attitude is captured in Leila's experience, whose contact with Unite left her feeling hopeless and disempowered.

> So, I joined this union. I never requested any help from them, they've never phoned me to tell me, 'Hi, this is us, would you like to join this meeting, so we can provide you some briefing about your basic rights and entitlements and all that.' Although, to become a member, you

need to give lots of information. So, they knew I was in a precarious job: that is why I was paying less money, because I was getting minimum wage. They never gave me any information. They have once invited me to a massive gathering, but it was more about, a general union gathering than a session to fucking empower people and tell them, 'Even though you are in a shithole because you are working in hospitality without a contract, these are your rights.' That was never provided.

Leila, Spanish/Tunisian woman, early 30s, hospitality

Most criticism of mainstream unions tends to progress along these lines: mainstream unions are seen as detached, not sufficiently involved in the lives of communities, not particularly keen to help precarious workers organize, and overwhelmingly rigid, bureaucratic and faceless (Angry Workers 2020; Bloodworth 2019; Roca and Martín-Díaz 2017; Tapia 2014). However, mainstream unions also have a darker history, characterized by racist and colonialist positions towards migrant workers.[5] In recent years, these tendencies have been significantly marginalized; however, they occasionally re-emerge on the forefront of public discourse, as occurred, for example, in the course of the 2009 wildcat Lindsey refinery strikes, where British workers rallied against migrant workers in their workplaces under GMB and Unite flags (Connolly and Sellers 2017) or when Unite General Secretary Len McCluskey came out in favour of restricting freedom of movement for EU workers (*The Guardian* 2019). Both cases reproduced the hegemonic xenophobic rhetoric which sees immigrants as parasites and tools in the hands of employers against the British working class (Virdee and McGeever 2018; Anderson 2013).

The effects of these mentalities were directly experienced by Arjun, an Indian worker who trained as a union representative. His involvement had the effect of permanently alienating him from union participation in the UK and is testament to how deeply discriminatory attitudes have pervaded British society. The trade union movement is a reflection of wider social processes; and, while anti-racist initiatives have occurred, this does not mean that every union member or official is actively anti-racist. In localized settings migrant workers may be exposed to the discriminatory attitudes of individual union officials, regardless of what processes exist at a national level.

Q: You have said a few things that I want to look at. You have said that there were a lot of ethnic minority people in this job. First of all, were you directly employed or through an agency?

Arjun: Directly.

Q: So there was a lot of people under the same contract but the rep was white British, even though he was a minority in that job?

Arjun: Because he don't want me to be the rep.

Q: Why?

Arjun: Because the thing was that he, there was only one rep. They don't want that other person to come there and represent ethnic minority. They were doing jobs which they were not supposed to do, it wasn't in the job description, but because they were not heard of, and because they were scared of their jobs, what would happen if they raise their voice, say something to manager? What I realized at that period. . . we still have the mentality that 'these people they have ruled us', we are still scared of it.

Q: So, you think for Indians and Pakistanis it is a direct colonial thought?

Arjun: Yeah, their mindset is like that. *[. . .]*

Q: Some of the other things that you said is that afterwards you started a dispute, you started complaining, and they suspended you for it with an allegation of gross misconduct and then you went to the union. But in the union, what happened?

Arjun: They refused to represent me. They told me, 'you don't have a strong case, we won't represent you. If you want to go of your own, you can go.'

Q: They basically left you alone to fight this. . .?

Arjun: Yeah.

[. . .]

Q: OK, did you try to follow up the case?

Arjun: I followed up with an appeal, but because of the limitation I couldn't proceed. Because the first question they raised in tribunal was, 'why union is not with you? You are representing yourself, why somebody from the union is not representing you?'

Q: And the allegation of gross misconduct, did they have any proof that. . .?

Arjun: There was no, it was telephonic communication only, the thing was that the manager, she said that I told her a 'bitch'.
Q: Really? And that was the case for an entire gross misconduct allegation?
Arjun: Yeah. I never did it, I never told her. And there was no evidence. There was no witness, nobody.
Q: So basically, it was your word against hers and the union basically supported the boss?
Arjun: Yeah, they said the manager is right.
Q: How does that make you feel about unions?
Arjun: I just left, I never joined union afterwards.

Arjun, Indian male, late 40s, care sector

Alongside the multiple blatantly problematic aspects highlighted in Arjun's experience, one crucial factor relating to barriers experienced by migrant workers in organizing with trade unions is the representational gap in their ranks. Arjun felt that it was difficult to find officials who could understand and assist with the issues faced by ethnic minority workers. It is precisely this representational gap that frequently forms a decisive factor in migrant workers organizing separately from mainstream unions (Alberti and Però 2018; Jayaraman and Ness 2005). Gabriella Alberti (2016) writes that, when unions have reached out to migrant workers, these initiatives have usually been spurred by a desire to attract new members rather than a commitment to intersectional organization and to the empowerment of migrant and Black and minority ethnic (BME) workers. Scholars have also noted unions' tendencies to use migrant workers instrumentally in order to achieve specific aims instead of attempting to organize horizontally alongside them (see, for example, Cappiali 2017).

Therefore, despite mainstream unions' official declarations of internationalism and solidarity with migrant workers, the translation of these declared principles into real, daily struggles is frequently contradictory and problematic. These combined concerns have led scholars and activists to advocate for semi-autonomous structures of migrant, BME and other marginalized workers within the union framework in order to ensure empowerment and substantial representation (Virdee and Grint 1994). A superficial establishment of contact between unions and migrant workers is not enough to meaningfully impact the conditions migrant workers experience or the wider structures that enable these conditions.

Distance and absence

Unions' withdrawal from precarious occupations is frequently explained in terms of procedural problems, such as the difficulty of securing union recognition agreements among a workforce that is constantly changing precisely due to the precarious nature of its employment (see, for example, Moore 2011). Other theorists have focused on problems within the union structure, such as how accessible they are for migrant workers and how well they deal with issues of intersectionality (for example, Alberti et al. 2013). Finally, as has been repeatedly analysed in the above pages, subjective elements that are frequently associated with the migrant condition have been shown to raise additional barriers for migrant workers in relation to unionization. However, my research indicates that all these analyses, while valuable, are examining issues that are already one step ahead of the actual reality on the ground: unions, and similar social movements, are almost entirely absent from the workplaces, lives and communities of migrant workers. It seems wishful thinking to endlessly deliberate on the shortcomings of unions or engage in deep analyses of the problems raised by language and cultural barriers when unions have not even managed to *exist* in most precarious workers' spheres of consciousness.

Before we continue, an important caveat: the nonexistence of unions from precarious workplaces does not mean that I am arguing that workers are powerless, or that an emancipatory process can only progress through official union activity. Suzan and her four Romanian colleagues managed to collectively bargain for more money by themselves; when workers are conscious of the power that they possess and get organized, they get results. However, the only reason that unions exist is *precisely* to provide workers with the resources and the knowledge to act upon their power; workers shouldn't have to do it alone. I am not saying that workers cannot organize without unions; I am arguing that their absence fuels the processes that foster the socialization of precarity, which in turn makes workers more likely to opt for individualized solutions to the collective and structural issues that they face. This absence goes beyond the workplace: it feeds into the wider retreat of social movements from working neighbourhoods and communities, as precarity increasingly permeates all aspects of our collective existence and neoliberalism is allowed to appear as an almost eternal and unchangeable reality.

Raquel and Charles, a mother and son from Lisbon that have both been working for years in the hospitality industry in Scotland, had absolutely no knowledge of unions or of their labour rights. Over the course of my interview with them it emerged that they had been subjected to various injustices that were fundamentally based on them not having access to a union. For Raquel, being bullied at work had become an accepted fact of life, and both mother and son mentioned attending disciplinary hearings without being informed of their right to be accompanied by a friend or union representative. The complete nonexistence of unions in their workplace had allowed management to cultivate a subtle but haunting environment of fear.

> *Q:* I want to ask you if you have ever considered speaking to a trade union. Is there a trade union in your workplace?
> *Raquel:* I don't know.
> *Charles:* I don't know.
> *Raquel:* I'm OK. I don't have that type of problem.
> *Q:* Is there even a presence of a trade union?
> *Raquel:* I don't know.
> *Q:* Fair enough. Has there ever been anyone that came up to you and introduced themselves as a union representative or anything similar?
> *Raquel:* Just the health and security department.
> *Q:* So, have you ever considered – for example, when you mentioned, Raquel, that you were bullied – to speak to a union, to find out what your rights are?
> *Raquel:* No, I have never thought about it. But even if I said that, it was my ticket to go out.
>
> Raquel and Charles. Both are Portuguese. Charles is a male in his early 20s. Raquel, his mother, is in her mid-40s. Both work in hospitality.

The degree of mistrust at any possibility of receiving support is expressed through Raquel's belief that, if she even spoke about her labour rights, it would be her 'ticket to go out'. This is the fear that sustains precarity; yet this fear has not spawned spontaneously. It has been *allowed* to exist precisely through the absence of unions from these workers' lives.

A similar scenario, but demonstrably worse, was experienced by Anna, the jurist from Guadeloupe, in the hotel she was working in. We met for our interview about half an hour after she had been issued her 'Final Warning Letter' from her – white South African – manager. After being repeatedly racially abused, overworked and saddled with impossible demands – a situation that was later confirmed through the written testimonies of some of her colleagues – she had refused to carry out an order. This had led to her manager reducing her hours to zero after issuing her with a 'First Warning Letter' and withholding a substantial amount of her wages. Prior to this final conflict, Anna had repeatedly notified her general manager of the discriminatory nature of the other manager's behaviour but was consistently ignored. The fact that an investigation into discrimination was not launched, alongside the procedural violations of labour law regarding Anna's disciplinary hearing, led me to believe that this was a winnable Employment Tribunal case under the UK's 2010 Equality Act. Anna was very distressed from her experiences and did not want to leave the job without at least trying to fight back. Since there was no union in her workplace, which was in a remote location that precluded any substantial union campaign (for example, a protest outside or a picket), Anna and I decided that, if negotiating proved unfruitful, we would proceed with a Tribunal process. The entire experience is exemplary of the ways in which – even with supposedly progressive legislation – the odds are stacked against migrant workers.

Upon lodging a tribunal claim, a mediator from the UK's Advisory, Conciliation and Arbitration Service (ACAS) gets in touch with both parties and attempts to settle the dispute informally. If this process is unsuccessful, the parties can proceed to a Tribunal.

In order to have a chance to win a discrimination case, the employee needs to prove that a discriminatory behaviour that they suffered was directly tied to a protected characteristic under the 2010 Equality Act. Crucially, where verbal statements are concerned, there needs to be a direct connection with the employee's protected characteristics (for example, 'you black people don't know how to work'), and where practices are concerned there needs to be evidence that the behaviour in question disproportionately impacted the individuals with that protected characteristic (for example, if the black workers are given the worst jobs while non-black workers are assigned more prestigious jobs). Finally, the claim needs to be connected to a single, measurable instance of discrimination which did not occur more than three months from the day the claim was made. In our case, this meant proving that the 'First Warning Letter' was issued because of Anna's protected characteristics of being a black, Muslim woman; our argument, however, was that the 'First Warning Letter' was but the culmination of a long process in which Anna was subjected to discriminatory behaviour from her manager.

These restrictions are made even more difficult to navigate by a range of factors. To begin with, lack of funds for a lawyer can play a significant role in hindering success. At the time I was a union representative in the IWW, which has an agreement with a legal firm that granted us a half-hour of free consultation per case. However, that limited amount of time is barely enough to scratch the surface of a complex case. Mainstream service unions like Unite have ample funds and lawyers at their disposal, but the IWW was too small to afford these provisions. Anna and I were obliged to do the research by ourselves, which involved many hours of phone calls and work on the internet around relevant labour and equalities legislation and case history. Anna compiled a list of every instance of discrimination she remembered and procured several witness statements from her colleagues that described in detail both what had occurred in her final conflict with the manager and the manager's general behaviour.

However, this was where the debilitating power of precarity was once again made evident: the statements we procured included very strong cases of discrimination from the manager's part, but their authors were too afraid to attach their names to them. Those that did, did so by significantly downplaying the severity of the situation in order to not provoke him. The single strong witness statement that was signed belonged to an individual *who no longer worked in the establishment. Furthermore, the informal environment fostered in the hotel meant that there was little formal written communication; Anna had raised her concerns about discrimination verbally, and there was no way to fully prove that she did so; her general manager's reassurance that he would launch an investigation was also verbal, and therefore the hotel denied that it was ever made; and the South African manager's discriminatory statements and behaviours were never reflected in writing.*

Once the ACAS mediator got in touch, it seemed that Anna's claims were not being taken seriously. The hotel's lawyers were denying every single one of our points. They claimed that Anna had not been punitively fired and was still employed, despite the fact that by this point a full month had passed and she had never been contacted for resuming her work. This constituted either an Unfair Dismissal or an improperly executed suspension process, but the law precludes workers from arguing these in a Tribunal when they have been employed for less than two years in an establishment. The hotel's lawyers further denied any knowledge of discrimination, and, taking advantage of the fact that Anna could not resort to an Unfair Dismissal claim, insinuated that she was claiming discrimination to vindictively get back at the establishment for disciplining her.

This was to be expected from the hotel's defence, but the strange thing was that the ACAS mediator seemed inclined to uncritically accept the hotel's position. For example, she kept on asking why Anna had not raised a formal grievance regarding discrimination, when it had already been explained to her that (1) there was no one in the workplace to advise Anna of that option, and (2) the climate of informality in the workplace was such that all such concerns were communicated verbally. Furthermore, she refused to acknowledge the continuity of Anna's experiences in the hotel, insisting that the dispute strictly concerned whether or not Anna's disciplinary constituted an instance of discrimination. For example, she told me that Anna 'did tell her manager to "fuck off and do his job", which is unacceptable', ignoring the fact that Anna did that following a long period of harassment. Speaking to the mediator felt like attempting to communicate with a lifeless robot, lacking in all empathy and concerned more with issues of etiquette rather than justice. She then told me that the hotel's lawyers were requesting to see our compiled evidence and advised us to hand it over, but that is a curious demand by a supposedly neutral arbiter to make in the stages preceding a Tribunal. With her prior legal experience in France, Anna refused to hand our evidence over to the other side, and we were gridlocked.

Since we could not agree on a resolution, the only option left was to proceed with a Tribunal. We agreed that Anna would consult a friend of hers who was working as a legal advisor in a Citizens Advice Bureau. She discouraged us from proceeding with the Tribunal. She advised that the anonymous witness statements, lack of written communication and lack of a single measurable instance which could be directly connected with Anna's protected characteristics would all be looked upon unfavourably in a Tribunal. Moreover, she said that the hotel could argue that our claim was vexatious, which, if accepted, could result in Anna being ordered to pay for the hotel's legal costs plus compensation. By this point more than a month had passed since we began the claim, and both Anna and I were emotionally drained from weeks of intense research, phone arguments with the mediator, and attempts to convince her colleagues to sign their witness statements. Anna decided to follow her friend's advice and drop the claim. However, the hotel did eventually pay her the money she was owed. Despite our relative failure, she was proud of us for having at least done something to combat the hotel's authority, and she told me that she was feeling empowered by her experience. She later joined the IWW and proceeded to attend organizer training and become active in the wider workings of the organization.

Even though Anna knew of the existence of unions and was a confident person thanks to her legal background prior to her arrival in Scotland, she nevertheless felt initially disempowered by their lack of presence and by the overwhelming pressures of precarity and abuse in her jobs. These burdens, combined with her feelings of insecurity and disorientation as a migrant worker, led to her being reticent to act before her final conflict with management. It turns out that she was correct: when she finally stood up for herself, she was promptly fired.

Q: Why did you not think about contacting a union when all of these things were happening in your working life?

Anna: Because the rights in the UK are completely different than France. I know that, as an immigrant, first of all, and then secondly as a worker, we don't have the same rights, same protection.

Q: That is false.

Anna: Yes! But that is what everyone said.

Q: So, was it other immigrants that were telling you that you don't have the same rights? This is basically exactly what I'm trying to find out.

Anna: Yeah. And also, to say that all the employers have such power on us. And that British people just stay quiet and don't say anything at all. So, for me I was just, I was thinking that we don't have a lot of rights.

Q: You saw the apathy and the lack of voice of the British and you kind of just fell in step?

Anna: Yes, yes. And I told them all, my co-workers, I said 'you so British, you like, you just double-face. You mumbling but you don't stand for your rights.' And now I'm fired! Because I stand for our rights. And, yeah...

Anna, Guadeloupean (French) woman, late 30s, hospitality

Here, Anna illuminates the erroneous ideas and narratives that are allowed to fester in the absence of the oppositional perspectives provided by unions and social movements. Such inaccurate views flourish in precarious workplaces because of the combination of the socialization of precarity, a lack of access to resources, and a variety of management scare tactics. Additionally, Anna refers to the wider socialization of precarity, expressed through the passivity and docility of the British workers, in limiting her confidence to pursue justice. It could reasonably be inferred that the docility Anna experienced, where workers were 'mumbling' but not standing up for their rights, is also related to the complete nonexistence of unions in that workplace. This nonexistence is self-perpetuating; as we saw from her colleagues' fears of reprisals, the more there is an absence of support in precarious workplaces, the more workers will be scared or unwilling to risk their jobs by acting. The socialization of precarity ensures its own reproduction.

Union absence was also confirmed through my own observations. Out of the six workplaces I entered in the course of conducting this research, only the fish factory had a union presence (and, paradoxically, the fish factory was the worst working environment out of all of them!). In the rest of the locations, including in Amazon, unions were nowhere to be seen. As was demonstrated in the above excerpt, this absence nurtured the emergence of a wider culture of resignation amongst the workforce, as the socialization of precarity was allowed to freely operate without challenge. This in turn allows blatant miscarriages of justice to be naturalized and accepted as 'just the way things are', which further enforces the socialization of precarity. This resignation was also observed in relation to dismissals. It was widely accepted that, if the superiors had a problem with a worker, they were fully within their rights to fire them on the spot. Anti-discrimination and equality legislations were completely ignored, and the word 'strike' was only ever mentioned as a joke – its very pronouncement indicating how utterly absurd it seemed in this context.

An additional factor that has seldom been considered in both movement and scholarly writing, and which is intimately connected to unions' absence from the lives of most migrant and precarious workers, concerns the vast cultural gap between these populations and social movements in the UK. This has little to do with ethnicity and language, and more to do with class, lifestyle and community. Simply put, the everyday realities of many migrant workers stand in stark opposition to the cultures that dominate many unions and other left-wing organizations. This creates a vicious cycle whereby the distance between movements and workers increases the more detached these movements are, eventually rendering translation across cultures and class positionalities almost impossible. This distance is statistically reflected in the much lower unionization density amongst precarious workers as opposed to those with more security. An example from La Dama encapsulates the chasm between precarious migrant workers and those that are meant to fight for their interests.

I overhear George [the Scottish head chef] *speaking to the main manager about some problems with the outside bins. I make sure to inform my Albanian colleagues, John and Manos, that they need to be careful about how they close the bins because he is complaining about them to the manager. They look scared; the overhanging threat of dismissal is omnipresent. Manos's eyes are wide open, and he is looking at the two much older, Scottish, hierarchically superior men talking in English about him, trying hard to pick up on a few words without being successful. I do my best to overhear, but the noise of the kitchen covers up most of what they are saying. I tell them that if anything happens my union will support them. The truth is, I worry about how accepted and welcome these people will feel as members of my union. We are talking about workers with very little knowledge of English, who work for most of their lives, and in their spare time take drugs, get rowdy, and go to strip clubs. From my experience of trade unions in the UK, it seems that they wouldn't fit in with many younger union members that attend meetings and dedicate time to political action. On the other hand, I could easily imagine British union members feeling uncomfortable with the migrants' differing performativity of masculinity, their expressiveness and their loud, confident demeanour. I have frequently been perceived as aggressive by British people because of the way I move my hands when I speak, which is something that I am culturally accustomed to from my Greek upbringing. How would an Albanian male worker with limited knowledge of British people's expectations feel in a union meeting mostly populated by British union members? This distance is something that we need to seriously look at. (Fieldnotes, 17 July 2019)*

Unions and social movements have a long road ahead of them if they desire to organize with migrant workers and address the wider phenomena associated with the socialization of precarity. From rectifying their deafening absence to cultivating cultures that are more accepting and tolerant of different backgrounds and socializations, these changes presuppose deep ideological and organizational reformations (Holgate 2021). However, despite their current overwhelming shortcomings, I agree with Jane Holgate and with Maite Tapia's (2014: 134) conclusions that 'immigrant workers both *need* and *want* to join unions [italics in original]'. Visibility and accessibility therefore emerge as the key barriers to migrant workers' participation.

Q: In all of these precarious jobs, was there ever a presence of a union?
Leila: No, never!
Q: There was never any leaflet or any. . .?

Leila: No, never! Never! And if there was, I would join! Like, if anybody from any union would have come, I know I would have joined! Unless it was like a Neo-Nazi or super conservative union, but any, even. . . yeah, Labour.[6]

Q: And you have changed a lot of jobs, so this is representative. So why do you think that there are so few migrants that are members of unions?

Leila: For many reasons, because unions are inexistent in our sector. They are never there. I barely see them, I barely see, like, a union member's protest. And any protest in this country about labour rights, and zero-hour contracts and all that, they just, they are just not there![7]

Q: They are not there. OK. And if they were more visible, and they made more attempts to be inside the community and talk to workers, do you feel that they would actually respond?

Leila: Yeah! Because the anger is there! People are not stupid, they know that they are taking advantage of them! You know, people don't have a distorted vision of reality, they know exactly what's going on, and they know is not normal that people have to work fucking 52 hours to make a fucking living and to provide for their kids!

Leila, Spanish/Tunisian woman, early 30s, hospitality

In a study of the US labour movement, Richard Sullivan (2010: 812) asks: 'What does that say about the efficacy of a working-class movement if its principal organizations are unable to organize workers in the greatest need?' This question is highly poignant. Every worker I interviewed spoke of the nonexistence of unions from their lives, workplaces and communities. Stefania Marino et al. (2017: 12) argue that specific union practices are 'a much better predictor of membership and active participation of migrant workers than the question of which country the migrant workers came from and whether they had experiences with trade unions before arrival'. More fundamentally, it emerges that union *in*action, as expressed through their almost complete lack of presence in workplaces and communities, is one of the strongest barriers to the empowerment and unionization of migrant workers. At the end of our interview, Suzan stopped speaking to me as a researcher, and began addressing the wider union movement:

I am telling you, you must try! I agreed to be interviewed today...
I didn't know what exactly would happen... But you must try to
become more powerful! You must be present, at this moment you are
too anonymous... You don't exist!

Suzan, Romanian woman, late 40s, hospitality and logistics
[translation mine from Greek]

The complex interplay of the various structural and subjective factors analysed in these pages pales in comparison with the significance of social movements' detachment from the lives and workplaces of the populations that are experiencing the brunt of precarious socioeconomic conditions. I am using 'trade unions' and 'social movements' interchangeably, as I believe that disempowerment – or its opposite – is fostered both in the workplace and in wider society. The socialization of precarity can only be ruptured through sustained action that highlights that alternatives are possible whilst empowering workers in tangible ways. For example, workers' fears that they might be fired for virtually anything must be assuaged through consistent engagement and the provision of information. The same applies to other subjective traits connected to migration such as the dual frame of reference or the lack of access to information about labour rights. Wider fears of feeling unsupported and alone can only be addressed through sustained community organizing. Ultimately, the more unions and social movements are *not* present, the more they do not directly engage with precarious migrant workers, the more the conditions that foster precarity will be allowed to worsen.

There is no way around the issue of presence. No matter how proficient unions become at using the language of intersectionality (which they generally aren't), no matter how many people from marginalized groups they elevate to positions of power (which they generally don't), and no matter how many resources are dedicated to supporting existing migrant members (which are generally lacking), unions will ultimately have to contend with the fact that a large proportion of migrant workers have never come across a union in the entirety of their working lives. Indeed, most of the people that I spoke to had never seen any form of social movement activity in their neglected Glasgow neighbourhoods – presumably, this is true across the UK. These absences do not mean that workers, by themselves, will not take the initiative to organize collectively.

They do mean, however, that for many insecure and exhausted workers – who are also lacking information on their labour rights and are feeling the added pressures of migration – the daily realities and demands of precarity may preclude thinking about engaging in oppositional action. Embeddedness, expressed primarily through being present, active and rooted in precarious workers' communities, thereby emerges as the main priority for social movements that are aiming to challenge the effects that precarity produces.

Conclusion:
Towards Community Embeddedness

The world is vastly different since I migrated to the UK more than a decade ago, with many trends worsening. Poverty, wars and climate crises mean that migration is on the rise all over the world, and the structural, economic and cultural processes that position migrant workers in the most precarious occupations are still operative. As workers continually leave their lands in search of a better life, the gears of international capital ensure that they will be used to create ever more profits, in ever deteriorating conditions.

In the UK, the results of Brexit mean that migrant workers are even more precarious, unprotected and subject to intensified immigration controls. While most EU workers had the privilege of not feeling the spectre of deportation breathing down their necks until 2021, this has now been rescinded. Even with the new – and ostensibly more attuned to human rights issues – Labour government, attacks on migration have not stopped; if anything, the new regime adds a veneer of humanitarianism to migrant criminalization, while fully subscribing to the myths that migration lowers wages and harms the local working class. Indeed, a big part of the new Labour government's stated migration policy involves strengthening border enforcement and making deportations easier. Such legislative measures simply mean that the migrant precarity will be accentuated as they are pushed into worse jobs, in shadier parts of the economy, with even fewer rights; they also mean that solidarity initiatives, developing coalitions and organizing alongside migrant communities become ever more vital.

In the United States, despite the existence of the strongest migrant-led movements in the hemisphere, racist and xenophobic attitudes have not been displaced, and the return of Trump to power is, at the time of writing, a strong possibility. Regardless of who wins the 2024 US election, the inequalities that migrant workers experience have not been addressed, and the proliferation of migration controls – through, for example, restricting access to asylum – is once again presented as the sole solution to dealing with the very profitable 'problem' of precarious and exploitable workers. In Europe, we are seeing further increases in hostility towards migrants and the adoption of ever-stricter border controls, with 'centrist' governments largely absorbing the same policies that were once derided as belonging to the far right. Within its borders, even the restrained and exclusionary 'freedom of movement' in the Schengen zone that was promoted as a key feature of European humanitarianism is increasingly being abandoned. In the meantime, thousands are still drowning in the Mediterranean as a direct result of European migration policies. Again, these developments do not spell the end of migration; they serve to create ever more precarious workers.

Our societies are becoming increasingly precarious *beyond* the scope of migration, with costs of living rising while the tatters that remain of welfare states are further eroded and privatized. In the absence of inspirational narratives and institutions that contest the desert of neoliberalism, workers from every walk of life are increasingly confronted with the realization that their survival is a matter of individual aptitude, entirely separated from the sphere of society – indeed, in the hypercompetitive context that precarity engenders, it often stands *in opposition* to it. In such a context, arguing for solidarity with migrant workers is perceived as ludicrous, because, apart from any racist or xenophobic attitudes that individuals may hold, solidarity *in itself* as a concept or a realizable goal is progressively pushed outside the horizon of possibilities. As theorists like Zygmunt Bauman, Bifo Berardi and Byung-Chul Han have warned for years, the neoliberal imaginary increasingly permeates all social relations in proportion to the retreat of oppositional narratives, further searing itself in the collective psyche. What's more, migration does not preclude migrant workers from subscribing to, and reproducing, these narratives. The socialization of precarity, forged in the pits of daily toil in precarious occupations while the subject simultaneously perceives, internalizes and negotiates the neoliberal dictums that are circulating in wider society, plays a critical role in the process by which collective problems are naturalized as individual struggles.

The purpose of this book was to use a sliver of our collective social reality to understand how this socialization develops in our daily lives as workers. More importantly, I aimed to understand what precisely prevents us from taking collective action to improve our labour conditions. While the springboard for this research was my own experience as a precariously employed migrant worker in the UK, I believe that the ways in which precarity socializes workers extend, to varying degrees, to everyone that is trying to make ends meet in an insecure environment that individualizes and exploits them.

I argue that this socialization reaches deep into the recesses of subjectivity and influences much more than simply workers' expectations of work. It interacts with wider social trends of individualization and the decline of class-based oppositional narratives and institutions to fortify overarching hegemonic social narratives that ground neoliberal economics as unchallengeable and unchangeable. This process ruptures the emergence of solidarities, obfuscates the power that workers inherently possess, fosters the emergence of individualist, survival-oriented attitudes, and can cumulate in a passive acceptance of the status quo. In conditions of intense exploitation and insecurity, even manifestations of solidarity become precarious.

The insidiousness of the socialization of precarity is that it feeds on our desires to feel dignity, autonomy, security and strength. This is one of the most essential points that I wish to underline. In its simplest iteration, it can be perceived as a set of dispositions that allow the individual to cope with the ceaseless and contradictory demands made upon them while developing the skills, comportments and performances required to survive precarity. Eventually this struggle may lead to workers crafting an identity of individual resilience that further enforces the ideological foundations of neoliberalism in daily life. Crucially, though, this means that despite the momentous obstacles they face in achieving precisely those needs of dignity, autonomy and strength, workers do *not* allow themselves to feel completely disempowered, and class consciousness is *not* entirely eroded in the fog of neoliberal identities. The socialization of precarity *does* mean that, as it proliferates uncontested, we are running the danger of completely losing sight of any capacity to imagine radical, liberating alternatives. However, it also means that the raw material for organizing – workers' hopes and desires for a fulfilling, secure life – survives. It is up to social movements to develop the resources and tactics that will steer these feelings towards a different path.

Migration and the socialization of precarity

Having traversed the realms of geopolitics, migration, neoliberalism, precarity, subjectivity, class consciousness and trade unions, it is important to briefly retrace the main points of this book in order to highlight the conceptual importance of the socialization of precarity, as well as to develop a foundation from which to challenge it.

Migrant labour does not exist on its own. It is situated in a wider socioeconomic context that is already characterized by weakening unions, the retreat of class-based oppositional narratives, and sustained, systemic assaults on workers' rights. In this context, migrant workers are positioned at the forefront of the precarious condition. Labour precarity has multiple manifestations, including illegal and semi-legal labour, the use of verbal contracts, agency work and zero-hours contracts. These jobs are usually underpaid, physically taxing, intensely alienating and quintessentially insecure. The needs of employers for flexible, obedient, exploitable labour interact with cultural and economic processes – such as deskilling or the perception that certain workers are 'naturally' suited for specific sectors – that push migrants precisely towards these jobs; simultaneously, migrants' own initial needs for quick jobs that pay the bills nurture a vicious cycle where a steady pool of exploitable immigrants exists to fill the staffing requirements of precarious occupations.

Most of the migrant workers that I spoke to explicitly stated that in the first stages of their migration they favoured the first jobs they could access. The operations of a significant segment of the UK economy are designed in such a way that they intimately depend on 'flexible' labour, and employers know that there is a steady supply of willing workers to fill their vacant positions; importantly, contractual precarity enables them to dispose of these workers when they are no longer required and absolves the employer of any long-term responsibilities towards the worker. As we saw in the previous chapters, these contracts are frequently used as a *management tool*, enabling employers to sort through workers until they find the individuals that best fit their requirements.

Over time, populations can become closely associated with the occupations they perform, in a process that essentially reproduces itself. This reality emerges out of a combination of different factors: for example, ethnic networks become embedded in certain sectors, continually

CONCLUSION: TOWARDS COMMUNITY EMBEDDEDNESS

attracting new migrant workers; on the other hand, agencies and employers in certain jobs have an interest in maintaining ethnic homogeneity, thereby creating a dynamic where both migrants and employers reproduce migrant workers' association with, and allocation to, specific precarious occupations. However, these two poles do not have equal power: while migrant workers may rely on ethnic networks to secure employment niches that counterbalance their wider disadvantage in the labour market, employers own the means of production, and their practices are ultimately borne out of considerations aiming to secure and augment profitability. This means that homogeneity is maintained purely where it is profitable to do so: my observations in Glasgow generally indicate that where high levels of communication are needed in the labour process (for example, in the radiator factory or La Dama), there is a tendency for employers to favour a concentration of specific migrant groups, whereas in largely atomized and impersonal jobs (such as in Amazon) the opposite tends to occur. In all cases, the precise ways that employers make use of the steadily available pool of migrant workers depend on the needs of each specific workplace to maintain profitability.

The workings of the national economic structure (legal processes such as the permittance of zero-hours contracts, the setting of the minimum wage, etc.) thus combine with migration law (such as minimum income thresholds, visa restrictions, restrictions on working hours, etc.), employer demands (flexibility, efficiency, productivity, specific orders) and subjective features that may be shared by migrant workers (from needing some quick money in the beginning, to gradually becoming socialized in precarity) to create, and reproduce, a complex of social and economic relations that, ultimately, reinforces its own neoliberal foundations. Migrant workers who do not have the privilege of a fully secure status are further disempowered, as their right to remain is directly connected with the job that they perform; as we saw from Arjun's testimony, the risk of losing an already precarious position carries significantly more weight than for relatively more secure workers. A plethora of factors thus intersect to create, and fortify, the exploitability of migrant workers.

How do migrant workers negotiate their precarity? Migrants' understandings of themselves as migrants, as workers, and as migrant workers are complex, contradictory and highly heterogeneous. For example, some migrants may present a strong class-focused analysis of exploitation but may nevertheless be fully invested participants in the narratives that make up Britain's conception of the 'community of value' (Anderson 2013), thereby accepting and reproducing the mystification of the conditions that enable their exploitation. Some, like Nicole, might try to empower themselves by investing in the development of a strong personality; others, like Felix, feel that their status as migrants essentially disempowers them relative to their peers. In every case, workers' everyday experiences play a foundational and formative role in how they perceive and frame their lives as migrants. In the wider absence of strong and socially embedded migrant workers' movements, the only migrant workers expressing a politicized migrant identity are usually those already active in such movements. It is therefore possible to argue that, in contrast with previous historical epochs of migrant struggles – and, perhaps, in contrast with the contemporary situation in the United States, where very strong migrant movements exist – and despite sustained attacks on migrant workers by the UK government, employers and the far right, a politicized migrant identity is *not* strongly developing in the UK.

This, however, does not mean that migrant workers are *not* conscious of their class status and of the role that migration plays in how it is lived. Borne of an experiential reflection on labour inequality, every migrant worker I spoke to was acutely aware of the hierarchical difference between them and their employers. This class consciousness also saturated my everyday experiences in precarious occupations. Indeed, the socialization of precarity *depends* upon workers' awareness of their precarious class position. Like all workers, migrant workers are not passive recipients of the conditions that are thrust upon them; nor, as traditional union wisdom would suggest, are they 'unorganizable' because of the various structural and subjective factors that are associated with their migration and precarious employment. It seems more accurate to argue that, in the absence of viable and inspiring alternatives, workers are compelled to address their precarity individualistically. Yet, as Ruth Milkman (2020) notes in relation to the US context, rarely have conditions been better for organizing migrant workers. Leila's exasperated proclamation in the previous chapter bears repeating: 'The anger is there! People are not stupid, they know that they are taking advantage of them! People don't have a distorted vision of reality, they know exactly what's going on.'

I therefore do not believe that factors such as precarity or migration are, in themselves, sufficient to explain the relative disempowerment and exploitability of migrant workers, or the wider lack of collective labour action emerging from migrant groups. As we saw, in specific conditions and depending on the resources that migrants have available to them in the new country of origin, the dual frame of reference can work both ways. Rather than exclusively functioning to disempower migrants or turn them into the *Homo economicus* discussed by Michael Piore (1979), it can sometimes *foster* political action. Those with experience of political mobilization in their home countries are highly likely to become active in their new setting. As such, while migrancy does generally play a significant role in fostering initial feelings of disempowerment, it is only through its wider interplay with the socialization of precarity and the wider social context – such as the complete absence of unions and social movements from most migrant workers' lives in the UK – that it contributes to an absence of resistance and the development of the traits associated with the socialization of precarity.

I have used the term 'socialization of precarity' to encapsulate the multiple complex mentalities, tendencies and behaviours that may emerge from migrant workers' prolonged interactions with the daily realities of precarious occupations. As their lives are constantly mediated by stress and insecurity, workers may become socialized in and through them. This socialization stems from multiple aspects that are inseparable features of precarious occupations, such as the lack of social bonds between workers, the 'agency arena' (the constant, underlying competition with other precarious workers in the same workplace and across society), the 'good worker paradox' (the knowledge that, as one is attempting to be as productive as possible in order to secure a job, one is also simultaneously at risk of reducing one's necessity to the employer), and the constant pressures to perform while knowing that labour security is far from guaranteed.

In such precarious workplaces, precarity permeates almost all interactions, significantly disrupting the potential for the formation of substantial bonds of affinity, mutuality and trust. The stress associated with precarious occupations, where one can be fired without any protection, induces an ever-present sense of anxiety and competition amongst workers; their interdependence and coexistence, instead of being tools of solidarity, can instead be a source of added pressure which distances workers from each other. Whether we are in a faceless and cold Amazon warehouse or in the bustling kitchen of La Dama, a precarious workplace is rarely warm and compassionate, and rarely fosters feelings of trust and solidarity.

Cumulatively, these experiences can lead to a wider fortification of the conditions that breed precarity. More precisely, workers are liable to internalize the conditions they face and reconstitute them into proud aspects of their identity: as we saw in La Dama, the fatigue, stress and scars that result from their precarity became badges of honour and ability rather than signs of an exploitative situation that must be overcome. This individual survivalism extends to further isolate workers. The nonexistence of bonds between workers, already a fundamental facet of precarious employment relations, is deepened. Perversely, precisely in attempting to wrest some degree of agency, autonomy and individuality from a social context that disempowers, marginalizes and exploits, the worker might actually be reinforcing the foundations of these malaises. This entails important complications in relation to the issue of collective action and organization, since the shared experiences of exploitation that, under different conditions, would lead to workers identifying with one another, are now interpreted as individual difficulties. Even more problematically, they are difficulties which may become intimately connected to workers' ideas of themselves, as one's ability to overcome them *by surviving through them* is the *measure of one's self-worth and dignity*. One's identity as a worker is therefore attached to *surviving* conditions rather than *changing* them.

In this context, while instances of resistance do occur with various degrees of tenacity and success, they mostly assume the form of individualized expressions of dissent rather than collective struggle. Occupational mobility emerges as the main technique that migrant workers use to improve their labour conditions; rather than focusing on changing a structure that is deemed unchangeable, migrant workers, especially those from the EU with some relative security in their right to remain in the UK, prefer to search for a 'better' job. However, escaping precarity, for most, remains an unfulfilled dream. Moreover, in their attempts to improve their conditions through relying predominantly on their individual capacity to switch jobs, workers reinforce the underlying

CONCLUSION: TOWARDS COMMUNITY EMBEDDEDNESS

foundations of both the precarious structure and the socialization of precarity.

While at this point precarity may seem like an overpowering cancer that relentlessly multiplies even through attempts to resist it, various workers proudly spoke to me of their labour victories. The stories of Lois, Suzan and Mateusz illustrate the power that migrant workers hold, even in the context of precarious employment, and even if unions may not be present in their workplaces. My own experience representing Anna, who, even though her Employment Tribunal claim was ultimately unsuccessful, went on to become an important organizer in her city, attests to the potential that workers have when in contact with contestational resources. These realizations were mirrored by the fact that virtually every worker I interviewed expressed a class-conscious understanding of their labour conditions. And, crucially, every migrant I spoke to responded that they would join and support a union if one were present in their workplace. Unfortunately, it emerges that the conditions that would encourage migrant workers towards collectively mobilizing are either uninspiring, alienating, or outright absent. Amongst the few workers I interviewed who have had contacts with trade unions, there were numerous reports of intensely alienating experiences.

The most significant obstacle to the organization of migrant workers – and, by extension, the most important source of the strength of the socialization of precarity – was the utter absence of unions and other emancipatory social movements from their workplaces and communities. I argue that this absence is directly responsible for nurturing and exacerbating attitudes of resignation and acceptance of the status quo, as the lack of any vocal and credible oppositional narrative allows the socialization of precarity to become hegemonic over workers' imaginations. The more the class imbalance between the employers and the employees is allowed to skew towards the side of the employers, the more inequality is solidified as a 'personal' struggle in the minds of workers. By consequence, personalized solutions to labour problems are increasingly viewed as the only plausible route of action. These avenues, however, culminate in reinforcing the foundations that breed precarity and migrant exploitation.

Ultimately, the weight of the interplay of the various structural and subjective factors that collectively uphold migrant precarity pales in comparison to the significance of unions' detachment from the lives and workplaces of the populations that are experiencing the brunt of precarious socioeconomic conditions. Unions – and social movements that intend to organize alongside migrant and marginalized groups – must contend with the fact that a large proportion of migrant workers have never come across them in the entirety of their working experience.[1] The socialization of precarity is a parasite that festers upon the space left empty by its opposite. Could this opposite be imagined as the 'socialization of solidarity'? And if this is the goal, then how do we embark upon nurturing this opposite in the desert of neoliberalism? In my view, community embeddedness is the key priority to reverse neoliberalism's stranglehold on the imagination and develop alternative modes of relating to ourselves and to each other: as workers, as migrants and as political subjects.

Notes towards embeddedness

Decades after what was one of the strongest migrant workers' movements in the UK's history, William Fishman (2004) tracked down some of its participants in order to understand, and salvage, their memories of organizing. In 1906, the *Arbeter Fraint* group, a coalition of radical thinkers and organizers that aimed to organize the precarious Jewish workers of London's East End, opened a social club in Jubilee Street. With an 800-capacity gallery, a library, and ample space for conducting meetings and getting together, it quickly became a central feature of the community's life. Cognizant that workers needed *more* than just political activities in order to emerge from the dregs of the alienation induced by their labour conditions, the group hosted cultural events like dances, live music and poetry readings, while also offering classes in history, sociology and even English literature. Access was open to anyone, regardless of club membership or background. An example of the club's scope that illustrates the depth to which it aimed to empower workers can be seen in the annual trip it organized to Epping Forest, which many workers remembered as the 'highlight of their lives' (Fishman 2004: 262). Workers would bring their families, and, following a long walk, would then congregate to listen to Rudolf Rocker lecture on topics ranging from literature to history and politics. These culturally-oriented initiatives were complemented by consistent organizing on the ground and in the sweatshops of London's East End.

Rather than simply viewing workers as faceless units in need of strict labour organization, the *Arbeter Fraint* group recognized that empowerment emerges out of experiences of beauty, mutuality, and the re-emergence of the humanity that alienation so mercilessly represses. Having a space in which workers could coalesce, escape, find themselves again, and ultimately organize in slowly led to sustained political action, including the momentous tailors' strike in 1912. Through these activities, beyond succeeding to abolish sweatshop labour in the East End, the Jewish workers were also able to forge strong connections of solidarity with the wider British working class. Crucially, these developments necessitated time. The *Arbeter Fraint* didn't impose itself upon workers, nor did it try to 'liberate' them; it did, however, provide resources and space that encouraged workers to critically reflect upon, and address, their experiences of exploitation. Rather than viewing the lack of organization as a confirmation of the difficulties of organizing, the group dynamically inserted themselves in the daily lives and neighbourhoods of migrant groups and developed institutions that both helped workers imagine a better *collective* life and convinced them of their *collective* power in bringing it about.

In contemporary society, the need for similar institutions, firmly embedded in social reality but offering windows that allow us to imagine beyond it, is of paramount importance. This need emerges from the understanding of how potent the socialization of precarity is, but also from understanding how current social conditions nurture it. This includes, for example, the temporariness associated with precarity, which prevents the establishment of long-lasting relationships in specific workplaces. It is hard to organize a strong union when significant sectors of the workforce are almost completely different every few months. It is even harder when these segments of the workforce have made their capacity to struggle individually into cornerstones of their identity and their methods of escape. This is a fundamental reason why, even though the socialization of precarity is produced in the sphere of labour, social movements must focus on the neighbourhood.

Scholarship examining migrant-focused union campaigns foregrounds the need for migrant-led strategies that are closely connected with migrant communities.[2] For example, Gabriella Alberti, Jane Holgate and Lowell Turner argue that campaigns have higher chances of success where they engage migrants specifically *as migrants*, operationalizing an intersectional analysis of the multiple oppressions that regulate their exploitation, rather than as members of the wider working class; they cite the CLEAN campaign in the US, where 'a broad understanding of oppression opened up the framing of the campaign and allowed organizers to talk about workers' rights alongside immigrant and social rights' (2014: 120). In Davide Però's (2014) examination of the Latin American Workers Association (LAWAS) in London, an intersectional approach connecting ethnicity, migrancy and class was found to be central to collective action, with LAWAS alternating between workplace organizing and the pursuit of wider demands around social recognition and rights. Significantly, LAWAS's strength fully matured only after people had solved more immediate issues such as housing, immigration and benefits. Furthermore, various studies (Alberti and Però 2018; Lopez and Hall 2015; Alberti et al. 2013; Jayaraman and Ness 2005) attest to the success and value of bottom-up, participatory organizing methods for attracting migrant workers and empowering them.

These approaches resonate with Satnam Virdee's (2000) writings on the unionization of racialized workers in the UK: together with Bob Miles (1982), he identifies racialized workers as a class 'fraction' that experiences similar but also divergent realities in comparison to white British workers. Virdee (2000) argues that these structural and subjective differences mean that the adequate representation of racialized workers requires the formation of semi-autonomous structures within the wider union framework. Such structures would allow migrant workers to self-organize whilst simultaneously feeding into, and strengthening, a wider working-class institution. These calls for unions to expand their spheres of operation recognize that migrant workers' relative disempowerment is not an exclusively economic concern, since the economy, culture and wider society intimately influence each other. The incorporation of intersectional methods in solidarity with migrant workers is therefore a precondition for empowering and organizing with migrant workers (Holgate 2021; Moore 2011). These conclusions have been reached by historical examples of migrant workers' movements in the UK such as the Indian Workers' Association, where the requirement of organizing simultaneously along the axes of race, ethnicity and class was a bare minimum in order to build towards the empowerment of migrant workers (Narayan 2019; Virdee 2014; Ramdin 2017).

In 2022, the Amazon Labor Union's (ALU) successful unionization drive in Amazon's JFK8 Staten Island warehouse demonstrated the importance of organizing along both class and migration lines. The ALU is an independent union, formed exclusively of workers and former workers employed in Amazon, and initially started without any external assistance. According to the testimonies of some of the organizers (Blanc 2022a, 2022b), the ALU maintaining a constant presence in the warehouses, established through engaging in conversations with workers, distributing union literature and speaking up at meetings, was paramount for winning the trust of the workforce. Organizers also spoke about tapping into the potential of ethnic networks to access larger pools of workers, using their community contacts to add more people to the WhatsApp chats they were using and relying on their proficiency in various languages to draw bridges and bring more people in. Having seen the foundations of its profitability creaking, Amazon is sure to go on the counteroffensive; nevertheless, the ALU's victory is momentous in terms of both its immediate and its long-term dimensions. Without significant resources beyond a commitment to long-term organizing, a workforce of precarious and mostly migrant workers defeated one of the biggest corporations of the world.

While tactics such as maintaining a presence in workplaces, foregrounding intersectional approaches, using participatory methods and securing the autonomy of existing groups of migrant workers in trade union structures potentially address some of the barriers to migrant worker unionization, they nevertheless encounter logistical problems when confronted with the issue of worker transience in precarious workplaces. Simply put, these tactics presuppose a relatively stable workforce, and they largely rely on the existence of homogeneous groups of migrant workers in specific workplaces (without this homogeneity, using ethnic networks is very difficult). Yet it has been established that many precarious occupations employing migrant workers are not characterized by these conditions. This is where community embeddedness comes to play a crucial role in our capacities to resist the socialization of precarity while also developing the foundations for organizing workers. Richard Sullivan

(2010) thus calls for a departure from traditional outlooks that consider trade unions as *the* constitutive organizations of labour struggles and urges us instead to focus on the actions and potentials of the spaces 'between' formal union structures.

Similarly, Beltrán Roca and Emma Martín-Díaz (2017) propose the term 'interstitial trade-unionism' to describe formations that resemble trade unions in their ultimate function but, rather than focusing on specific workplaces, are organized in the form of networks that span multiple worksites and neighbourhoods. They present the case study of the Solidarity Federation in Bristol and its Hospitality Workers Campaign, which successfully organized migrant workers. Characterized by de-centred, non-hierarchical and democratic structures, these networks 'operate in the margins of national systems of labour relations' and 'can have a variety of dimensions, relationships with existing trade unions and other civil society organizations, ethnic composition, and degree of formalization. They can also perform multiple functions for their members and pursue different ends. In some cases, these networks do not pursue an explicit labour goal, but in addressing the needs of their members, they end up carrying out some sort of industrial action' (Roca and Martín-Díaz 2017: 1201). Simply put, the barriers to organizing formal union structures in many precarious workplaces do not mean that organizing is doomed. They mean that movements must find alternative routes for reaching workers.

An example of such an effort can be found in London and Bristol, where the Angry Workers group attempts to organize with precarious and migrant workers by purposefully targeting jobs that are considered precarious and unorganizable. They circulated a newspaper aiming to connect and publicize dispersed experiences of class struggle in order to combat the socialization of precarity. They also operated weekly, neighbourhood-based open meetings connected to a 'solidarity network' that encourage workers to engage with each other and try to look for collective solutions to the problems they experience (Angry Workers 2020). Eschewing traditional trade union formations, these groups prefer to immerse themselves inside the class and the communities they aim to work alongside; the use of formal trade union structures emerges as epiphenomenal and purely based on the circumstances at hand, while their main priorities converge around embeddedness and mutual

CONCLUSION: TOWARDS COMMUNITY EMBEDDEDNESS

empowerment. In 2024, the Angry Workers inserted themselves in the care sector in Bristol and are currently circulating a magazine called *Vital Signs* that is addressed to the workers of the industry (Vital Signs 2024).

In other parts of the West, the establishment of autonomous social spaces and workers' centres has been a significant development in social movements' attempts to counteract the multiple barriers that exist in organizing alongside precarious and undocumented, migrant workers.[3] These realizations hark back to those reached by historical migrant workers' movements, such as the Jewish workers' movement in London in the 1900s (Rocker 2005). In discussing politically oriented squats in Europe, Miguel Martínez López (2012: 882) writes that they 'constitute accessible, free and independent meeting spaces for many individuals, groups and movements', enabling the cultivation of participatory, community-oriented political activity. Autonomous community spaces, whether they be squatted or not, are central components of social movement infrastructure in Europe, particularly important in organizing with populations such as migrants and refugees who have unstable living conditions (Raimondi 2019; King 2016).

In North America, the emergence of workers' centres since the early 2000s provides examples of how such structures embedded in migrant communities could operate. Janice Fine (2005: 3) defines workers' centres as 'community-based and community-led organizations that engage in a combination of service, advocacy, and organizing to provide support to low-wage workers. The vast majority of them have grown up to serve predominantly or exclusively immigrant populations.' These centres are largely heterogeneous and can be directly connected to trade unions, tied to NGOs, or be completely autonomous institutions. However, they all share the central characteristic of community embeddedness. The strong, physical community presence of such centres is important for counteracting the atomization fostered by the occupational precariousness and transience migrant workers experience. Furthermore, these centres engage in a range of activities that address the various intersectional oppressions migrant workers experience: whilst the reclamation of stolen wages is a key concern (Fine 2005), they also operate language and other types of classes and engage in a variety of services such as assisting people with their immigration forms (Fine 2011) or providing classes of political education (Sullivan 2010). Member participation and empowerment, as opposed to passive acceptance of assistance, fosters sustainability and engagement.

These examples across the West attest that social movements have already begun searching for, and operationalizing, solutions. I am not arguing that these initiatives should be uncritically replicated; indeed, activists such as Natasha King (2016) have demonstrated how even such community spaces may become embroiled in the reproduction of a range of problematic tendencies, eventually entrenching disempowerment rather than radically organizing to overcome it.[4] However, they are presented here as potent examples of the possibilities that emerge when social movements establish a steady presence in the communities they aim to organize with.

It is beyond the scope of this book to go deeper into an analysis of what these structures could look like. Yet it is clear that community embeddedness emerges as one of the prerequisites to any type of effort to address the structural and subjective effects of precarity. This is not simply an abstract call to engage in more community work; indeed, I would argue that we must steer as far away from NGOs and charities as possible. It is a call to organize specific institutions in neighbourhoods and communities that will be connected – as much as possible – to people's workplaces, in a process that is conscious of the precise ways in which contemporary capitalism in the West destroys our capacities to conceive alternative modes of living and working.

Establishing identifiable and accessible physical centres allows transient and precarious workers to access information and become involved in their own time in a safe environment. As worker transience through the proliferation of companies like Amazon expands, we will become increasingly dispersed, atomized and powerless; and as the socialization of precarity is allowed to proliferate in the absence of alternatives, this absence will become insuperable. Physical institutions that nurture contact, community, and that can serve as bases through which to explore new ways of existing beyond the socialization of precarity are no longer simply an ideological dream. They are necessary in order to connect the vastly heterogeneous social groups – including migrant workers – that are experiencing the debilitation engendered by precarity. As the socialization of precarity is nurtured and reproduced through workers' everyday experiences with their labour, each other, their own selves and wider society, it makes sense that any organized responses should themselves be deeply rooted in the material conditions of precarity.

The initiatives briefly outlined above go beyond the domain of traditional trade unions, instead implementing multi-scalar, intersectional approaches that are attentive to the multiplicity of socioeconomic forces that collectively maintain the precarity of migrant workers (and, indeed, precarity in general). The ideas, and the blueprints, already exist. On a theoretical level, these begin with a firm commitment to organize alongside migrant workers on the basis of their migration *and* their class status. On a practical level, community embeddedness emerges as one of the fundamental ways to counteract the most insidious effects of the socialization of precarity, and nurture the relationships that will allow us to imagine beyond it.

Notes

Introduction

1 At the time, it was £6.50 an hour.
2 At this point, it is important to state that the theory behind this book owes a lot to many important scholars that have worked on the topic of migration. The biggest debts, though, are to Bridget Anderson (2013), Zygmunt Bauman (2012), John Berger and Jean Mohr (2010), Abdelmalek Sayad (2004) and Sandro Mezzadra and Brett Neilson (2013). Alongside them, anarchist and Marxist theory forms the philosophical and political bedrock upon which everything else stands.
3 The amount of writing on the unjust geopolitical and economic relations that create this phenomenon is too vast to adequately encapsulate. However, the reader is advised to read Ian Sanjay Patel (2021), Walter Rodney (2018 [1976]), Satnam Virdee (2014), David Harvey (2005) and Costas Lapavitsas (2012).
4 This argument is also made in relation to lifestyle by Jarness et al. (2019).
5 This line of thought is fully indebted to Pierre Bourdieu's (2010) theories around habitus, Richard Sennett and Jonathan Cobb's (1972) explorations on pride associated with ability, and Andrew Smith's (2016) ideas on how the everyday structures the ways that we perceive our world.
6 The early to mid-2010s was the period where Latin American workers were engaged – and still are – in momentous labour victories in London, and many pages were written about how *they did it*. However, the reality in most of the shop floors of the UK was vastly different. Studies exploring these mobilizations include Alberti and Però (2018), Lagnado (2015) and Però (2014).
7 Here it is important to highlight that, while this book formally draws on research conducted during my PhD, it is *not* intended as an academic contribution. The PhD was the culmination of more than a decade of working and organizing alongside other migrants, and gave me the privilege to explore deeply questions that I was already immersed in. The book intends to present these explorations as coherently as possible, for a wider audience beyond and outside of academic circles. Thus, scholarly and theoretical work is cited only where I felt that it would provide important contextual information for the points being made. An academic reader might find that the book does not directly speak to extant academic debates in the fields of migration, precarity and resistance; similarly, a non-academic reader might find some passages too theory-heavy and dense. I tried to strike a balance where I use the relevant theory to inform my arguments and make them accessible for as wide a readership as possible.
8 Following Bloodworth (2019), this was done covertly. Managers and most fellow workers were unaware that I was conducting research. This choice was made in order to protect my access to the job: since bypassing employment law was an inseparable characteristic of

most of the jobs I accessed – and, even where rights were observed, the labour situation was still far from agreeable – it was highly unlikely that any of these companies would give me access to observe their operations as a researcher. Moreover, I wanted to observe people's unfiltered interactions and negotiations of precarity; this would immediately have been lost if they knew that they were being observed by a researcher. Most importantly, I was a longtime precarious worker, and as soon as my PhD funding ran out, I worked at Amazon separately from any research purposes; it was simply done in order to have a salary. In this context, while covert research always involves a degree of deception, in my case it significantly involved a degree of a worker simply taking notes about his labour environment.

9 A fuller discussion of the methods that inform this book is available on the Polity website, here: https://www.politybooks.com/bookdetail?book_slug=the-precarious-migrant-worker-the-socialization-of-precarity--9781509564989.

10 All the companies other than Amazon, as well as all interview participants, have had their names changed, in keeping with the confidentiality demands that underpinned the approval of my research by the University of Glasgow.

11 The utterances of interview participants are mostly presented as they were uttered; I wanted to represent their voices as closely as possible to the original recordings. However, in the interests of not losing the meaning of their words and allowing some degree of readability, slight edits have been made alongside Polity's editors.

12 An incredibly important exploration into how work is experienced by illegalized groups has been conducted by Hsiao-Hung Pai (2008). The role of borders in the lives of migrants has also been extensively analysed by Bridget Anderson (2013, 2010). The lives of Black workers in the UK, including their migratory struggles, have been comprehensively explored by Ron Ramdin (2017).

13 Guy Standing's (2011) use of 'precarity' as a qualitatively new iteration of capitalism in the West and of the emergent class that he argues is associated with it – the 'Precariat' – has triggered lengthy debate amongst scholars. I concur with Jan Breman (2013) and Ronaldo Munck (2016) that precarity should not be seen as a novel stage of capitalism, that the 'Precariat' is not a distinct class, and that precarious relations should be instead perceived as the rule, rather than the exception, of capitalism. Indeed, most of the world has never known anything other than precarity. This book, however, is not the forum to engage in such a debate. I use the word 'precarity' as a shorthand to refer to the combination of labour relations that characterize insecure jobs in the West, as well as to refer to the anxiety and compulsion to overexert oneself that it produces on the part of the workers.

14 A debate on the EU is outside the scope of this book. I would simply like to note that solidarity with migrants must surely involve more than supporting a structure that is directly responsible for the drowning of thousands of migrants in the Mediterranean.

15 Except where otherwise indicated, the statistics used come from the Migration Observatory at the University of Oxford. See Fernández-Reino and Brindle (2024) and Sumption et al. (2024). The statistic on union participation comes from the Department for Business, Energy and Industrial Strategy (2017).

16 For a discussion of precarious migrant workers in the US labour market, the reader is encouraged to read Milkman (2020).

17 Essentialization refers to the process where specific characteristics are associated

with specific groups of people, as if stemming from their *essential*, 'natural' qualities. For example, Polish workers in the UK have been essentialized as being 'good workers'.
18 This is fully explored in Theodoropoulos (2023).

Chapter 1: 'We Were Always Migrants'

1 When using the word 'subject' in this book, I may be referring to two things. One can be subject *to* something; for example, migrants can be subject to migration controls. The other use of the word refers to one being *a* subject: an agent, a personality, an amalgamation of thoughts, experiences and histories that coalesces in a sense of self, a personhood. That is the sense in which the word subjectivity is used: beyond simply 'personality', it connotes this mixture of personal history, social structures, power relations, externally-imposed categorizations, cultures, thoughts and self-identifications that make up one's conception of oneself.
2 Every name of every worker that is mentioned in this book is a pseudonym, and various identifying details have been slightly changed to ensure anonymity.
3 Bauder (2006) is a good source to begin thinking about the non-recognition of foreign credentials. In the UK, the study by Johnston et al. (2015) convincingly demonstrates the 'migration penalties' that foreign workers (specifically from Eastern Europe) are subject to; they are underpaid relative to their existing qualifications, and over-concentrated in less favourable jobs. Similarly, Oikelome and Healy (2013) have explored these trends in relation to doctors. See also Sirkeci et al. (2018).

Chapter 2: The Precarious Condition

1 I am indebted to Professor Andrew Smith for highlighting this point explicitly.
2 I am once again indebted to Professor Andrew Smith for explicitly teasing out this point.

Chapter 3: The Socialization of Precarity

1 As the conditions in Amazon have been extensively analysed in mainstream, academic and social movement platforms, there is no need to repeat them here. Indicatively, the reader is encouraged to read Delfanti (2021), Bloodworth (2019), Briken and Taylor (2018) and Harvey (2019).

Chapter 5: Solidarities and Resistances

1 See Mbembe (2019), Bradley (2016), Han (2015), Bourgeois and Schonberg (2009), Wacquant (2008) and Bauman (2004).
2 A comprehensive history of migrant workers' movements would necessitate – at the very least – a whole book dedicated to it. The reader is invited to read a brief history of the aforementioned struggles in the UK in chapter 1 of my PhD thesis (https://theses.gla.ac.uk/82275/). For examples in the US, a starting point is Loza (2016), Adler et al. (2014), Jayaraman and Ness (2005) and Goldberg and Griffey (2010). See also Choudry and Henaway (2016).
3 This is the Solidarity union, the key social force behind the collapse of the authoritarian 'communist' regime in Poland. Supported by the West, their activity peaked in the late 1980s and led to the 1989 elections, whereupon a coalition government led by Solidarity

oversaw a transition to liberal 'democracy'. The promise of workers' rights was ultimately not delivered, as the coalition oversaw the introduction of a plethora of neoliberal market reforms that led to a collapse of its membership. As Kris mentioned in the first chapter, these same reforms resulted in the destruction of previously secure occupations and led millions of Polish workers to migrate to the United Kingdom and other European nations.
4 At that point of the story, the company had declared bankruptcy.
5 The history of unions' hostility to migrant groups in the UK and the US is extensive and is comprehensively covered in the sources on migrant movements provided above. Since around the 1970s, we see a general trend towards unions recognizing that the rights of migrant workers are an inseparable aspect of the fight for the rights of workers as a whole. However, this change has still been interspersed with various forms of covert or overt hostility and exclusion towards precarious migrant workers.
6 Readers interested in working-class movements might want to note the reticence that this precarious worker displayed towards accepting support from a Labour-affiliated union.
7 I feel compelled to anticipate union members' indignant defence at this accusation. It is true that recent years have seen momentous activities by unions in support of migrant workers on both sides of the Atlantic. Yet, are we confident that these are generalizable and consistent enough for workers to recognize them as elements of their lives? As someone who has spent many hours in public union activities in the UK, with friends who have dedicated their entire lives to these endeavours, I felt a slap in the face every time a worker told me that we simply 'were not there' (and this was basically every worker I interviewed). Yet, these are the workers that we claim to represent. If they perceive us as nonexistent, it probably means that we are. I would be extremely happy to stand corrected.

Conclusion

1 Of course, this claim is specific to the UK, as it is based on my research in Glasgow and my experiences – for varying amounts of time – as a worker and organizer in other cities in these islands. Metropoles such as London, New York or Paris feature completely different relations between migrants and social movements. However, I believe that the argument that the socialization of precarity festers precisely where movements are either nonexistent, detached or unable to empower precarious workers, still stands.
2 See Lopez and Hall (2015), Fine and Holgate (2014), Alberti et al. (2014, 2013), Moore (2011) and Jayaraman and Ness (2005).
3 See King (2016), Choudry and Henaway (2016), Martínez López (2012), Milkman (2011), Fine (2011) and Jayaraman and Ness (2005).
4 See also Frantz and Fernandes (2018).

References

Acker, J. (2006) Inequality regimes: Gender, class, and race in organizations. *Gender & Society*, 20(4), pp. 441–64.

Adler, L.H., Tapia, M. and Turner, L. (eds.) (2014) *Mobilizing Against Inequality: Unions, Immigrant Workers, and the Crisis of Capitalism*. New York: Cornell University Press.

Alberti, G. (2016) Moving beyond the dichotomy of workplace and community unionism: The challenges of organizing migrant workers in London's hotels. *Economic and Industrial Democracy*, 37(1), pp. 73–94.

Alberti, G. (2014) Mobility strategies, 'mobility differentials' and 'transnational exit': The experiences of precarious migrants in London's hospitality jobs. *Work, Employment and Society*, 28(6), pp. 865–81.

Alberti, G. and Però, D. (2018) Migrating industrial relations: Migrant workers' initiative within and outside trade unions. *British Journal of Industrial Relations*, 56(4), pp. 693–715.

Alberti, G., Holgate, J. and Turner, L. (2014) Opportunity and choice for unions organizing immigrant workers: A comparison across countries and industries. In: Adler, L.H., Tapia, M. and Turner, L. (eds.) *Mobilizing Against Inequality: Unions, Immigrant Workers, and the Crisis of Capitalism*. New York: Cornell University Press.

Alberti, G., Holgate, J. and Tapia, M. (2013) Organizing migrants as workers or as migrant workers? Intersectionality, trade unions and precarious work. *The International Journal of Human Resources Management*, 24(22), pp. 4132–48.

Anderson, B. (2013) *Us and Them? The Dangerous Politics of Immigration Control*. Oxford: Oxford University Press.

Anderson, B. (2010) Migration, immigration controls and the fashioning of precarious workers. *Work, Employment and Society*, 24(2), pp. 300–17.

Anderson, B., Sharma, N. and Wright, C. (2011) Editorial: Why no borders? *Refuge: Canada's Journal on Refugees*, 26(2), pp. 5–18.

Angry Workers (2020) *Class Power on Zero-Hours*. London: PM Press.

REFERENCES

Balani, S. (2023) *Deadly and Slick: Sexual Modernity and the Making of Race.* London: Verso.

Balibar, E. and Wallerstein, I. (1991) *Race, Nation, Class: Ambiguous Identities.* London: Verso.

Barnard, C., Ludlow, A. and Fraser Butlin, S. (2018) Beyond employment tribunals: Enforcement of employment rights by EU-8 migrant workers. *Industrial Law Journal*, 47(2), pp. 226–62.

Bauder, H. (2006) *Labor Movement: How Migration Regulates Labor Markets.* New York: Oxford University Press.

Bauman, Z. (2012) *Liquid Modernity.* Cambridge: Polity Press.

Bauman, Z. (2004) *Wasted Lives: Modernity and its Outcasts.* Cambridge: Polity Press.

Berardi, B. (2017) *Futurability: The Age of Impotence and the Horizon of Possibility.* London: Verso.

Berger, J. and Mohr, J. (2010) *A Seventh Man: A Book of Images and Words about the Experience of Migrant Workers in Europe.* London: Penguin.

Berntsen, L. (2016) Reworking labour practices: On the agency of unorganized mobile migrant construction workers. *Work, Employment and Society*, 30(3), pp. 472–88.

Blanc, E. (2022a) Here's how we beat Amazon. [Online] *Jacobin.* Available at: https://jacobin.com/2022/04/amazon-labor-union-alu-staten-island-organizing [Accessed 23 June 2022].

Blanc, E. (2022b) How Amazon's immigrant workers organized to win a union on Staten Island. [Online] *Jacobin.* Available at: https://jacobin.com/2022/04/amazon-warehouse-alu-staten-island-immigrant-workers [Accessed 23 June 2022].

Bloodworth, J. (2019) *Hired: Undercover in Low-Wage Britain.* London: Atlantic Groups.

Boswell, C. and Geddes, A. (2011) *Migration and Mobility in the European Union.* New York: Palgrave Macmillan.

Bourdieu, P. (2010) *Distinction: A Social Critique of the Judgement of Taste.* Abingdon: Routledge.

Bourgeois, P. and Schonberg, J. (2009) *Righteous Dopefiend.* Berkeley: University of California Press.

Bradley, H. (2016) *Fractured Identities: Changing Patterns of Inequality*, 2nd edn. Cambridge: Polity Press.

REFERENCES

Breman, J. (2013) A bogus concept? [Online] *New Left Review*. Available at: https://newleftreview.org/issues/ii84/articles/jan-breman-a-bogus-concept [Accessed 21 June 2018].

Briken, K. and Taylor, P. (2018) Fulfilling the 'British way': Beyond constrained choice – Amazon workers' lived experience of workfare. *Industrial Relations Journal*, 49(5), pp. 438–58.

Cappiali, T. (2017) 'Whoever decides for you without you, s/he is against you!' Immigrant activism and the role of the Left in political racialization. *Ethnic and Racial Studies*, 40(6), pp. 969–87.

Casas-Cortés, M. (2014) A genealogy of precarity: A toolbox for rearticulating fragmented social realities in and out of the workplace. *Rethinking Marxism*, 26(2), pp. 206–26.

Castells, M. (1975) Immigrant workers and class struggles in advanced capitalism: The Western European experience. *Politics & Society*, 5(1), pp. 33–66.

Castles, S. (2000) *Ethnicity and Globalization*. London: Sage.

Choudry, A. and Henaway, M. (2016) Temporary employment agency workers in Montreal: Immigrant and migrant workers' struggles in Canada. In: Choudry, A. and Hlatshwayo, M. (eds.) *Just Work? Migrant Workers' Struggles Today*. London: Pluto Press.

Connolly, H. and Sellers, B. (2017) Trade unions and migrant workers in the UK: Organizing in a cold climate. In: Marino, S., Penninx, R. and Roosblad, J. (eds.) *Trade Unions and Migrant Workers: New Contexts and Challenges in Europe*. Cheltenham: Edward Elgar.

Datta, A. and Brickell, K. (2009) 'We have a little bit more finesse, as a nation': Constructing the Polish worker in London's building sites. *Antipode*, 41(3), pp. 439–64.

Delfanti, A. (2021) Machinic dispossession and augmented despotism: Digital work in an Amazon warehouse. *New Media & Society*, 23(1), pp. 39–55.

Department for Business and Trade (2023) Trade union statistics 2022. [Online] Available at: https://www.gov.uk/government/statistics/trade-union-statistics-2022 [Accessed 17 May 2024].

Department for Business, Energy and Industrial Strategy (2017) *Trade union membership 2016: Statistical bulletin*. [Online] Available at: https://www.gov.uk/government/uploads/system/uploads/attachment_data/file/616966/trade-union-membership-statistical-bulletin-2016-rev.pdf [Accessed 10 July 2017].

REFERENCES

Ehrenreich, B. (2021 [2001]) *Nickel and Dimed: Undercover in Low-Wage America*. London: Granta Publications.

Engels, F. (1952) *The Condition of the Working-Class in England in 1844*. London: George Allen and Unwin Ltd.

Eni-D (2016) Συμμόρφωση. Ο Χάρτης. Digital music album. Available at: https://www.youtube.com/watch?v=RIg4wq81xZk&list=PLqTny6p2icoQn9M1g9RXqEi5Zzwta03U8&index=9

Federici, S. (2012) *Revolution at Point Zero: Housework, Reproduction, and the Feminist Struggle*. Oakland, CA: PM Press.

Fernández-Reino, M. and Brindle, B. (2024) *Migrants in the UK labour market: An overview*. [Online] The Migration Observatory. Available at: https://migrationobservatory.ox.ac.uk/wp-content/uploads/2019/07/MigObs-Briefing-Migrants-in-the-UK-labour-market-an-overview-2024.pdf [Accessed 17 May 2024].

Fine, J. (2011) Worker centers: Entering a new stage of growth and development. *New Labor Forum*, 20(3), pp. 45–53.

Fine, J. (2005) *Worker centers: Organizing communities at the edge of the dream*. [Online] Economic Policy Institute. Available at: https://www.policyarchive.org/handle/10207/8085 [Accessed 20 June 2020].

Fine, J. and Holgate, J. (2014) The countermovement needs a movement (and a counterstrategy). In: Adler, L.H., Tapia, M. and Turner, L. (eds.) *Mobilizing Against Inequality: Unions, Immigrant Workers, and the Crisis of Capitalism*. New York: Cornell University Press.

Fisher, M. (2009) *Capitalist Realism: Is There No Alternative?* Winchester: O Books.

Fishman, J. (2004) *East End Jewish Radicals*. Nottingham: Five Leaves Publications.

Forde, C., MacKenzie, R., Ciupijus, Z. and Alberti, G. (2015) Understanding the connections between temporary employment agencies and migration. *International Journal of Comparative Labour Law and Industrial Relations*, 31(4), pp. 357–70.

Foucault, M. (2020) *Discipline and Punish: The Birth of the Prison*. London: Penguin.

Foucault, M. (2010) *The Birth of Biopolitics: Lectures at the Collège de France, 1978–79*. New York: Palgrave Macmillan.

Fox, J.E., Moroşanu, L. and Szilassy, E. (2012) The racialization of the new European migration to the UK. *Sociology*, 46(4), pp. 680–95.

REFERENCES

Frantz, C. and Fernandes, S. (2018) Whose movement is it? Strategic philanthropy and worker centers. *Critical Sociology*, 44(4–5), pp. 645–60.

Freire, P. (1993 [1970]) *Pedagogy of the Oppressed*. London: Penguin Books.

Garland, D. (2001) *The Culture of Control: Crime and Social Order in Contemporary Society*. Oxford: Oxford University Press.

Gemi, E. (2017) Albanian migration in Greece: Understanding irregularity in a time of crisis. *European Journal of Migration and Law*, 19, pp. 12–33.

Goldberg, D. and Griffey, T. (eds.) (2010) *Black Power at Work: Community Control, Affirmative Action, and the Construction Industry*, 1st edn. New York: Cornell University Press.

Gomberg-Muñoz, R. (2010) Willing to work: Agency and vulnerability in an undocumented immigrant network. *American Anthropologist*, New Series, 112(2), pp. 295–307.

Greene, A. (2019) Low-skilled employment in a new immigration regime: Challenges and opportunities for business transition. *National Institute Economic Review*, 248, pp. 17–27.

Han, B. (2017) *Psychopolitics*. London: Verso.

Han, B. (2015) *The Burnout Society*. Stanford, CA: Stanford University Press.

Hardt, M. and Negri, A. (2017) *Assembly*. New York: Oxford University Press.

Hardy, J. (2014) Transformation and crisis in Central and Eastern Europe: A combined and uneven development perspective. *Capital and Class*, 38(1), pp. 143–55.

Harvey, D. (2005) *A Brief History of Neoliberalism*. New York: Oxford University Press.

Harvey, M. (2019) A union at Amazon? Organize the class, not the shop. [Online] Notes from Below. Available at: https://notesfrombelow.org/article/a-union-at-amazon [Accessed 24 June 2019].

Holgate, J. (2021) Trade unions in the community: Building broad spaces of solidarity. *Economic and Industrial Democracy*, 42(2), pp. 226–47.

Holgate, M. (2005) Organizing migrant workers: A case study of working conditions and unionization in a London sandwich factory. *Work, Employment and Society*, 19(3), pp. 463–80.

Holmes, S. (2013) *Fresh Fruit, Broken Bodies: Migrant Farmworkers in the United States*. London: University of California Press.

REFERENCES

Jarness, V., Flemmen, M.P. and Rosenlund, L. (2019) From class politics to classed politics. *Sociology*, 53(5), pp. 879–99.

Jayaraman, S. and Ness, I. (2005) Models of worker organizing. In: Jayaraman, S. and Ness, I. (eds.) *The New Urban Immigrant Workforce: Innovative Models for Labor Organizing*. New York: M.E. Sharpe.

Johnston, R., Khattab, N. and Manley, D. (2015) East versus West? Over qualification and earnings among the UK's European migrants. *Journal of Ethnic and Migration Studies*, 41(2), pp. 196–218.

Jørgensen, M.B. (2016) Precariat – What it is and isn't – Towards an understanding of what it does. *Critical Sociology*, 42(7–8), pp. 959–74.

King, N. (2016) *No Borders: The Politics of Migration Control and Resistance*. London: Zed Books.

Kukreja, R. (2021) Recouping masculinity: Understanding the links between macho masculinity and self-exploitation among undocumented South Asian male migrants in Greece. *Geoforum*, 122, pp. 164–73.

Lagnado, J. (2015) Towards a history of the Latin American Workers Association 2002–12. In: Choudry, A. and Hlatshwayo, M. (eds.) *Just Work? Migrant Workers Struggles Today*. London: Pluto Press.

Lapavitsas, C. (2012) *Crisis in the Eurozone*. London: Verso.

Lazzarato, M. (2015) *Governing by Debt*. South Pasadena, CA: Semiotexte.

Lever, J. and Milbourne, P. (2017) The structural invisibility of outsiders: The role of migrant labour in the meat-processing industry. *Sociology*, 51(2), pp. 306–22.

Levi, P. (1988) *The Drowned and the Saved*. London: Penguin.

Lopez, A. and Hall, T. (2015) Organizing migrant workers: The living wage campaign at the University of East London. *Industrial Relations Journal*, 46(3), pp. 208–21.

Loza, M. (2016) *Defiant Braceros: How Migrant Workers Fought for Racial, Sexual, and Political Freedom*. Chapel Hill: The University of North Carolina Press.

MacKenzie, R. and Forde, C. (2009) The rhetoric of the 'good worker' versus the realities of employers' use and the experiences of migrant workers. *Work, Employment and Society*, 23(1), pp. 142–59.

Majumdar, N. (2017) Silencing the subaltern. [Online] *Catalyst: A Journal of Theory and Strategy*. Available at: https://catalyst-journal.com/2017/11/silencing-the-subaltern [Accessed 30 June 2017].

REFERENCES

Marcuse, H. (1991 [1964]) *One-Dimensional Man: Studies in the Ideology of Advanced Industrial Society*. Boston: Beacon Press.

Marino, S., Penninx, R. and Roosblad, J. (2017) Introduction: How to study trade union action towards immigration and migrant workers? In: Marino, S., Penninx, R. and Roosblad, J. (eds.) *Trade Unions and Migrant Workers: New Contexts and Challenges in Europe*. Cheltenham: Edward Elgar.

Martínez López, M.A. (2012) The squatters' movement in Europe: A durable struggle for social autonomy in urban politics. *Antipode*, 45(4), pp. 866–87.

Marx, K. (1844) Comments on James Mill. [Online] Marxists Internet Archive. Available at: https://www.marxists.org/archive/marx/works/1844/james-mill/ [Accessed 10 April 2020].

Mayo, P. (2016) Hegemony, migration and misplaced alliances: Lessons from Gramsci. In: Agustín, O.G. and Jørgensen, M.B. (eds.) *Solidarity without Borders: Gramscian Perspectives on Migration and Civil Society Alliances*. London: Pluto Press.

Mbembe, A. (2019) *Necropolitics*. Theory in Forms. Durham, NC: Duke University Press.

McAlevey, J. (2016) *No Shortcuts: Organizing for Power in the New Gilded Age*. New York: Oxford University Press.

McCollum, D. and Findlay, A. (2015) 'Flexible' workers for 'flexible' jobs? The labour market function of A8 migrant labour in the UK. *Work, Employment and Society*, 29(3), pp. 427–43.

McKay, S, and Markova, E, (2010) The operation and management of agency workers in conditions of vulnerability. *Industrial Relations Journal*, 41(5), pp. 446–60.

Melossi, D. (2008) *Controlling Crime, Controlling Society: Thinking about Crime in Europe and America*. Cambridge: Polity Press.

Mezzadra, S. and Neilson, B. (2013) *Border as Method: Or, the Multiplication of Labour*. London: Duke University Press.

Migration Observatory (2022) *EU migration to and from the UK*. [Online]. Migration Observatory at the University of Oxford. Available at: https://migrationobservatory.ox.ac.uk/resources/briefings/eu-migration-to-and-from-the-uk/ [Accessed 8 June 2022].

Miles, R. (1982) *Racism and Migrant Labour*. London: Routledge.

Miles, R. and Brown, M. (2003) *Racism*, 2nd edn. London: Routledge.

REFERENCES

Milkman, R. (2020) *Immigrant Labour and the New Precariat.* Cambridge: Polity Press.

Milkman, R. (2011) Immigrant workers, precarious work, and the US labor movement. *Globalizations*, 8(3), pp. 361–72.

Moore, P. and Robinson, A. (2016) The quantified self: What counts in the neoliberal workplace. *New Media & Society*, 18(11), pp. 2774–92.

Moore, S. (2011) *New Trade Union Activism: Class Consciousness or Social Identity?* Basingstoke: Palgrave Macmillan.

Munck, R. (2016) Globalization, labour and the 'precariat': Old wine in new bottles? In: Schierup, C. and Jørgensen, M.B. (eds.) *Politics of Precarity: Migrant Conditions, Struggles and Experiences.* Chicago: Haymarket.

Narayan, J. (2019) British Black Power: The anti-imperialism of political blackness and the problem of nativist socialism. *The Sociological Review*, 67(5), pp. 945–67.

Oikelome, F. and Healy, G. (2013) Gender, migration and place of qualification of doctors in the UK: Perceptions of inequality, morale and career aspiration. *Journal of Ethnic and Migration Studies*, 39(4), pp. 557–77.

Pai, H.-H. (2008) *Chinese Whispers: The True Story behind Britain's Hidden Army of Labour.* London: Penguin.

Papadopoulos, D., Stephenson, N. and Tsianos, V. (2008) *Escape Routes: Control and Subversion in the 21st Century.* London: Pluto.

Paret, M. and Gleeson, S. (2016) Precarity and agency through a migration lens. *Citizenship Studies*, 20(3–4), pp. 277–94.

Patel, I.S. (2021) *We're Here Because You Were There: Immigration and the End of Empire.* London: Verso.

Però, D. (2014) Class politics and migrants: Collective action among new migrant workers in Britain. *Sociology*, 48(6), pp. 1156–72.

Piore, M.J. (1979) *Birds of Passage: Migrant Labor and Industrial Societies.* New York: Cambridge University Press.

Raimondi, V. (2019) For 'common struggles of migrants and locals': Migrant activism and squatting in Athens. *Citizenship Studies*, 23(6), pp. 559–76.

Ramdin, R. (2017) *The Making of the Black Working Class in Britain.* London: Verso.

Recchi, E. and Triandafyllidou, A. (2010) Crossing over, heading west and south: Mobility, citizenship, and employment in the enlarged Europe. In: Menz, G. and Caviedes, A. (eds.) *Labour Migration in Europe.* Basingstoke: Palgrave Macmillan.

Roca, B. and Martín-Díaz, E. (2017) Solidarity networks of Spanish migrants in the UK and Germany: The emergence of interstitial trade unionism. *Critical Sociology*, 43(7–8), pp. 1197–212.

Rocker, R. (2005) *The London Years*. Nottingham: Five Leaves Publications.

Rodney, W. (2018 [1976]) *How Europe Underdeveloped Africa*. London: Verso.

Roediger, D.R. (2007) *The Wages of Whiteness: Race and the Making of the American Working Class*, revised edn. London: Verso.

Ruhs, M. and Anderson, B. (2010) Introduction. In: Ruhs, M. and Anderson, B. (eds.) *Who Needs Migrant Workers? Labour Shortages, Immigration, and Public Policy*. New York: Oxford University Press.

Rzepnikowska, A. (2019) Racism and xenophobia experienced by Polish migrants in the UK before and after Brexit vote. *Journal of Ethnic and Migration Studies*, 45(1), pp. 61–77.

Samaluk, B. (2016) Migrant workers' engagement with labour market intermediaries in Europe: Symbolic power guiding transnational exchange. *Work, Employment and Society*, 30(3), pp. 455–71.

Sayad, A. (2004) *The Suffering of the Immigrant*. Cambridge: Polity Press.

Scottish Government (2019) *Non-UK nationals in Scotland's workforce: Statistics from the annual population survey 2018*. [Online] Scottish Government. Available at: https://www.gov.scot/binaries/content/documents/govscot/publications/statistics/2018/12/labour-market-by-country-of-birth-and-nationality/documents/2018/non-uk-nationals-in-scotlands-workforce-jan-2018---dec-2018-published-may-2019/non-uk-nationals-in-scotlands-workforce-jan-2018---dec-2018-published-may-2019/govscot%3Adocument/non%2Buk%2Bjan-dec%2B2018.pdf [Accessed 10 October 2025].

Sennett, R. and Cobb, J. (1972) *The Hidden Injuries of Class*. London: W.W. Norton & Co.

Shubin, S. and McCollum, D. (2021) Migrant subjectivities and temporal flexibility of East-Central European labour migration to the United Kingdom. *Population, Space and Place*, 27, pp. 1–11.

Sirkeci, I., Acik, N., Saunders, B. and Přívara, A. (2018) Barriers for highly qualified A8 immigrants in the UK labour market. *Work, Employment and Society*, 32(5), pp. 906–24.

Sivanandan, A. (1990) *Communities of Resistance: Writings on Black Struggles for Socialism*. London: Verso.

REFERENCES

Sivanandan, A. (1983) *A Different Hunger*. London: Pluto Press.

Smith, A. (2016) *Racism and Everyday Life: Social Theory, History and 'Race'*. Basingstoke: Palgrave Macmillan.

Sonovate (2019) 46% increase in number of UK recruitment agencies. [Online] Sonovate. Available at: https://www.sonovate.com/press/46-increase-in-number-of-uk-recruitment-agencies/ [Accessed 23 April 2020].

Sporton, D. (2013) 'They control my life': The role of local recruitment agencies in East European migration to the UK. *Population, Space and Place*, 19, pp. 443–58.

Standing, G. (2011) *The Precariat: The New Dangerous Class*. London: Bloomsbury.

Sullivan, R. (2010) Organizing workers in the space between unions: Union-centric labor revitalization and the role of community-based organizations. *Critical Sociology*, 36(6), pp. 793–819.

Sumption, M., Walsh, P. and Brindle, B. (2024) *Net migration to the UK*. [Online] The Migration Observatory. Available at: https://migrationobservatory.ox.ac.uk/resources/briefings/long-term-international-migration-flows-to-and-from-the-uk/ [Accessed 10 October 2024].

Tabili, L. (1994) *'We Ask for British Justice': Workers and Racial Difference in Late Imperial Britain*. New York: Cornell University Press.

Tapia, M. (2014) United Kingdom: Dialectic approaches to organizing immigrant workers, postwar to 2012. In: Adler, L.H., Tapia, M. and Turner, L. (eds.) *Mobilizing Against Inequality: Unions, Immigrant Workers, and the Crisis of Capitalism*. New York: Cornell University Press.

The Guardian (2019) McCluskey sparks Labour backlash over tough line on free movement. [Online] *The Guardian*. Available at: https://www.theguardian.com/politics/2019/nov/13/mccluskey-tells-corbyn-defy-calls-extend-freedom-of-movement [Accessed 13 November 2019].

Theodoropoulos, P. (2023) The thief and the cash cow: Twins from a union of enemies. [Online] Interregnum. Available at: https://interregnum.ghost.io/the-thief-and-the-cash-cow-twins-from-a-union-of-enemies/ [Accessed 10 May 2024].

Theodoropoulos, P. (2021) Rituals of submission: Amazon's creation of the neoliberal worker. [Online] *ROAR Magazine*. Available at: https://roarmag.org/essays/amazon-neoliberal-worker/ [Accessed 2 September 2023].

Topak, Ö. (2021) Border violence and migrant subjectivities. *Geopolitics*, 26(3), pp. 791–816.

Trimikliniotis, N., Parsanoglou, D. and Tsianos, V.S. (2016) Mobile commons and/in precarious spaces: Mapping migrant struggles and social resistance. *Critical Sociology*, 42(7–8), pp. 1035–49.

UK Government (2020) National minimum wage and national living wage rates. [Online] Gov.uk. Available at: https://www.gov.uk/national-minimum-wage-rates [Accessed 30 April 2020].

US Bureau of Labor Statistics (2023) Union members – 2023. [Online] US Bureau of Labor Statistics. Available at: https://www.bls.gov/news.release/pdf/union2.pdf [Accessed 24 May 2024].

Vasey, H. (2017) The emergence of a low-skill migrant labour market: Structural constraints, discourses of difference and blocked mobility. *International Migration & Integration*, 18, pp. 863–79.

Virdee, S. (2014) *Racism, Class and the Racialized Outsider*. London: Palgrave Macmillan.

Virdee, S. (2000) A Marxist critique of Black radical theories of trade-union racism. *Sociology*, 34(3), pp. 545–65.

Virdee, S. and Grint, K. (1994) Black self-organization in trade unions. *The Sociological Review*, 42(2), pp. 202–26.

Virdee, S. and McGeever, B. (2018) Racism, crisis, Brexit. *Ethnic and Racial Studies*, 41(10), pp. 1802–19.

Vital Signs (2024) *Vital Signs No. 1*. [Online] Available at: https://www.vitalsignsmag.org/posts/issue-1-pdf [Accessed 5 September 2024].

Wacquant, L. (2008) *Urban Outcasts: A Comparative Sociology of Advanced Marginality*. Cambridge: Polity Press.

World Employment Confederation (2023) *Economic report 2023*. [Online] World Employment Confederation. Available at: https://wecglobal.org/uploads/2023/04/WEC-Economic-Report-2023.pdf [Accessed 18 May 2024].

Wu, B. and Liu, H. (2014) Bringing class back in: Class consciousness and solidarity among Chinese migrant workers in Italy and the UK. *Ethnic and Racial Studies*, 37(8), pp. 1391–408.

Young, I.M. (1990) *Justice and the Politics of Difference*. Princeton, NJ: Princeton University Press.

Index

absence; *see* narrative (oppositional), union (lack of presence)
abuse, 68–72, 117–20, 139, 144, 166–9, 180
acceptance, 127–8, 131, 136, 183
accommodation, 27, 38, 40–1; *see also* housing
advantage / disadvantage, 73, 77, 102, 126, 129, 191
Advisory, Conciliation and Arbitration Service (ACAS), 177, 179
African workers, 23, 60, 161, 177–9
agency, 16, 24, 38, 52, 91–6, 125
   arena, 93, 96, 103, 164
   worker, 53, 69, 79–80, 93–4, 170–1
agency (personal), 49, 97, 113, 130, 147, 164, 170
Albanians, 38–40, 59–62, 134, 154–7, 160
Algeria, 37, 40
alienation, 78–82, 101, 106, 138, 195–7
Amazon Labor Union (ALU), 199
Amazon, 84–91, 101, 108, 147, 191
anarchism / anarcho-syndicalism, 83, 108, 119, 148

anger, 40, 55, 148, 184
Angry Workers, 153, 164, 170–1, 200–1
anxiety, 37, 82, 88, 95–6, 107, 112
Arbeter Fraint, 196–7
Asian workers, 30
assistance, 41, 62, 201–2; *see also* training (for new workers)
associate (Amazon), 85, 90, 115, 145
asylum, 188
atomization, 86–8, 108, 157, 164, 201–2
Auschwitz concentration camp, 107
austerity, 11, 15, 32
authority, 62–4, 86, 119, 139, 153–5, 160–1
automation, 85, 191; *see also* mechanization
autonomist movements, 148
autonomy
   organizational; *see* organizing (in autonomous structures)
   personal, 36, 50, 84–5, 97, 131, 138
availability
   of jobs, 15–16, 93, 111–12, 114
   of resources, 115, 144, 148–9
   of workers, 69, 93, 112–13, 190–1

INDEX

availability (*cont.*)
  required of workers, 64, 96, 155

Bakers, Food and Allied Workers Union, 74
Bangladeshi workers, 109
banking, 42, 63, 138, 156
barriers, 49, 68, 100, 142; *see also* language (barrier)
  to organizing migrant workers, 97, 152, 174, 183–4, 199–201
  to solidarity, 105–10, 113, 133–6, 152, 162
bartending, 46, 72
Bauman, Zygmunt, 87, 99
belonging, 131, 141, 148
benefits, 126–8, 131–3, 198
Black Power, 11, 140, 151
Black workers / blackness, 31, 63, 137–8, 161, 174, 178
body, 57, 64, 73, 89, 127
border / bordering, 21–2, 24, 30, 37, 126–7, 187–8
boss; *see* manager
Bradford, 1, 9, 11
brain, 89, 152
break, 56, 79–80, 88, 90, 100–1
Brexit, 19–20, 22, 31, 45–6, 132
British workers, 31, 44, 55, 133, 148, 172, 181, 197
Bulgaria, 22
business (migrants opening), 41, 50

cafe, 69–70, 168
camaraderie, 160

camera (surveillance), 3, 71, 86, 88, 147
capital, 15, 32, 91, 169
  cultural, 63, 73, 111–12, 123, 144
  socioeconomic, 44, 72, 121
capitalism, 15, 29–31, 71, 78–80, 87, 99–100, 134
care; *see* children (providing for), health and care (sector)
Caribbean and West Indians, 30–1, 45
charity, 17–18, 202
chef / sous-chef, 51, 59–65, 109, 117–18, 137–8, 154–6
children, 82, 134
  providing for, 48, 56, 75–8, 112, 114, 184
Chinese workers, 30, 73, 146
Citizens Advice Bureau, 72, 180
citizenship, 21–2, 63, 131–4, 136–8, 165; *see also* 'good citizen'
class, 15–19, 116, 138, 142, 144–9, 151–3, 157, 182
  conflict, 87, 93, 95
  middle, 37, 123
  ruling (bourgeoisie), 29, 58, 84, 87
  working, 55, 58, 99, 108, 123, 164, 197–200
CLEAN campaign (US), 198
collective action; *see* resistance (collective)
collective bargaining, 15, 18, 87, 163–4, 175
Colonial Seamen's Movement, 151

colonialism, 29–33, 138, 172–3
communication, 37, 62, 105–6, 160, 179–80, 191
communist movement / regime, 31, 39, 84
community, 17, 87, 125, 151–3, 165, 175–6
  of resistance, 141
  of value, 131–5, 149, 192
community embeddedness, 125, 149, 184–6, 196–203
community spaces, 201–2
competition, 21
  migrants vs. locals, 25, 73, 128–30, 133, 172
  with the self, 57, 82, 93, 97
  between workers, 70, 82, 93, 101, 108–9, 162–4
competitiveness, 88, 91–3, 100, 107, 145, 152–4
concentration (of specific migrant groups), 22, 24, 191
confidence, 70–1, 111, 125, 137–9, 164, 180–1
conflict, 107–10, 148, 177–80
construction (sector), 22, 44, 111
contract; *see also* precarity (contractual)
  agency; *see* agency (worker)
  permanent, 57, 69, 89–91, 93–4, 108, 163
  temporary, 16, 92
  verbal, 57, 70, 190
  zero-hours, 50–1, 70–1, 93, 98, 114, 117, 190–1
control, 18, 21, 81, 91, 93–6, 101, 103; *see also* border

/ bordering, migration (controls)
cost
  legal, 166, 180
  of living, 167, 184, 188
  production, 15–16, 66, 80, 101, 103
country
  host, 29–30, 48, 97, 116
  of origin, 34, 36–7, 49, 116, 122–4, 128–9
creativity, 78, 81, 138
criminalization, 131, 187
culture, 84, 107, 127, 135, 139, 141, 182–3

death, 27, 58, 84
debt
  national, 31–3
  personal, 112–13, 155
democracy, 150, 200
dependency
  on migrant labour, 24, 111, 134, 163, 169
  of migrant workers, 21, 101, 126, 155
deportation, 21, 109, 126, 135, 187
deskilling, 23, 47–8, 137–8, 142
development, 29–34
difference, 25, 126–30, 138, 142–3, 152, 148, 198
dignity, 40, 58, 69, 97, 102–3, 165
disciplinary process, 53, 71, 74, 161, 166–8, 176–9
discipline, 33, 86–7, 135
discrimination, 46–7, 128–30, 138–40, 172, 177–9

INDEX

disempowerment, 17, 84, 96–7, 120, 135–6, 140, 150–1
dismissal
   threat of, 74, 105–6, 146–7, 161–2, 182
   unfair, 50, 168, 179
disorientation, 7, 54, 97, 120, 125, 169
disrespect; *see* respect
distance (between social movements & workers), 182–83
division (among migrants), 21, 62, 134, 156–7, 162
drugs, 57–8, 63, 134, 150, 160, 183
dual frame of reference, 49–51, 68, 83, 121–4, 185
dysregulation, 16, 58, 150

eating, 100, 105, 117–18, 156
economic crisis (2008), 15–16, 32, 39, 121–3, 129
economy, 24–5, 30, 33, 132–4
education, 32, 116, 124, 201; *see also* studying
election, 29, 187
emancipation, 8, 108, 150–2, 195
embeddedness; *see* community embeddedness
emigration (culture of), 33, 37–40
employer, 23–24, 44, 47, 91–4, 112–14, 120, 139; *see also* responsibilities (employer)
employment
   illegal, 43, 57, 190
   informal; *see* informality
   normal (full-time), 98–9

Employment Tribunal, 50, 70, 72, 78, 120, 177–80
empowerment, 11, 38–40, 143, 151, 163, 174, 196–201
endurance, 40, 51, 64, 105
Engels, Friedrich, 58
environmental catastrophes, 150
Equality Act (2010); *see* legislation (anti-discrimination/equality)
essentialization, 24–5, 47, 91, 102, 125, 127–8, 135
Estonia, 22
ethnicity, 21–2, 41, 62, 127–8, 152–3, 173–4, 198–200; *see also* network (ethnic)
Europe, 33, 188
   Central and Eastern, 31–2, 83
   Southern, 31
European Central Bank, 31
European Union (EU), 20, 24, 31–2
European workers / EU nationals, 19–20, 44–5, 112, 125–8, 136–7, 172
   Eastern, 22–3, 40, 71, 128–9
(the) everyday, 82, 127–30, 140, 149, 162, 182
exclusion, 18–19, 21, 30, 60, 126, 128, 130
exhaustion, 57, 78, 89, 120
exploitability, 23, 29–31, 112, 132, 141–3
exploitation, 78, 85, 102, 111, 148–9, 198
   awareness of, 38, 51, 68, 121, 145
   naturalization of, 67, 98, 125, 138–9

INDEX

by other migrants, 41–2, 71, 154–7
self-, 97, 100–1

factory, 36, 58, 44, 80–1
  cake, 74, 165–7
  fish, 52–7, 69, 73, 106, 158, 182
  printing, 1–4, 80, 94–5, 171
  radiator, 34–6, 69, 81–2, 92, 105, 158–9, 191
  shelf-making, 48
familiarity
  with the labour market, 23, 68, 111, 113
  among workers, 60–2, 85
family, 27–8, 69, 77, 127, 167, 196; *see also* network (familial)
fatigue, 13, 57, 64–6, 97, 102
fear, 21, 91, 100, 109, 154, 176–7, 185
Fisher, Mark, 100
flexibility, 15–16, 23–4, 64, 85, 93–4, 99, 114
food (preparation), 53, 109, 129, 137; *see also* eating, kitchen
Fordism, 15, 17, 87, 93
foreigner / foreignness, 15, 22, 124–6, 130, 169
Foucault, Michel, 21, 84, 86–7
France, 29, 33, 37
Frankfurt School, 84
freedom of movement, 172, 188
freedom, 36, 131
French (Guadeloupean), 45–6, 137–9

friendship
  with fellow workers, 62, 72, 110, 163–4, 176
  with superiors, 145–6, 154–5, 158

gender, 24, 54, 77, 116, 151
genocide, 150
Glasgow, 38–9, 57–8, 85, 112, 117, 127, 185
globalization, 19–20, 150
'good citizen', 131
'good migrant', 130–6
'good worker', 64–5, 92–6, 101–3, 130–1, 153–5, 159–61, 164
government, 31–2, 72, 150, 187–8, 192
Gramsci, Antonio, 84
Greek workers / Greece, 10–11, 32, 36, 38–9, 50, 122–3, 127–8
Grey Zone (Primo Levi), 107, 110, 157

habitus, 102–3, 107
health and care (sector), 22, 43–4, 80–1, 141, 201
health and safety (workplace), 34, 52–3, 70, 73–9, 167
hegemony, 84
hierarchy, 18, 170, 200
  labour, 44, 46, 62–3, 116, 145, 152–7, 164
  between/within migrant groups, 42, 128, 132, 162
hire and fire, 24, 160–2; *see also* dismissal
holiday pay, 71, 120, 169

holidays, 38, 76, 93, 122–3, 127
Homo economicus, 115
homogeneity (ethnic), 14, 191, 199
hope, 27–8, 33–7, 48–50, 65, 94
hospitality (sector), 15, 22, 46, 58, 69, 106, 200
hostility, 19–20, 109, 119, 130, 134, 140
hotel, 75, 110, 117–20, 136–9, 177–80
hours, 42, 75, 95–6, 122, 167
  long, 58, 64–6, 67, 100–1, 155
  securing more, 64–5, 88, 95, 101
  zero; *see* contract (zero-hours)
housing, 36, 63, 198
human rights, 98, 187
humanitarianism, 187–8
humiliation, 4, 69, 166
humour, 60, 147–8; *see also* sarcasm
Hungarian workers, 22, 42

identification, 8, 18–19, 134, 141–4, 151
identity politics, 151
identity, 115–16, 121
  class, 19, 87, 144, 148, 151
  collective, 8, 18, 87, 151
  of hard work & resilience, 63, 97, 102, 114, 197
  migrant, 40, 47, 60, 133–4, 149
  politicized migrant, 140–4, 149, 151, 192
(the) Illegal Immigrant, 135
immigration controls; *see* migration (controls)

immigration, 19, 37, 134, 138, 201
imperialism, 19, 29–31, 57–8
inclusion, 21–2, 106, 130, 135, 170
  differential, 30, 43, 126, 132
Indian Workers' Association, 151, 198
Indian workers / India, 30–1, 46–7, 172–3
individualism / individualization, 74, 85–7, 93, 99–100, 107–8, 131–6, 175; *see also* resistance (individualized)
Industrial Revolution, 7, 31
Industrial Workers of the World (IWW), 117, 124, 168, 178, 180
inequality, 29, 56, 71, 74, 125, 144, 195
  language/narratives obscuring, 69, 85, 131, 145–6
informality, 41–3, 57–8, 68–70, 74, 161–2, 179
injury, 58, 64, 66
insecurity, 57, 70, 78, 87, 95, 99–100, 126
institutions, 17–18, 140, 151, 164, 197–8, 201–2
intensity, 64–8, 73, 106
interconnectedness, 148, 160
interdependence, 108, 159, 162
interests, 44, 47, 84, 108–9, 114, 153, 159
internalization, 51, 86–7, 91, 97, 103–7, 130
International Monetary Fund (IMF), 31–2

internationalism, 174
interpersonal relations; *see* relationship
intersectionality, 142, 174–5, 185, 198–9, 201
Irish workers, 14, 30, 58
isolation, 54, 84–7, 100, 105–9, 136
Italians / Italy, 32, 58–9, 129–30, 142–3

Japan, 16
Jewish workers, 30–1, 83, 141, 151, 196–7
job switching; *see* mobility (occupational)

kitchen (La Dama), 57–68, 101, 103–4, 109, 147, 154–6, 161–2
kitchen porter, 58–9, 65–6, 118, 137, 156

La Dama; *see* kitchen (La Dama)
labour
   academic, 81
   reproductive, 77
   skilled, 32, 35, 44, 64, 137–8, 141
   unskilled, 35, 43, 47–8, 64
   wage, 98–9
labour conditions; *see* working conditions
labour power, 29, 33–4
labour regime, 15, 58, 98–9, 104, 108, 125, 153
labour rights, 20, 71, 190, 198
   difficulty claiming, 75–7, 93, 100, 119–23
   lack of information on, 120–22, 166, 171–2, 176, 181, 184–6
language, 51, 55, 62
   barrier, 23, 29, 97, 105, 111, 175, 199
   classes, 201
   test, 46
Latin American Workers' Association (LAWAS), 124, 198
law; *see* legislation
lawyer, 45–6, 178–9
leadership, 90, 139, 153
leafleting, 42
legislation, 30, 44
   anti-discrimination/equality, 177–8, 182
   employment/labour, 72, 114, 120, 161, 177–9, 191
   migration, 19, 45, 187, 191
leisure, 58, 66, 77
lifestyle, 182
Lithuanian workers, 22, 37–8, 49, 158
logistics sector, 15, 22
London, 31, 83, 141, 196–8, 200–1
loss, 28
loyalty, 99, 155, 157

Macedonia, 134
machine, 54, 74, 80, 86–9, 109, 163
management, 68, 92, 153, 157, 176, 181

INDEX

management-speak, 145; *see also* inequality (language/narratives obscuring)
manager, 71, 74, 86–8, 90, 105, 145–6
  challenging the, 71–2, 113, 119–20, 138–9, 165–9, 173–4, 177–80
  locals as, 34, 70, 148
  migrant as, 54–5, 63, 74, 116, 145, 153, 158
Manchester, 31
marginalization, 11, 30, 130–1, 134–5, 141–2, 150–1, 174
market liberalization, 32
Marx, Karl, 78, 84, 93
Marxism, 20, 108, 162
masculinity, 62, 127, 183
McCluskey, Len, 172
means of production, 84, 93, 191
mechanization, 54, 85, 95; *see also* automation
media, 10, 130, 140; *see also* newspaper
Merkel, Angela, 133
Mexican workers / Mexico, 33, 73, 102, 160
migrancy, 67, 100, 143, 152, 193, 198
migrant; *see* 'good migrant', subjectivity (migrants')
  becoming a, 28–9
Migrant Workers' Network; *see* Industrial Workers of the World (IWW)
migration, 27–34, 40–1, 51
  controls, 20–1, 43, 126, 187
  regime, 26, 125
mindset, 83, 122–3, 173
minority groups, 15, 30, 152, 173
mobility
  occupational, 110–14, 194
  upward, 154
mobilization, 10–11, 18–19, 140–2, 153, 169, 193, 195
Moldovan workers, 129
money
  need for quick, 40, 97
  saving to return home, 36, 49–50, 68, 115–16
  spending vs. sending abroad, 132
  supporting family; *see* children (providing for)
mother, 76–7, 111
motivation (behind migration), 49–51, 68, 97
mutuality / mutual aid, 16, 18, 108, 157–9, 193, 197, 200
mystification, 149, 192

narrative
  dominant/hegemonic, 16, 25, 129–30, 135, 140, 148
  oppositional, 51, 96, 102, 116, 164, 197
nation(-state), 19–20, 29–33, 40, 131, 148
National Health Service (NHS), 80, 128
nationalism, 10, 19
naturalization, 33, 37, 48, 67, 100, 125, 139

INDEX

neighbourhood, 127, 176, 197, 200–2
neoliberalism, 15–18, 20–1, 57, 93, 99, 115, 176
network
   ethnic, 37, 41, 146, 155–6, 164–5, 190–1, 199
   familial, 29, 33, 62, 146, 154
   support, 72, 77, 117, 200
newspaper (workers' organization), 200–1
NGOs, 17–18, 201–2
nomination (of colleagues), 89
non-recognition of foreign credentials; *see* qualifications (recognition of)
normalization (of precarious working conditions), 100–3
nursing; *see* health and care (sector)

objectification, 52, 81
occupation, 31, 44, 73, 70, 104, 190
Occupy movements, 144
oppression, 11, 21–2, 102, 140–1, 143, 151, 198
organizing, 97, 141, 150–3, 164, 170–1, 183–6, 196–203
   in autonomous structures, 124, 150–1, 163, 171, 174, 198–200
   barriers to; *see* barriers (to organizing migrant workers)
othering, 29, 141–2
overexertion, 57, 91, 101–2, 109, 163
overtime, 74, 88, 91, 93, 101

pain, 13, 66–7, 101–3, 156
Pakistani workers, 23, 31, 173
participation
   political, 84, 144, 148
   social, 30, 127
   union; *see* union (migrant engagement)
participatory methods, 198–9, 201
partner (business), 145
partner (family), 36, 56, 82
partying, 63, 160; *see also* club
passivity, 114, 135, 181, 189, 192, 202
paternalism, 64, 154–5
performance, 22, 86, 100, 136, 158–9
   monitoring, 3, 16, 71, 85–90
   over-, 57, 78, 82, 85, 97
   under-, 106, 109, 161
performance (of certain traits), 47–8, 89–91, 93, 101, 153–4
Philippines, 33
Piore, Michael, 49, 115, 121
Polish workers / Poland, 22, 33–6, 38, 54–5, 102, 127–9, 165
political party, 10, 19, 150, 187–8, 192
politicization, 18, 83, 123–4, 141–4, 148–9, 192
Portugal, 29, 32
poverty, 16, 18, 21, 32, 112, 145, 150
power, 71, 74, 84, 86, 145
   of the State, 20–1
   of unions, 16–17, 165–9, 175
   of workers, 55, 113, 150, 153, 163–5, 175, 197

powerlessness, 57, 77, 113, 125, 139, 151
precariat, 99
precarity, 15–17
  contractual, 57, 68, 74, 81, 105–8, 110, 190
  interrelational, 105
  as management tool, 68, 92
  psychological, 17
  reproduction of, 104, 115, 135–6, 181
  socialization of, 51, 82, 96–107, 113–14, 162, 181–2, 202–3
presence; *see* community embeddedness, union (lack of presence)
pride
  in achievements, 35, 63, 132–3, 137, 165, 180
  in enduring precarious conditions, 97, 102, 105, 115
privilege, 29, 55–6, 128, 136–8, 153, 155–7, 159
production
  line, 1–3, 54–6, 87, 95
  rate / target, 85, 88–91, 108, 163
productivity, 7, 62, 84–6, 91–3, 105–6, 164
profit / profitability, 6, 21, 64, 79, 93–4, 145, 191
promotion, 90–1, 137
prosperity, 29, 58
protest, 5, 177, 184
psyche, 79, 83–4, 87, 110, 188
public infrastructure, 32
public spending, 32
public sphere, 14, 18

qualification(s)
  non-recognition of, 23, 43–7, 68, 141–2
  over-, 23, 45, 48
race, 116, 138, 151, 153, 199
racialization, 47, 91, 128, 130, 134, 140–1, 198
racism, 18–19, 55, 60, 127–8, 134–5, 140, 172
rate (pick / production); *see* production (rate/target)
recognition, 198; *see also* qualifications (non-recognition of)
refugee, 5, 131, 134, 201
relationship; *see also* precarity (interrelational)
  with fellow workers, 62, 103, 109, 162
  with superiors, 43, 69, 74, 85, 154–8, 161
remuneration, 13, 17, 35, 68, 147; *see also* wage
replaceability, 94–6, 105, 113
representation, 17–18, 96, 161, 167, 173–4
residence status; *see* right to remain
resignation, 40, 54, 58, 79, 121, 125, 182
resilience, 57, 63, 113, 189
resistance, 18, 83, 120, 147
  collective, 97, 116, 141–3, 150–3, 162–9, 197–9
  communities of, 141
  individualized, 62, 71–2, 110–14, 139, 175

INDEX

respect, 69–70, 79–80, 137–8, 154–5, 165, 168
responsibilities
    caring/family, 77, 111–13; *see also* children (providing for)
    employer, 71, 85, 190
responsibilization, 16, 87, 99
restaurant, 25, 41, 71, 136–7; *see also* kitchen (La Dama)
retail, 22
revolution, 83, 99, 108
're-working', 147
right; *see also* human rights, labour rights
    of free entry, 31
    to remain, 24, 112, 126, 191, 194
riot, 19
Rocker, Rudolf, 83, 196
Roma, 134
Romanian workers, 22, 110, 133–4, 163
rule of law, 33

safety; *see* health and safety (workplace)
sarcasm, 53, 107, 147
Schengen zone, 188
science & research, 19, 81
security, 64–5, 69–70, 85, 89–90, 116, 132, 164
self-worth, 62, 97
sense of self, 26, 56, 79, 86
service sector, 15, 31
settled status; *see* right to remain
sexuality, 151
shift; *see* hours

shipyard, 58
sickness, 93
Sikhs, 46–7
skill; *see* labour (skilled/unskilled)
slavery, 137–8
Slovakia, 22
Slovenia, 22
Small Claims Court, 120
smoking, 65, 106
sociability, 90–1, 107
social body, 20–2, 73, 93, 127
social bonds, 97, 99, 105–8, 113, 143, 151–2, 160–4
social justice, 7, 146, 162
social movement, 102–3, 116, 175–6, 182–6, 197, 201–2
socialists, 83
socialization, 123, 183, 196; *see also* precarity (socialization of)
socializing (with fellow workers), 83, 106
Solidarity Federation (Bristol), 200
solidarity, 17–18, 146–7, 151, 158–64, 198–200; *see also* barriers (to solidarity)
Solidarnosc, 165
South Africans (white), 60, 177–9
Spanish workers / Spain, 29, 32–3, 37–8, 117–24, 142–3
squatting, 201
stability, 33, 40, 51, 80, 96, 112
(the) State, 17–18, 20–2
stealing jobs; *see* competition (migrants vs. locals)
stereotype, 24, 33, 47, 128–9

INDEX

Stirling, 136–7
stress, 57, 66, 88–9, 97, 100, 107, 112
strike, 64, 172, 182, 197
studying, 36–7, 45–6, 123
subjectivity, 140
   migrants', 116, 123, 125, 134, 136
   workers', 86–7, 97–9, 102, 105, 122
supermarket, 47, 53, 87
supervisor, 86, 89, 133, 153, 167
surveillance; *see* camera
survivalism, 40, 51, 70, 97, 107–8, 120
sweatshop, 83, 197

tax, 34, 132–5, 145; *see also* wage (untaxed)
team leader, 95, 139, 153
temporariness, 68, 97, 111, 121, 171, 197
textile industry, 31
Thatcher, Margaret, 55
tips, 70, 139, 156–7
tourist (vs. migrant), 126, 129, 142
trade union; *see* union
training (for new workers), 34, 69, 86, 92, 137, 146, 158–9
transience, 99, 113, 171, 199, 201–2
transport and storage sector, 15, 22
trial shift, 58–9
Trump, Donald, 19, 45, 187
turnover, 69, 92, 106

UKIP, 10
underdevelopment, 29–34
understaffing, 64, 66, 85, 101
undocumented migrant worker, 30, 73, 102, 201
unemployment, 32–3, 94–5, 112, 147
unfairness, 104, 133; *see also* dismissal (unfair)
union, 16–21, 146
   appeal to, 119–20, 156, 165–9, 178
   busting, 85
   lack of presence, 63, 119–120, 161, 175–7, 180–5
   migrant engagement, 23, 151–3, 162–3, 170–5, 183–4, 197–8, 200
   spaces between, 164, 200
United Kingdom, 16, 19–24, 29–31, 72, 150–1, 170, 192
United States, 16–17, 19, 73, 138, 187, 201
university; *see* studying

vigilance, 21, 77, 91, 94
violence (physical), 14, 19, 166
visa, 21–2, 30, 37, 191
vulnerability, 17, 21, 30, 40, 162

wage
   migrants vs. locals, 24, 67, 122, 187
   migration in search of better, 32, 36, 49, 121–2
   minimum, 35, 43, 65, 91, 114, 121

negotiation, 163–4
theft, 3, 10, 71, 117–20, 177, 201
untaxed, 41–3, 156–7
warehouse, 44, 52–4, 87–8, 105–7, 163, 199
welfare / welfare state, 18, 32–3, 87, 98, 188
white immigrant workers / whiteness, 14, 63, 128, 138, 148
women, 77, 133–4, 178
work experience, 36, 44–5, 48

worker; *see* 'good worker', subjectivity (workers')
workers' centres, 201–2
workers' rights; *see* labour rights
working conditions, 83–4
   acceptance of, 51, 86, 98, 100–4, 114, 122–3
   improvement of, 65, 110–11, 113, 122–3, 145, 150, 154, 168

xenophobia, 18–19, 39, 55, 130–1, 134–5, 172